P-H 12.95

W9-AZW-641

WHO'S RUNNING AMERICA?

HN
90
E4
D93
1983

WHO'S RUNNING AMERICA?

The Reagan Years

third edition

THOMAS R. DYE

Florida State University

PRENTICE-HALL, INC., ENGLEWOOD CLIFFS, NJ 07632

Library of Congress Cataloging in Publication Data

Dye, Thomas R.
   Who's running America?—the Reagan years.

    Rev. ed. of: Who's running America?: The Carter years.
2nd ed. c1979.
   Includes bibliographical references and index.
   1. Elite (Social sciences)—United States. 2. United
States—Politics and government—1981-
I. Title.
HN90.E4D93 1983   305.5'2   82–3853
ISBN 0–13–958470–6 (pbk.)   AACR2

©1983, 1979, 1976 by Prentice-Hall, Inc., Englewood Cliffs, N.J. 07632

*All rights reserved. No part of this book
may be reproduced in any form or
by any means without permission in writing
from the publisher.*

Printed in the United States of America

10 9 8 7 6 5 4 3 2 1

Editorial/production supervision and interior design: Marina Harrison
Cover design: Karolina Harris
Manufacturing buyer: Edmund W. Leone and Ron Chapman

ISBN 0-13-958470-6

PRENTICE-HALL INTERNATIONAL, INC., *London*
PRENTICE-HALL OF AUSTRALIA PTY. LIMITED, *Sydney*
PRENTICE-HALL CANADA, INC., *Toronto*
PRENTICE-HALL OF INDIA PRIVATE LIMITED, *New Delhi*
PRENTICE-HALL OF JAPAN, INC., *Tokyo*
PRENTICE-HALL OF SOUTHEAST ASIA PTE. LTD., *Singapore*
WHITEHALL BOOKS LIMITED, *Wellington, New Zealand*

Contents

PART TWO
Institutional leadership in America

4 THE NEWSMAKERS, 119

5 THE CIVIC ESTABLISHMENT, 135

PART THREE
The structure of institutional elites

6 INTERLOCKING AND SPECIALIZATION AT THE TOP, 169

10   INSTITUTIONAL ELITES IN AMERICA, 265

Preface

Who's Running America? The Reagan Years was *not* supported by any grant or contract from any institution, public or private. It grew out of the graduate seminar "Research on Power and Elites" at Florida State University in the spring of 1972. Biographical data for over 5,000 members of various institutional elites was painstakingly collected and coded by students. These computerized biographies constituted the original data base for the continuing project *Who's Running America?* The data base was revised in 1980–81 by students at Florida State University, and data on over 7,000 institutional elites was collected and coded.

Two articles based on this data from the early 1970s were published in social science journals:

> Thomas R. Dye, Eugene R. DeClercq, and John W. Pickering, "Concentration, Specialization, and Interlocking among Institutional Elites," *Social Science Quarterly* (June 1973), pp. 8–28.

> Thomas R. Dye and John W. Pickering, "Governmental and Corporate Elites: Convergence and Specialization," *Journal of Politics* (November 1974), pp. 900–925.

We are indebted to a number of commentators who wrote to us before and after publication of these articles, including scholars G. William

Domhoff, Suzanne Keller, John Walton, Robert Lineberry, and Victor Reinemer of the staff of the Senate Committee on Government Affairs.

The First Edition of this book was published in 1976 and described national leadership in the Nixon-Ford years. The First Edition was subtitled "Institutional Leadership in the United States."

The Second Edition of this volume, "The Carter Years," reflected changes in national leadership which occurred with the election of Jimmy Carter to the presidency and the advent of a new Democratic administration. The year 1977 brought many "new faces" into power in Washington, not only in the executive branch, but in Congress as well. The Second Edition updated many of the original observations, but the statistical analysis was still based upon the original data collected from 1970–71 sources.

The Third Edition of this book, "The Reagan Years," involved the collection of an entire new data base for national leaders in 1980–81. Special topics were addressed in several articles in professional journals, including:

Thomas R. Dye, "Oligarchic Tendencies in National Policy-Making: The Role of the Private Policy-Planning Organization," *Journal of Politics,* 40 (May 1978), 309–331.

Thomas R. Dye and Julie Strickland, "Women At the Top," *Social Science Quarterly,* 63 (March 1982).

This volume is divided into three parts. Part I, Power in American Society, sets forth our questions for research, defines terms and concepts, and explains our method of identifying the nation's institutional elite. Part II, Institutional Leadership in America, describes concentration of power in industry, banking, insurance, utilities, government, the news media, the law, investment finance, foundations, civic and cultural organizations, and universities. It also describes the type of persons who occupy top institutional leadership positions in these various sectors of society; it "names names," and in so doing, makes use of brief biographical sketches. These sketches are designed to give us a general introduction to the characteristics of elites: the schools they attend, their early careers, their records of achievement, and the multiple positions of leadership they occupy. These sketches are derived from a wide variety of sources: *Who's Who in America, Current Biography, Forbes, Fortune, Congressional Quarterly,* and individual articles and books.[1] The sketches in Part II are designed to

---

[1] *Who's Who in America,* published biannually by Marquis Who's Who, Inc., Chicago; *Current Biography,* published monthly and annually by H.L. Wilson Co., New York; *Forbes,* published biweekly by Malcom S. Forbes, New York; *Fortune,* published monthly by Time-Life, Inc., New York; *Congressional Quarterly Weekly Report,* published weekly by Congressional Quarterly, Inc., Washington, D.C.

pave the way for more systematic analysis of biographical data, which follows in Part III.

Part III, The Structure of Institutional Elites, is a systematic investigation of interlocking and specialization among elites, overlapping elite membership, recruitment paths, socioeconomic backgrounds, previous experience, racial and sexual bias, club memberships and life styles, attitudes and opinions, competition and consensus, factionalism, and patterns of interaction in policy-making. Part III relies heavily on the computerized biographical files which we compiled at Florida State University on thousands of top institutional elites in 1970–71 and in 1980–81. What is suggested in a general way about characteristics of America's elites in Part II is subject to more careful systematic analysis in Part III.

The decision to "name names" was carefully considered. We know that occupants of top institutional positions change over time, and that some of our information will be out of date by the time of publication. And with thousands of names, some mistakes are inevitable. However, the biographical sketches provide "flesh and bones" to the statistical analysis; they "personalize" the numbers and percentages in our research. The people who run America *are* real people, and we know of no better way to impress this fact upon our readers.

THOMAS R. DYE
Tallahassee, Florida

WHO'S RUNNING AMERICA?

PART ONE

Power
in
American society

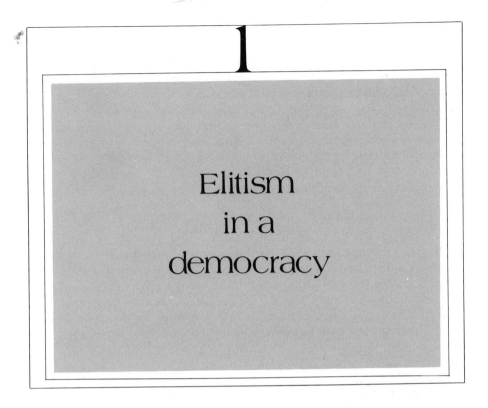

Elitism in a democracy

Great power in America is concentrated in a tiny handful of people. A few thousand individuals out of 220 million Americans decide about war and peace, wages and prices, consumption and investment, employment and production, law and justice, taxes and benefits, education and learning, health and welfare, advertising and communication, life and leisure. In all societies—primitive and advanced, totalitarian and democratic, capitalist and socialist—only a few people exercise great power. This is true whether or not such power is exercised in the name of "the people."

Who's Running America? is about those at the top of the institutional structure in America—who they are, how much power they wield, how they came to power, and what they do with it. In a modern, complex industrial society, power is concentrated in large institutions: corporations, banks, utilities, insurance companies, broadcasting networks, the White House, Congress and the Washington bureaucracy, the military establishment, the prestigious law firms, the large investment houses, the foundations, the universities, and the private policy-planning organizations. The people at the top of these institutions—the presidents and principal officers and directors, the senior partners, the governing trustees, the congressional committee chairpersons, the department heads, the senior advisers, the supreme court justices, the top generals and admirals—are the objects of our study in this book.

We want to ask questions such as: Who occupies the top positions of authority in America? How concentrated or dispersed is power in this nation? How do these institutional leaders attain their positions? What are their backgrounds, attitudes, and goals? Can we distinguish between leaders in corporations, government, broadcasting, law, foundations, investments, universities, or private civic and cultural organizations in terms of their class backgrounds or recruitment paths? What relationships exist among these people of power? How much cohesion or competition characterizes their relationships? Do they agree or disagree on crucial issues confronting the nation? How do they go about making important decisions or undertaking new programs or policies?

We also want to ask about stability and change: Is America's leadership changing over time? Is there a true "changing of the guard" occurring at the top of the nation's institutional structure, or do top leaders today resemble those of a decade or more ago in terms of social origins, education, attitudes, and experiences? Is power gradually dispersing over time to larger and more diverse leadership groups, or do we find even greater concentrations of power today than a decade ago? Are women and blacks making significant inroads into top positions in America, or are "the higher circles" still nearly all male and all white? And what about those who drop from the ranks of the nation's elite; where are they now?

THE INEVITABILITY OF ELITES

The *elite* are the few who have power in society; the *masses* are the many who do not. We shall call our national leaders "elites" because they possess formal authority over large institutions which shape the lives of all Americans.

America is by no means unique in its concentration of great power in the hands of a few. The universality of elites has been a prominent theme in the works of scholars throughout the ages. The Italian sociologist Vilfredo Pareto put it succinctly: "Every people is governed by an elite, by a chosen element of the population."[1]

Traditional social theorizing about elites views them as essential, functional components of social organization. The necessity of elites derives from the general need for *order* in society. Whenever human beings find themselves living together, they establish a set of ordered relationships so that they can know how others around them will behave. Without ordered behavior, the concept of society itself would be impossible. Among these ordered relationships is the expectation that a few people will make decisions on behalf of the group. Even in primitive societies someone has to

---

[1] V. Pareto, *Mind and Society* (New York: Harcourt Brace Jovanovich, 1935), p. 246.

decide when the hunt will begin, how it will proceed, and what will be done with the catch.

Nearly two centuries ago Alexander Hamilton defended the existence of the elite by writing:

> All communities divide themselves into the few and the many. The first are the rich and well-born, the other the masses of people. The voice of the people has been said to be the voice of God; and however generally this maxim has been quoted and believed, it is not true in fact. The people are turbulent and changing, they seldom judge or determine right.[2]

The Italian political scientist Gaetano Mosca agreed:

> In all societies—from societies that are very underdeveloped and have largely attained the dawnings of civilization, down to the most advanced and powerful societies—two classes of people appear—a class that rules and a class that is ruled. The first class always the less numerous, performs all of the political functions, monopolizes power, and enjoys the advantages that power brings, whereas the second, the more numerous class, is directed and controlled by the first, in a manner that is now more or less legal, now more or less arbitrary and violent.[3]

Contemporary social scientists have echoed the same theme. Sociologist Robert Lynd writes:

> It is the necessity in each society—if it is to be a society, not a rabble—to order the relations of men and their institutional ways of achieving needed ends.... Organized power exists—always and everywhere, in societies large or small, primitive or modern—because it performs the necessary function of establishing and maintaining the version of order by which a given society in a given time and place lives.[4]

Political scientists Harold Lasswell and Daniel Lerner are even more explicit: "The discovery that in all large-scale societies the decisions at any given time are typically in the hands of a small number of people, confirms a basic fact: Government is always government by the few, whether in the name of the few, the one, or the many."[5]

Elitism is *not* a result of inadequate education of the masses, or of poverty, or of a "military-industrial complex," or of capitalist control of the mass media, or of any special problem in society. The necessity for

[2]A. Hamilton, *Records of the Federal Convention* of 1797.

[3]G. Mosca, *The Ruling Class* (New York: McGraw-Hill Book Co., 1939), p. 50.

[4]Robert Lynd, "Power in American Society," in *Problems of Power in American Society*, ed. Arthur Kornhauser (Detroit: Wayne State University Press, 1957), pp. 3–4.

[5]Harold Lasswell and Daniel Lerner, *The Comparative Study of Elites* (Stanford, Calif.: Stanford University Press, 1952), p. 7.

leadership in social organizations applies universally. Robert Michels, who as a student was active in socialist politics in Europe in the early 1900s, concluded reluctantly that elitism was *not* a product of capitalism. *All* large organizations—political parties, labor unions, governments—are oligarchies, even radical *socialist* parties. In Michels' words, "He who says organization says oligarchy." Michels explains his famous "iron law of oligarchy" as a characteristic of *any* social system.[6]

Thus, the elitist character of American society is not a product of political conspiracy, capitalist exploitation, or any specific malfunction of democracy. *All* societies are elitist. There cannot be large institutions without great power being concentrated within the hands of the few at the top of these institutions.

THE INSTITUTIONAL BASIS OF POWER

Power is not an attribute of individuals, but of social organizations. Power is the potential for control in society that accompanies certain roles in the social system. This notion reflects Max Weber's classic formulation of the definition of power:

> In general, we understand by "power" the *chance* of a number of men to realize their own will in a communal act even against the resistance of others who are participating in the action.[7]

"Chance" in this context means the opportunity or capacity for effecting one's will. Viewed in this fashion, power is not so much the *act* of control as the *potential to act*—the social *expectation* that such control is possible and legitimate—that defines power.

Power is simply the capacity or potential of persons in certain roles to make decisions that affect the conduct of others in the social system. Sociologist Robert O. Schultze puts it in these words:

> ... a few have emphasized that *act as such* rather than the *potential to act* is the crucial aspect of power. It seems far more sociologically sound to accept a Weberian definition which stresses the potential to act. Power may thus be conceived as an inherently group-linked property, an attribute of social statuses rather than of individual persons.... Accordingly, power will denote the *capacity* or *potential* of persons *in certain statuses* to set conditions, make decisions, and/or take actions which are determinative for the existence of others within a given social system.[8]

[6]Robert Michels, *Political Parties: A Sociological Study of the Oligarchical Tendencies of Modern Democracy* (1915) (New York: Free Press, 1962), p. 70.

[7]Hans Gerth and C. Wright Mill, eds., *From Max Weber* (New York: Oxford University Press, 1946), p. 180.

[8]Robert O. Schultze, "The Bifurcation of Power in a Satellite City," in *Community Political Systems*, ed. Morris Janowitz (Glencoe: Free Press, 1961), p. 20.

Thus, elites are people who occupy power roles in society. In a modern, complex society, these roles are institutionalized; the elite are the individuals who occupy positions of authority in large institutions. Authority is the expected and legitimate capacity to direct, manage, and guide programs, policies, and activities of the major institutions of society.

It is true, of course, that not all power is institutionalized. Power can be exercised in transitory and informal groups and in interpersonal interactions. Power is exercised, for example, when a mugger stops a pedestrian on the street and forces him to give up his wallet, or when a political assassin murders a President. But great power is found only in institutional roles. C. Wright Mills, a socialist critic of the structure of power in American society, observed:

> No one...can be truly powerful unless he has access to the command of major institutions, for it is over these institutional means of power that the truly powerful are, in the first instance, powerful.[9]

Adolf A. Berle, who spent a lifetime studying private property and the American corporation, was equally impressed with the institutional basis of power:

> Power is invariably organized and transmitted through institutions. Top power holders must work through existing institutions, perhaps extending or modifying them, or must at once create new institutions. There is no other way of exercising power—unless it is limited to the range of the power holder's fist or his gun.[10]

Individuals do not become powerful simply because they have particular qualities, valuable skills, burning ambitions, or sparkling personalities. These assets may be helpful in gaining positions of power, but it is the position itself that gives an individual control over the activities of other individuals. This relationship between power and institutional authority in modern society is described by Mills:

> If we took the one hundred most powerful men in America, the one hundred wealthiest, and the one hundred most celebrated away from the institutional positions they now occupy, away from their resources of men and women and money, away from the media of mass communication... then they would be powerless and poor and uncelebrated. For power is not of a man. Wealth does not center in the person of the wealthy. Celebrity is not inherent in any personality. To be celebrated, to be wealthy, to have power, requires access to major institutions, for the institutional positions men occupy determine in large part their chances to have and to hold these valued experiences.[11]

---

[9]C. Wright Mills, *The Power Elite* (New York: Oxford University Press, 1956), p. 9.

[10]Adolph A. Berle, *Power* (New York: Harcourt Brace Jovanovich, 1967), p. 92.

[11]Mills, *The Power Elite*, p. 9.

Power, then is an attribute of *roles* in a social system, not an attribute of individuals. People are powerful when they occupy positions of authority and control in social organizations. Once they occupy these positions, their power is felt as a result not only in their actions but in their failures to act as well. Both have great impact on the behaviors of others. Elites "are in positions to make decisions having major consequences. Whether they do or do not make such decisions is less important than the fact that they do occupy such pivotal positions: their failure to act, their failure to make a decision, is itself an act that is often of greater consequence than the decisions they do make."[12]

Political scientists Peter Bachrach and Morton S. Baratz have argued persuasively that individuals in top institutional positions exercise power whether they act overtly to influence particular decisions or not.[13] They contend that when the social, economic, and political values of elite groups, or, more importantly, the structure of the institutions themselves, limit the scope of decision-making to only those issues which do not threaten top elites, then power is being exercised. Bachrach and Baratz refer to this phenomenon as *"non*-decision making." A has power over B when he or she succeeds in suppressing issues that might in their resolution be detrimental to A's preferences. In short, the institutional structure of our society (and the people at the top of that structure) encourages the development of some kinds of public issues, but prevents other kinds of issues from ever being considered by the American public. Such "non-decision making" provides still another reason for studying institutional leadership.

POWER AS DECISION-MAKING:
AN ALTERNATIVE VIEW

It is our contention, then, that great power is institutionalized—that it derives from roles in social organizations and that individuals who occupy top institutional positions possess power whether they act directly to influence particular decisions or not. But these views—often labeled as "elitist"—are not universally shared among social scientists. We are aware that our institutional approach to power conflicts with the approach of many scholars who believe that power can only be viewed in a decision-making context.

This alternative approach to power—often labeled as "pluralist"—defines power as *active participation in decision-making.* Persons are said to

---

[12]*Ibid.,* p. 4.

[13]Peter Bachrach and Morton S. Baratz, "Decisions and Non-Decisions," *American Political Science Review,* 57 (September 1963), pp. 632–642.

have power *only* when they participate directly in particular decisions. Pluralist scholars would object to our presumption that people who occupy institutional positions and who have formal authority over economic, governmental, or social affairs necessarily have power. Pluralists differentiate between the "potential" for power (which is generally associated with top institutional positions) and "actual" power (which assumes active participation in decision-making). Political scientist Robert A. Dahl writes:

> Suppose a set of individuals in a political system has the following property: there is a high probability that if they agree on a key political alternative, and if they all act in some specified way, then that alternative will be chosen. We may say of such a group that it has a high *potential* for control.... But a *potential* for control is not, except in a peculiarly Hobbesian world, equivalent to *actual* control.[14]

Pluralists contend that the potential for power is not power itself. Power occurs in individual interactions: "A has power over B to the extent that he can get B to do something that B would not otherwise do."[15] We should not simply assume that power attaches to high office. Top institutional officeholders may or may not exercise power—their "power" depends upon their active participation in particular decisions. They may choose not to participate in certain decisions; their influence may be limited to specific kinds of decisions; they may be constrained by formal and informal checks on their discretion; they may be forced to respond to the demands of individuals or groups within or outside the institutions they lead; they may have little real discretion in their choice among alternative courses of action.

Pluralists would argue that research into institutional leadership can describe at best only the *potential* for control that exists within American society. They would insist that research on national leadership proceed by careful examination of a series of important national decisions—that the individuals who took an active part in these decisions be identified and a full account of their decision-making behavior be obtained. Political scientist Nelson Polsby, a former student of Robert A. Dahl at Yale, reflects the interests of pluralists in observing specific decisions:

> How can one tell, after all, whether or not an actor is powerful unless some sequence of events, competently observed, attests to his power? If these events take place, then the power of the actor is not "potential" but actual. If these events do not occur, then what grounds have we to suppose that the actor is powerful?[16]

[14]Robert A. Dahl, "Critique of the Ruling Elite Model," *American Political Science Review,* 52 (June 1958), p. 66 [Italics mine.]

[15]Robert A. Dahl, "The Concept of Power," *Behavioral Science,* 2 (1957), p. 202.

[16]Nelson Polsby, *Community Power and Political Theory* (New Haven: Yale University Press, 1963), p. 60.

And, indeed, much of the best research and writing in political science has proceeded by studying specific cases in the uses of power.

Pluralism, of course, is more than a definition of power and a method of study—it is an integrated body of theory that seeks to reaffirm the fundamental democratic character of American society. Pluralism arose in response to criticisms of the American political system to the effect that individual participation in a large, complex, bureaucratic society was increasingly difficult. Traditional notions of democracy had stressed individual participation of all citizens in the decisions that shape their own lives. But it was clear to scholars of all persuasions that relatively few individuals in America have any *direct* impact on national decision-making.

Pluralism developed as an ideology designed to reconcile the *ideals* of democracy with the *realities* of a large-scale, industrial, technocratic society. Jack L. Walker writes that the "principal aim" of the pluralists "has been to make the theory of democracy more realistic, to bring it into closer correspondence with empirical reality. They are convinced that the classical theory does not account for 'much of the real machinery' by which the system operates."[17]

Pluralists recognize that an elite few, rather than the masses, rule America and that "it is difficult—nay impossible—to see how it could be otherwise in large political systems."[18] However, they reassert the essentially democratic character of America by arguing that:

1. While individuals do not participate directly in decision-making, they can join organized *groups* and make their influence felt through group participation.
2. Competition between leadership groups helps protect the individual—that is, countervailing centers of power check each other and guard against abuse of power.
3. Individuals can choose between competing groups in elections.
4. Leadership groups are not closed; new groups can be formed and gain access to the political system.
5. The existence of multiple leadership groups in society gives rise to a "polyarchy." Leaders who exercise power over some kinds of decisions do not necessarily exercise power over other kinds of decisions.
6. Public policy may not be majority preference, but it is the rough equilibrium of group influence and therefore a reasonable approximation of society's preferences.

We are committed in this volume to the study of the institutional structure of American society, for the reasons cited earlier. It is *not* our purpose to assert the superiority of our approach to power in America over

---

[17]Jack L. Walker, "A Critique of the Elitist Theory of Democracy," *American Political Science Review*, 60 (June 1966), p. 286.

[18]Robert A. Dahl, "Power, Pluralism and Democracy," paper delivered at the Annual Meeting of the American Political Science Association, 1966, p. 3.

the approaches recommended by others. We do *not* intend to debate the merits of "pluralism" or "elitism" as political philosophies. Abstract arguments over conceptualizations, definitions, and method of study already abound in the literature on power. Rather, working within an *institutional* paradigm, we intend to present systematic evidence about the concentration of resources in the nation's largest institutions, to find out who occupies top positions in these institutions, to explore interlocking and convergence among these top position-holders, to learn how they rose to their positions, to investigate the extent of their consensus or disagreement over the major issues confronting the nation, to explore the extent of competition and factionalism among various segments of the nation's institutional leadership, and to learn how institutional leadership interacts in national policy-making.

We hope to avoid elaborate theorizing about power, pluralism, and elitism. We propose to present what we believe to be interesting data on national institutional elites and to permit our readers to relate it to their own theories of power.

IDENTIFYING POSITIONS OF POWER

A great deal has been said about "the power elite," "the ruling class," "the liberal establishment," "the military-industrial complex," "the rich and the super-rich," and so on. But even though many of these notions are interesting and insightful, we never really encounter a systematic definition of precisely *who* these people are, how we can identify them, how they came to power, and what they do with their power.

Admittedly, the systematic study of power and elites is a frustrating task. Political scientists Herbert Kaufman and Victor Jones once observed:

> There is an elusiveness about power that endows it with an almost ghostly quality. It seems to be all around us, yet this is "sensed" with some sixth means of reception rather than with the five ordinary senses. We "know" what it is, yet we encounter endless difficulties in trying to define it. We can "tell" whether one person or group is more powerful than another, yet we cannot measure power. It is as abstract as time yet as real as a firing squad.[19]

We agree that power is elusive and that elites are not easy to identify, particularly in a society like ours. Scholars have encountered great difficulty in finding a specific working definition of a national elite—a definition that can be used to actually identify powerful people. However, this is the necessary starting place for any serious inquiry into power in America.

[19]Herbert Kaufman and Victor Jones, "The Mystery of Power," *Public Administration Review,* 14 (Summer 1954), p. 205.

Our first task, therefore, is to develop an operational *definition* of a national elite. We must formulate a definition that is consistent with our theoretical notions about the institutional basis of power and that will enable us to identify, by name and position, those individuals who possess great power in America.

Our institutional "elites" will be individuals who occupy *the top positions in the institutional structure of American society.* These are the individuals who possess the formal authority to formulate, direct, and manage programs, policies, and activities of the major corporate, governmental, legal, educational, civic, and cultural institutions in the nation. Our definition of a national elite, then, is consistent with the notion that great power in America resides in large institutions.

For purposes of analysis, we have divided American society into twelve sectors: (1) industrial corporations, (2) utilities, transportation, and communications, (3) banking, (4) insurance, (5) investments, (6) mass media, (7) law, (8) education, (9) foundations, (10) civic and cultural organizations, (11) government, and (12) the military. In the corporate sectors, our operational definition of the elite is *those individuals who occupy formal positions of authority in institutions which control over half of the nation's total corporate assets.* Our procedure in identifying the largest institutions was to rank corporations by the size of their assets, and to cumulate these assets, moving from the top of the rankings down, until at least 50 percent of the nation's total assets in each sector are included (see Tables 2–1, 2–2, 2–3, and 2–4 in the next chapter). We also identified the nation's fifteen largest Wall Street investment firms (see Table 2–5). Then we identified by name the presidents, officer-directors, and directors of these corporations.

We also included in our definition of the elite *those individuals who occupy formal positions of authority in the mass media, the large prestigious New York and Washington law firms, the well-endowed private universities, the major philanthropic foundations, and the most influential civic and cultural organizations.* The identification of these institutions involved some subjective judgments. These judgments can be defended, but we recognize that other judgments could be made. In the *mass media,* we include the three television networks (CBS, ABC, and NBC); the *New York Times;* Time, Inc.; *The Washington Post* and *Newsweek;* Associated Press and United Press International wire services; and ten newspaper chains which account for over one third of the nation's daily newspaper circulation. Because of the rapidly growing influence of the news media in America's elite structure, we have devoted a special chapter to "The Newsmakers."

Leadership in a variety of sectors is considered under the general heading of "The Civic Establishment." These leaders include the senior partners or directors of the nation's fifteen largest Wall Street *investment* firms. In *education,* we identify the twenty-five colleges and universities with the largest private endowment funds; we exclude public universities. Our 25 universities, however, control over 50 percent of all private endowment funds in higher education, and they are consistently ranked among the nation's most "prestigious" private colleges and universities. Our leadership group includes their presidents and trustees. Our selection of foundations is based on *The Foundation Directory*'s data on the nation's fifty largest foundations. These foundations, and their trustees/directors, control over 50 percent of all foundation assets. Identifying top positions in the *law* was an even more subjective task. Our definition of positions of authority in the law includes the senior partners of twenty-five large and influential New York and Washington law firms. Top positions in *civic and cultural affairs* were identified by qualitative evaluations of the prestige and influence of various well-known organizations. The civic organizations are the Council on Foreign Relations, Brookings Institution, the Committee for Economic Development, the Business Roundtable, the National Association of Manufacturers, the American Red Cross, and the American Assembly. The cultural organizations are the Metropolitan Opera, the National Gallery of Art, the John F. Kennedy Center for Performing Arts, the Museum of Modern Art, and the Smithsonian Institute. The members of the governing boards of trustees or directors were included in our definition of institutional leadership.

In the governmental sectors, the operational definition of the elite is *those individuals who occupy formal positions of authority in the major civilian and military bureaucracies of the national government.* Positions of authority in government were defined as the President and Vice-President; secretaries, under secretaries, and assistant secretaries of all executive departments; Senior White House presidential advisers and ambassadors-at-large; congressional committee chairpersons and ranking minority committee members in the House and Senate; House and Senate majority and minority party leaders and whips; Supreme Court Justices; and members of the Federal Reserve Board and the Council of Economic Advisers. Positions of authority in *the military* include both civilian offices and top military commands: secretaries, under secretaries, and assistant secretaries of the Departments of the Army, Navy, and Air Force; all four-star generals and admirals in the Army, Navy, Air Force, and Marine Corps, including the chairperson of the Joint Chiefs of Staff; and the chiefs of staff and vice-chiefs of staff of the Army and Air Force, the chief and vice-chief of Naval Operations, and the commanding officers of the major military commands.

Any effort to operationalize a concept as broad as a national institutional elite is bound to generate discussion over the inclusion or exclusion of specific sectors, institutions, or positions. (Why law, but not medicine? Why not law firms in Chicago, Houston, or Atlanta? Why not religious institutions or labor unions? Why not governors or mayors of big cities?) *Systematic* research on national elites is still in the exploratory stage, and there are no explicit guidelines. Our choices involve many subjective judgments. Let us see, however, what we can learn about concentration, specialization, and interlocking using the definitions above; perhaps other researchers can improve upon our attempt to operationalize this elusive notion of a national institutional elite. In the analysis to follow, we will present findings for our aggregate elites, and for specific sectors of these elites. Clearly, findings for specific sectors will be free of whatever bias might exist in the aggregate elite as a result of our inclusion or exclusion of specific sectors.

DIMENSIONS OF AMERICA'S ELITE:
THE TOP SEVEN THOUSAND

Our definition of a national institutional elite results in the identification of 7,314 elite positions:

Corporate Sectors	Number of Leadership Positions
1. Industrial corporations (100)	1,475
2. Utilities, communications, transportation (50)	668
3. Banks (50)	1,092
4. Insurance (50)	611
5. Investments (15)	479
Total	4,325
Public Interest Sectors	
6. Mass media (18)	220
7. Education (25)	892
8. Foundations (50)	402
9. Law (25)	758
10. Civic and cultural organizations (12)	433
Total	2,705
Governmental Sector	
11. Legislative, executive, judicial	236
12. Military	48
Total	284
Total	7,314

These top positions, taken collectively, control half of the nation's industrial assets; half of all assets in communication, transportation, and utilities; half of all banking assets; two thirds of all insurance assets; and they direct Wall Street's largest investment firms. They control the television networks, the influential news agencies, and the major newspaper chains. They control nearly 40 percent of all the assets of private foundations and half of all private university endowments. They direct the nation's largest and best-known New York and Washington law firms as well as the nation's major civic and cultural organizations. They occupy key federal governmental positions in the executive, legislative, and judicial branches. And they occupy all the top command positions in the Army, Navy, Air Force, and Marines.

These aggregate figures—roughly 7,000 positions—are themselves important indicators of the concentration of authority and control in American society. Of course, these figures are the direct product of our specific definition of top institutional positions.[20] Yet these aggregate statistics provide us with an explicit definition and quantitative estimate of the size of the national elite in America.

SOME QUESTIONS FOR RESEARCH

Our definition of America's institutional elite provides a starting place for exploring some of the central questions confronting students of power. How concentrated are institutional resources in America? How much concentration exists in industry and finance, in government, in the mass media, in education, in the law, in the foundations, and in civic and cultural affairs? Who are the people at the top of the nation's institutional structure? How did they get there? Did they inherit their positions or work their way up through the ranks of the institutional hierarchy? What are their general attitudes, beliefs, and goals? What do they think about their own power? Do elites in America generally agree about major national goals and the general directions of foreign and domestic policy, and limit their disagreements to the *means* of achieving their goals and the details of policy implementation? Or do leaders disagree over fundamental *ends* and values and the future character of American society?

Are institutional elites in America "interlocked" or "specialized"? That is, is there convergence at the "top" of the institutional structure in America, with the same group of people dominating decision-making in industry, finance, education, government, the mass media, foundations, law, investments, and civic and cultural affairs? Or is there a separate elite in each sector of society with little or no overlap in authority? Are there opportunities to rise to the top of the leadership structure for individuals from both sexes, all classes, races, religions, and ethnic groups, through multiple career paths in different sectors of society? Or are opportunities

---

[20]In earlier editions of this volume, using data from 1970–71, we included only 5,416 positions. In this volume, using data from 1980–81, we added the investment firms and expanded the number of utilities, insurance companies, universities, and foundations. This produced 7,314 positions. Thus, even minor changes in the definition of an elite can produce substantial differences in the overall size of the elite.

to acquire key leadership roles generally limited to white, Anglo-Saxon, Protestant, upper- and upper-middle class males whose careers are based primarily in industry and finance? Is the nation's institutional leadership recruited primarily from private "name" prep schools and "Ivy League" universities? Do leaders join the same clubs, intermarry, and enjoy the same life styles? Or is there diversity in educational backgrounds, social ties, club memberships, and life styles among the elite?

How much competition and conflict takes place among America's institutional elite? Are there clear-cut factions within the nation's leadership struggling for preeminence and power, and if so, what are the underlying sources of this factionalism? Do different segments of the nation's institutional elite accommodate each other in a system of bargaining, negotiation, and compromising based on a widely shared consensus of values?

How do institutional elites make national policy? Are there established institutions and procedures for elite interaction, communication, and consensus building on national policy questions? Or are such questions decided in a relatively unstructured process of competition, bargaining, and compromise among a large number of diverse individuals and interest groups? Do the "proximate policy makers"—the President, Congress, courts—respond to mass opinion, or do they respond primarily to initiatives originating from the elite policy-planning organizations?

Is America's leadership changing over time, and if so, how? Is power becoming more or less concentrated or dispersed over time? Is there more or less "interlocking" today than a decage ago? Do the same types of people occupy top leadership positions today as compared to a decade ago? Have blacks and women gained significant representation among top positions over the last ten years?

These are the questions that we will tackle in the pages to follow. In Part II, Institutional Leadership in America, we will describe the concentration of power in a limited number of institutions in various sectors of society. We will also describe in general terms the type of individuals who occupy top positions in these institutions; we will provide a number of brief biographical sketches suggestive of the characteristics of these elites—who they are and how they got there. These sketches are designed to "personalize" the statistical analysis that follows. In Part III, The Structure of Institutional Elites, we will examine the questions posed above in a more systematic fashion, employing computerized data files on our top 7,000 elites.

PART TWO

Institutional leadership
in
America

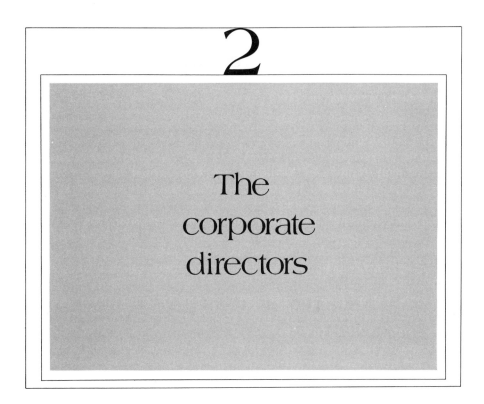

2

The corporate directors

A great deal of power is organized into large economic institutions—industrial corporations, banks, utilities, insurance companies, and invest-ment firms. Control of economic resources provides a continuous and important base of power in any society. Economic organizations decide what will be produced, how it will be produced, how much will be produced, how much it will cost, how many people will be employed, and who will be employed and what their wages will be. They determine how goods and services will be distributed, what technology will be developed, what profits will be made and how they will be distributed, how much money will be available for loans, how much money will be available for capital investment and under what terms it will be made available, what interest rates will be charged, and many similarly important questions.

Obviously, these decisions affect our lives as much as, or perhaps even more than, those typically made by governments. We cannot draw inferences about a "national power structure" from studies of governmen-tal decision-making alone. Studies of power in society must include economic power.

THE CONCENTRATION OF ECONOMIC POWER

Economic power in America is highly concentrated. Indeed, only about 4,500 individuals—two one-thousandths of 1 percent of the population—exercise formal authority over half of the nation's industrial assets, over half of all banking assets, over half of all assets in communications, transportation, and utilities, and over two thirds of all insurance assets. These individuals are the presidents, officer-directors, and directors of the largest corporations in these fields. The reason for this concentration of power in the hands of so few people is found in the concentration of industrial and financial assets in a small number of giant corporations. The following statistics can only suggest the scale and concentration of modern corporate enterprise in America.

There are about 200,000 *industrial corporations* in the United States with total assets in 1980 of about $1.2 trillion. The 100 corporations listed in Table 2–1 control 55.0 percent ($683 billion) of all industrial assets. The five largest industrial corporations—Exxon (formerly Standard Oil of New Jersey), General Motors, Mobil, IBM, and Ford—control 13 percent of all industrial assets.

The concentration of resources among a relatively few industrial corporations is slowly increasing over time. In a 38-year period, the proportion of all industrial assets controlled by the top 100 corporations grew as follows:

1950	1955	1960	1965	1970	1976	1980
39.8%	44.3%	46.4%	46.5%	52.3%	54.9%	55.0%

Concentration in *transportation, communications,* and *utilities* is even greater than in industry. Fifty corporations (see Table 2–2), out of 67,000 in these fields, control over two-thirds of the nation's assets in airlines and railroads, communications, and electricity and gas. This sector of the nation's economy is dominated by the American Telephone and Telegraph Company (AT&T)—the single largest private corporation in the world. AT&T has over 100 billion dollars in assets, 70 million customers, and a work force larger than the U.S. Army—over one million employees. Although AT&T is now divesting itself of 22 subsidiary Bell companies, this giant utility company will remain America's largest corporation.

The financial world is equally concentrated. The 50 largest *banks* (see Table 2–3), out of 17,700 banks serving the nation, control 61.3 percent of all banking assets. Three banks (Bank America, Citicorp, and Chase Manhattan) control 19.4 percent of all banking assets.

In the *insurance* field, 50 companies (see Table 2–4) out of 1,890 control over 75 percent of all insurance assets. Two companies (Prudential and Metropolitan) control nearly one quarter of all insurance assets.

Table 2–1 The 100 Largest Industrial Corporations (Ranked by assets)

Rank	Corporation	Assets (B$)	Cumulative Percent*
1	Exxon	49.5	4.0
2	General Motors	32.2	6.6
3	Mobil	27.5	8.8
4	International Business Mach.	24.5	10.8
5	Ford Motor	23.5	12.7
6	Texaco	23.0	14.9
7	Standard Oil of California	18.1	16.4
8	Gulf Oil	17.3	17.8
9	Standard Oil (Ind.)	17.1	19.2
10	General Electric	16.6	20.5
11	Shell Oil	16.1	21.8
12	Intl. Telephone & Telegraph	15.1	23.0
13	Atlantic Richfield	13.8	24.1
14	Tenneco	11.6	25.1
15	U.S. Steel	11.0	25.9
16	Dow Chemical	10.3	26.8
17	Conoco	9.3	27.5
18	Standard Oil (Ohio)	9.2	28.3
19	E.I. du Pont de Nemours	8.9	29.0
20	Union Carbide	8.8	29.7
21	Phillips Petroleum	8.5	30.4
22	Eastman Kodak	7.6	31.0
23	Sun	7.5	31.6
24	Western Electric	7.1	32.2
25	Westinghouse Electric	6.8	32.7
26	Chrysler	6.7	33.2
27	Xerox	6.6	33.8
28	United Technologies	6.4	34.3
29	R.J. Reynolds	6.4	34.8
30	Philip Morris	6.4	35.3
31	Getty Oil	6.0	35.8
32	Union Oil of California	6.0	36.3
33	RCA	6.0	36.8
34	Procter & Gamble	5.7	37.2
35	Occidental Petroleum	5.6	37.7
36	Monsanto	5.5	38.1
37	Caterpillar Tractor	5.4	38.6
38	Goodyear	5.4	39.0
39	International Harvester	5.2	39.4
40	Bethlehem Steel	5.2	39.8
41	Gulf & Western	5.2	40.3
42	Union Pacific	5.1	40.7
43	Weyerhaeuser	4.9	41.1
44	Amerada Hess	4.9	41.5
45	Boeing	4.9	41.9
46	International Paper	4.8	42.2
47	Cities Service	4.8	42.6
48	Aluminum Co. of America	4.7	43.0
49	Minnesota Mining & Manufacturing	4.6	43.4
50	Marathon Oil	4.3	43.7
51	Allied Chemical	4.2	44.1
52	Deere	4.2	44.4
53	Rockwell International	4.1	44.7

Table 2–1   The 100 Largest Industrial Corporations (Ranked by assets) (continued)

Rank	Corporation	Assets (B$)	Cumulative Percent*
54	Georgia-Pacific	4.1	45.1
55	AMAX	3.9	45.4
56	LTV	3.9	45.7
57	W.R. Grace	3.7	46.0
58	Sperry	3.7	46.3
59	American Brands	3.7	46.6
60	Beatrice Foods	3.7	46.9
61	IC Industries	3.7	47.2
62	Continental Group	3.6	47.5
63	Firestone	3.5	47.8
64	Burroughs	3.7	48.0
65	McDonnell Douglas	3.4	48.3
66	Honeywell	3.3	48.6
67	J.Ray McDermott	3.3	48.8
68	Armco	3.3	49.1
69	National Steel	3.2	49.4
70	Ashland Oil	3.1	49.6
71	Pfizer	3.0	49.8
72	Champion International	3.0	50.1
73	Kaiser Aluminum	3.0	50.3
74	Coca-Cola	2.9	50.6
75	Reynolds Metals	2.9	50.8
76	NCR	2.9	51.0
77	Owens-Illinois	2.9	51.3
78	PepsiCo	2.9	51.5
79	Johnson & Johnson	2.9	51.7
80	Warner-Lambert	2.9	52.0
81	Litton	2.9	52.2
82	Signal Companies	2.8	52.3
83	American Cyanamid	2.8	52.4
84	Kennecott Copper	2.4	52.6
85	Republic Steel	2.7	52.8
86	Inland Steel	2.7	53.1
87	Superior Oil	2.7	53.3
88	American Can	2.7	53.5
89	PPG Industries	2.6	53.7
90	TRW	2.6	53.9
91	Merck	2.6	54.1
92	General Foods	2.6	54.3
93	Kraft	2.5	54.5
94	Dresser	2.5	54.7
95	Borden	2.5	54.9
96	FMC	2.4	55.1
97	Colgate-Palmolive	2.4	55.3
98	Diamond Shamrock	2.4	55.5
99	Esmark	2.4	55.7
100	Norton Simon	2.4	55.9

Total Industrial Assets: $1,241 B
Total Number of Industrial Corporations: 197,807

*In this table, and in Tables 2–3 and 2–4, cumulative percent refers to the total percentage of the nation's assets in, for example, industrial enterprise at a specific ranking. Thus, the first ten corporations (through General Electric) account for 20.5 percent of the nation's industrial assets. All figures are for 1980.

Table 2–2   The 50 Largest Utilities, Transportation, and Communication Companies (Ranked by assets)

Rank	Company	Assets (B$)
1	AT&T (American Telephone & Telegraph)	113.8
2	General Telephone & Electronics	18.4
3	Southern Company	10.6
4	Pacific Gas & Electric	10.3
5	Commonwealth Edison	9.2
6	American Electric Power	8.8
7	Consolidated Edison	7.1
8	Southern California Edison	7.0
9	Middle South Utilities	6.5
10	Public Service Electric & Gas	6.1
11	Virginia Electric & Power	6.0
12	Texas Utilities	5.8
13	Duke Power	5.6
14	Consumers Power	5.6
15	Philadelphia Electric	5.3
16	Detroit Edison	5.1
17	Southern Pacific	5.0
18	General Public Utilities	5.0
19	Florida Power & Light	4.8
20	Burlington Northern	4.2
21	American National Resources	3.9
22	Santa Fe Industries	3.9
23	United Telecommunications	3.9
24	REAL	3.9
25	Houston Industries	3.8
26	Pennsylvania, Power & Light	3.8
27	Central & South West	3.6
28	Carolina Power & Light	3.6
29	Columbus Gas System	3.6
30	El Paso	3.6
31	Niagara Mohawk Power	3.5
32	Long Island Lighting	3.5
33	Ohio Edison	3.4
34	Chessie System	3.4
35	Seaboard Coastline Industries	3.4
36	Texas Eastern Corp.	3.2
37	Northeast Utilities	3.2
38	American Airlines	3.2
39	Union Electric	3.2
40	Pacific Power & Light	3.1
41	Ohio Pipe Line	3.1
42	Peoples Gas	3.0
43	Continental Telephone	2.9
44	Southern Ry.	2.9
45	Baltimore Gas & Electric	2.9
46	Allegheny Power System	2.9
47	Northern Natural Gas	2.8
48	Transco Companies	2.8
49	Cleveland Electric Illuminating	2.7
50	Panhandle Eastern Pipe Line	2.6

Table 2–3   The 50 Largest Commercial-Banking Companies (Ranked by assets)

Rank	Corporation	Assets (B$)	Cumulative Percent
1	BankAmerica Corporation (San Francisco)	108.3	7.5
2	Citicorp (New York)	106.3	14.9
3	Chase Manhattan Corporation (New York)	64.7	19.4
4	Manufacturers Hanover Corp. (New York)	47.7	22.7
5	J.P. Morgan & Co. (New York)	43.5	25.8
6	Chemical New York Corporation	39.4	28.5
7	Continental Illinois Corporation (Chicago)	35.8	31.0
8	Bankers Trust New York	31.0	33.2
9	First Chicago Corporation	30.1	35.3
10	Western Bancorp. (Los Angeles)	29.7	37.3
11	Security Pacific Corporation (Los Angeles)	24.9	39.0
12	Wells Fargo & Co. (San Francisco)	20.6	40.5
13	Irving Bank Corporation (New York)	16.7	41.6
14	Crocker National Corp. (San Francisco)	16.1	42.8
15	Marine Midland Banks (Buffalo)	15.7	43.9
16	First National Boston Corporation	13.8	44.8
17	Mellon National Corporation (Pittsburgh)	13.5	45.8
18	Northwest Bancorp. (Minneapolis)	12.4	46.6
19	First Bank System (Minneapolis)	12.1	47.5
20	First International Bancshares (Dallas)	11.5	48.3
21	Republic of Texas Corporation (Dallas)	10.8	49.0
22	National Detroit Corporation	9.5	49.7
23	First City Bancorp. of Texas (Houston)	9.5	50.3
24	Texas Commerce Bancshares (Houston)	9.3	51.0
25	Bank of New York Co.	9.0	51.6
26	First Pennsylvania Corp. (Philadelphia)	9.0	52.2
27	Seafirst Corporation (Seattle)	8.4	52.8
28	European American Bancorp. (New York)	7.8	53.4
29	Harris Bankcorp (Chicago)	7.1	53.8
30	Union Bank (Los Angeles)	6.6	54.3
31	NCNB Corporation (Charlotte)	6.4	54.8
32	Philadelphia National Corporation	5.9	55.2
33	Pittsburgh National Corporation	5.6	55.6
34	AmeriTrust Corporation (Cleveland)	5.4	55.9
35	Michigan National Corporation	5.4	56.3
36	Northern Trust Corporation (Chicago)	5.4	56.7
37	Valley National Bank of Arizona	5.2	57.0
38	First Wisconsin Corporation	5.1	57.4
39	Wachovia Corporation (Winston-Salem)	5.1	57.8
40	Detroitbank Corporation	5.1	58.1
41	Southeast Banking Corporation (Miami)	5.0	58.5
42	BancOhio Corporation (Columbus)	5.0	58.8
43	National Cit Corporation (Cleveland)	5.0	59.2
44	National Bank of North America (New York)	4.8	59.5
45	Mercantile Texas Corporation (Dallas)	4.7	59.8
46	Manufacturers National Corporation (Detroit)	4.5	60.1
47	Rainier Bancorp. (Seattle)	4.5	60.4
48	U.S. Bancorp. (Portland)	4.4	60.7
49	Republic New York Corporation	4.4	61.0
50	Girard Co. (Philadelphia)	4.4	61.4

Total Commercial Banking Assets: 1,437.7 B$
Total Number of Commercial Banks: 14,738

Table 2–4   The 50 Largest Life-Insurance Companies (Ranked by assets)

Rank	Company	Assets (B$)	Cumulative Percent
1	Prudential (Newark)	54.7	12.7
2	Metropolitan (New York)	45.0	23.1
3	Equitable Life Assurance (New York)	30.8	30.2
4	Aetna Life (Hartford)	18.6	34.5
5	New York Life	18.5	38.8
6	John Hancock Mutual (Boston)	17.3	42.8
7	Connecticut General Life (Bloomfield)	12.2	45.6
8	Travelers (Hartford)	11.8	48.3
9	Northwestern Mutual (Milwaukee)	10.6	50.8
10	Massachusetts Mutual (Springfield)	8.3	52.7
11	Teachers Insurance & Annuity (New York)	8.3	54.6
12	Mutual of New York	7.4	56.3
13	Bankers Life (Des Moines)	6.8	57.9
14	New England Mutual (Boston)	6.3	59.4
15	Mutual Benefit (Newark)	5.2	60.6
16	Connecticut Mutual (Hartford)	5.0	61.7
17	Lincoln National Life (Fort Wayne)	4.7	62.8
18	Penn Mutual (Philadelphia)	3.7	63.7
19	Continental Assurance (Chicago)	3.0	64.4
20	Western & Southern (Cincinnati)	2.9	65.0
21	State Farm Life (Bloomington, Ill.)	2.9	65.7
22	National Life & Accident (Nashville)	2.8	66.3
23	Phoenix Mutual (Hartford)	2.8	67.0
24	Pacific Mutual (Newport Beach, Calif.)	2.6	67.6
25	Occidental of California (Los Angeles)	2.6	68.2
26	Franklin Life (Springfield, Ill.)	2.3	68.7
27	American National (Galveston)	2.3	69.3
28	National Life (Montpelier)	2.3	69.8
29	State Mutual of America (Worcester, Mass.)	2.2	70.3
30	Southwestern Life (Dallas)	1.8	70.7
31	Provident Mutual (Philadelphia)	1.8	71.1
32	Guardian of America (New York)	1.8	71.5
33	Home Life (New York)	1.8	72.0
34	Provident Life & Accident (Chattanooga)	1.7	72.4
35	Nationwide Life (Columbus)	1.7	72.8
36	Union Mutual (Portland, Me.)	1.6	73.1
37	United Benefit (Omaha)	1.6	73.5
38	Minnesota Mutual (St. Paul)	1.6	73.9
39	Jefferson Standard (Greensboro, N.C.)	1.6	74.2
40	Northwestern National (Minneapolis)	1.5	74.6
41	Liberty National (Birmingham, Ala.)	1.5	74.9
42	General American Life (St. Louis)	1.5	75.3
43	Aetna Life & Annuity (Hartford)	1.4	75.6
44	Anchor National (Phoenix)	1.4	75.9
45	Life Insurance of Virginia (Richmond)	1.4	76.2
46	Capitol Life (Denver)	1.4	76.6
47	Variable Annuity Life (Houston)	1.3	76.9
48	IDS Life (Minneapolis)	1.3	77.2
49	American United Life (Indianapolis)	1.3	77.5
50	Bankers Life & Casualty (Chicago)	1.3	77.8

Total Life Insurance Assets: 432.3 B$
Total Number of Companies: 1,890

Finally, in the field of *investment* banking, we have identified fifteen major Wall Street firms (see Table 2–5). These firms are in a central strategic position in the American economy. They decide whether, when, and under what terms American corporations (and state and local governments) can sell stocks, bonds, and other securities. These firms "underwrite" the sale of new securities, usually joining together in a large syndicate to do so. They then sell these stocks, bonds, and securities to their own individual and institutional client-investors.

Table 2–5   The Investment Firms

Brown Brothers Harriman & Company
Dean Witter Reynolds Incorporated
Dillon, Read & Company, Inc.
Drexel Burnham Lambert, Inc.
First Boston Corporation
Goldman, Sachs and Company
E. F. Hutton & Company, Inc.
Kidder, Peabody and Company, Inc.
Lehman Brothers Kuhn Loeb, Inc.
Merrill Lynch, Pierce, Fenner and Smith, Inc.
Morgan Stanley and Company, Inc.
Paine Webber Jackson and Curtis, Inc.
Bache Halsey Stuart Shields, Inc.
Salomon Brothers
Lazard Freres and Company

THE MULTINATIONALS: WORLDWIDE BIG BUSINESS

The concentration of industrial power in a relatively few large institutions is not an exclusively American phenomenon. On the contrary, since World War II the growth of world trade, increasing overseas investments, and international corporate mergers all have combined to create giant multinational corporations whose operations span the globe. The trend toward corporate concentration of resources is worldwide. It is not only large American corporations which have expanded their markets throughout the world, invested in overseas plants and banks, and merged with foreign countries. Large European and Japanese firms compete very effectively for world business. Just as American companies have greatly expanded investments abroad, so too have foreign companies sharply increased their business in the United States. The result is the emergence of truly supranational corporations, which not only trade worldwide, but which also build and operate plants in many nations.

The fifty largest industrial corporations *in the world* are listed by their total assets in Table 2–6. Ranked at the top of the list is Royal Dutch Shell,

Table 2–6   The World's Largest Industrial Corporations (Ranking by assets)

Company and Nationality	Industry	Assets in Millions
1. Royal Dutch Shell, U.K. and Neth.	Oil	59,717
2. Exxon, U.S.A.	Oil	49,489
3. British Petroleum, U.K.	Oil	34,779
4. General Motors, U.S.A.	Autos	32,215
5. Mobil, U.S.A.	Oil	27,505
6. IBM, U.S.A.	Business Machines	24,529
7. Ford, U.S.A.	Autos	23,524
8. Texaco, U.S.A.	Oil	22,991
9. ENI, Italy	Oil	19,547
10. Mitsubishi, Japan	Machinery	18,824
11. Phillips Lamp, Neth.	Electrical	18,447
12. Standard Oil of California, U.S.A.	Oil	18,102
13. Gulf Oil, U.S.A.	Oil	17,265
14. Siemens, Germany	Electrical	17,012
15. General Electric, U.S.A.	Electrical	16,644
16. Nippon Steel, Japan	Steel	16,440
17. ELF Aquitane, France	Oil	15,841
18. ITT, U.S.A.	Electronics	15,091
19. Marubeni, Japan	Wholesaler	14,322
20. Francaise de Petroles	Oil	14,279
21. VEBA, Germany	Oil	14,080
22. Atlantic Richfield, U.S.A.	Oil	13,833
23. Bayer, Germany	Drugs	13,775
24. Hatachi, Japan	Electrical	13,308
25. C Itoh, Japan	Wholesaler	13,214
26. Petroles de Venezuela	Oil	13,092
27. Imperial Chemicals, U.K.	Chemicals	12,800
28. Hoechst, Germany	Chemicals	12,710
29. Volkswagenverk, Germany	Autos	12,508
30. Unilever, U.K.	Consumer Goods	12,389
31. Peugeot-Citroen, France	Autos	12,266
32. Renault, France	Autos	11,700
33. Tenneco, U.S.A.	Oil	11,631
34. U.S. Steel, U.S.A.	Steel	11,029
35. Petroleo Brasileiro, Brazil	Oil	11,023
36. RWE, Germany	Oil	11,000
37. British Steel	Steel	10,800
38. Nestlé, Switzerland	Food	10,322
39. Dow Chemical, U.S.A.	Chemicals	10,251
40. BASF, Germany	Chemicals	10,045
41. Nissan, Japan	Autos	10,028
42. Ciba-Geigy, Switzerland	Drugs	9,827
43. Montedison, Italy	Chemicals	9,750
44. Canadian Pacific, Canada	Transportation	9,419
45. Conoco, U.S.A.	Oil	9,311
46. Standard Oil of Ohio, U.S.A.	Oil	9,209
47. Thyssen, Germany	Steel	9,200
48. Sumitomo, Japan	Steel	9,055
49. B.A.T. Industries, U.K.	Multi	9,007
50. E.I. du Pont de Nemours, U.S.A.	Chemicals	8,940

Source: *Forbes*, July 7, 1980.

the giant British-Dutch conglomerate. America's largest industrial corporation, Exxon, is second, and Britain's British Petroleum (BP) is third. General Motors is fourth; Mobil, IBM, Ford, and Texaco are also listed in the top ten. However, most giant multinationals are *not* American. In all, thirty-five of the fifty largest industrial corporations in the world are headquartered *outside* the United States. Indeed, the percentage of total sales of the fifty largest multinationals going to American companies has been steadily declining over time.[1] Finally, we should know that international trade accounts for only about twelve percent of the GNP of the United States. Our dependency on foreign trade is less than that of most other nations.

Thus, critics of American capitalism are incorrect if they charge or imply that corporate multinationalism is strictly an American invention. A careful review of the list also reveals that oil companies are disproportionately represented among the multinationals. The reason is simple: Most of the world's oil is used by nonproducers of oil. This means that multinationalism in the oil industry is essential in getting the oil from producers to users. Seventeen of the world's largest industrial corporations are oil companies. However, international corporate mergers and overseas plant investments by *non-oil* companies have also contributed to multinational concentrations of corporate power. For example, General Motors builds Opels in Germany, Vauxhalls in Great Britain, and Frigidaire products in ten countries. Volkswagenwerk not only sells imports in the United States, but it now builds autos in Pennsylvania.

Foreign corporations sell their products in the United States (steel, automobiles, chemicals, electrical products) and also buy American corporations, which become subsidiaries of the foreign multinationals. For example, Royal Dutch Shell (Netherlands) owns Shell Oil; British Petroleum (U.K.) owns Standard Oil of Ohio; Tengelmann (Germany) owns A & P supermarkets; Nestle´ (Switzerland) owns the Libby, Stouffer, and Beech-Nut corporations; Unilever (U.K.) owns the Lever Brothers and Lipton companies; Bayer (Germany) owns Miles and Cutter Laboratories (Bayer Aspirin); and so on.

Large international banks are also involved in this worldwide network of business and finance. Multinational corporations have access to the world's largest banks. Table 2–7 lists the world's ten largest banks. Note that only three of the world's largest banks are American: BankAmerica (3), Citicorp (4), and Chase Manhattan (8). The others are French, German, or British. In 1980, Midland Bank Ltd. of London took over

---

[1] See *Fortune*, August 1976, p. 243; *Forbes*, July 17, 1980.

Crocker National Bank, the fourteenth largest bank in the United States. This is the first large U.S. bank to be acquired by a foreign bank.

While a great deal has been written about the "dangers" of multinationalism in subverting the national interest, in most cases the opposite is true. The multinational corporation is in a very exposed position vis-à-vis its investments overseas. These investments may be confiscated by revolutionary governments without notice; may be subject to discriminatory taxes, duties, or quotas; or may be forced to be sold or transferred to new foreign owners. The multinational corporation is at the mercy of the host government. Multinationals must conform to the conflicting laws of many nations. On the other hand, the legal maze in which multinationals operate leaves cracks in which clever managers can walk; shifting resources or profits to the lowest tax countries in which they operate; avoiding antitrust laws with international mergers; obscuring corporate reporting through foreign subsidiaries; shifting cash revenues from one currency to another; and so on.

Table 2-7   The World's Largest Banks (Ranking by assets)

Bank and Nationality	Assets (B$)
1. Credit Agricole, France	$104.9
2. Banque National de Paris, France	98.8
3. BankAmerica, U.S.A.	94.3
4. Citicorp, U.S.A.	94.2
5. Deutsche Bank, Germany	91.3
6. Credit Lyonnais, France	91.1
7. Societe Generale, France	85.0
8. Chase Manhattan, U.S.A.	64.7
9. Barclays, U.K.	64.5
10. National Westminster, U.K.	64.4

Source: *Forbes*, July 7, 1980.

In brief, the central feature of the American economy is the concentration of resources in relatively few large corporations. Most of this concentration occurred many years ago. "The long-established norm of market structure and behavior is that of oligopoly, that is, the constrained rivalry of a few interdependent sellers who compete mainly by means of product differentiation."[2] In recent years concentration has increased very

---

[2]Edward S. Herman, *Corporate Control, Corporate Power* (Cambridge: Cambridge University Press, 1981), p. 1.

slowly, if at all.[3] Nonetheless, society is *not* going to return to a small, romanticized, perhaps mythical, world of individual enterprise.

WHO CONTROLS THE CORPORATION

In the formal, legal sense, the board of directors "controls" the modern corporation. The average number of board members in the 100 largest industrial corporations is 14. However, "inside" directors—those who are also top management officers in the corporation—usually dominate board decision-making and even the process of choosing directors. Inside directors usually include the president and the top senior vice-presidents. About 44 percent of corporate directors are inside directors. "Outside" directors—persons who serve on the board but who take no direct part in managing the corporation—usually defer to the judgment of the inside officer–directors. About 56 percent of all directors are "outside" directors. However, *all* directors have a legal responsibility to the owners (stockholders) of the corporation to protect their investment. All directors are formally elected by the stockholders, who cast their votes on the basis of one share equals one vote.

The power of stockholders, however, is a legal fiction. The millions of middle-class Americans who own corporate stock have virtually no influence over the decisions of directors. When confronted with mismanagement, the stockholders simply sell their stock, rather than try to challenge the powers of the directors. Indeed, most stockholders sign over "proxies" to top management so that top management may cast these proxy votes at the annual meetings of stockholders. Management itself usually selects its own "slate" for the board of directors and easily elects them with the help of "proxies."

While a majority of large corporations are controlled by their own top management, some corporations are dominated by a small "control bloc" of stock owners in cooperation with top management. The stock of large corporations is widely distributed among the stock-owning public. This sometimes enables small "control blocs" of only 1 or 2 percent of the total stock of the corporation to hold a strategic position—electing its own directors and influencing corporate decisions. Adolf A. Berle Jr., a corporate lawyer and corporate director who wrote extensively on the modern corporation, explains:

---

[3]The merger of Dupont (19th largest U.S. industrial) and Conoco (17 largest) in 1981, together with a relaxation of antitrust rules by the Reagan Administration, suggest the possibility of another round of corporate mergers in the 1980s.

The control system in today's corporations, when it does not lie solely in the directors as in the American Telephone and Telegraph Company, lies in a combination of the directors and a so-called control block [of stock] plus the directors themselves. For practical purposes, therefore, the control or power element in most large corporations rests in its group of directors, and it is autonomous—or autonomous if taken together with a control block.... This is a self-perpetuating oligarchy.[4]

Thus, some outside directors may represent the interest of "control blocs" of stock on the board. These directors usually do not take a direct role in decision-making, but their presence on the board ensures good communication with top management.

Another type of outside corporate director is one representing financial interests (banks, insurance companies, investment firms). These financial interests wish to oversee the use of their funds by the corporation. Sometimes part of the price of a large loan from a major bank or insurance company to an industrial corporation will include a seat on the board of directors of that corporation. Outside directors representing financial interests do not usually take a direct role in decision-making; they perform a general watch-dog role over their investment.

A few outside directors of large corporations represent public relations efforts by top management to improve the image of the corporation. For example, a few corporations have selected civil-rights activists, blacks, women, and consumer activists for their boards. (When the Chrysler Corporation faced the prospect of bankruptcy, it ceded a seat on its board to the president of the United Automobile Workers, Douglas Fraser, in exchange for union acceptance of a less costly contract.) It may be true that these corporations really want the counsel of these people; however, one suspects that they also want to promote an image of social responsibility. It is doubtful that these particular people are influential in corporate decision-making.

Finally, there are the corporate directors—whether inside officers or outsiders—who represent family owners. Family ownership and domination of large corporations has not yet disappeared in America despite marked decline in family control of corporations over the last several decades.

Thus, corporate board members can be divided into types. The following percentage approximations of various types of corporate directors are estimated for the 1,475 members of the 100 largest industrial corporations:[5]

[4]Adolf A. Berle, Jr., *Economic Power and a Free Society* (New York: Fund for the Republic, 1958), p. 10.
[5]Estimates from materials presented in Herman, *Corporate Control, Corporate Power*, Chap. 2.

INSIDERS
Manager-directors	44%

OUTSIDERS
Former managers	6%
Financial representatives	8%
Ownership representatives	13%
Substantial business with corporation	11%
Charitable, civic, or educational representatives	5%
Other	<u>13%</u>
OUTSIDER TOTAL	56%

Managers usually triumph in the boardroom. The "managerial revolution"—the displacement of owners as corporate decision-makers by professional managers—has become part of our conventional wisdom, accepted by liberals and conservatives alike.[6] The inside directors, although only a minority of most boards, usually vote as a solid, unified block under the direction of the president. Their block voting strength on the board is augmented by their greater depth of knowledge of the organization, its technology, and its business problems. Insiders work full time on corporate affairs, continuously communicating with each other. Outsiders have no such information or communication base.

Outside directors, with some exceptions, are "invited" to serve on boards by the managers. They are "guests" in the boardroom. They usually have a sense of loyalty to the president who put them on the board. They are passive on most management decisions. They may advise on special areas of competence; they may help coordinate decision-making with major suppliers or buyers; and by their presence on the board they may help assure the outside world that the organization is in good hands. The only important exceptions to these usually passive outside managers are those who still represent large stockholder interests.

This does not mean that management never loses. Indeed, management ousters do occur. But the publicity given to management defeats makes the control of large corporations appear more "up for grabs" than is really the case. Great size is a major obstacle to involuntary ouster of management. Because of their size, AT&T, Exxon, General Motors, Mobil Oil, and so on, are out of reach of the takeover process. When ousters occur, they usually do so in response to very poor business performance or the retirement or sudden death of a dominant manager.

[6]For some Marxists and others on the left, managerialism is still denied, because it complicates the theory of class struggle in a capitalist society. They still argue that great families, or banking empires, have retained latent power—power to be exercised when something goes seriously wrong. Some Marxists, however, have accepted the managerial thesis and simply focus on managers as "the leading echelon of the capitalist class." See Paul A. Baran and Paul M. Sweezy, *Monopoly Capital*, (Newark: Monthly Review Press, 1966).

Adolf A. Berle, Jr. summarizes the dominance of managers in corporate America:

> Management control is a phrase meaning merely that no large concentrated stockholding exists which maintains a close working relationship with the management or is capable of challenging it, so that the board of directors may regularly expect a majority, composed of small and scattered holdings, to follow their lead. Thus, they need not consult with anyone when making up their slate of directors, and may simply request their stockholders to sign and send in a ceremonial proxy. They select their own successors.... Nominal power still resides in the stockholders; actual power in the board of directors.[7]

Admittedly, there are limits on corporate power-holders. What appears to be decisions by top corporate officers may be dictated by pressure from below—unions bargaining on wages and working conditions; various levels of government taxes, subsidies, and regulation; community pressures; and interactions with other corporations that lend money, sell securities, buy goods, and supply materials.

INSIDE EXXON

Exxon is America's largest industrial corporation. Its annual revenues are larger than those of any state in the nation—indeed larger than the gross national product of Sweden. Exxon operates in 100 countries. It owns 70 refineries and operates 195 ocean-going tankers—more ships than the British navy. Its decisions affect energy, transportation, prices, and economic growth in America. Yet, because it is not a "government," political scientists do not study its policy-making process nor the impact of its policies on the nation.

Exxon is the descendant of the original Standard Oil Company, which was incorporated by John D. Rockefeller in 1882 as the Standard Oil Company of New Jersey. "Exxon" was adopted as its American name in 1972; overseas it is labeled "Esso." It was in 1911 that the U.S. Supreme Court delivered one of its most sweeping decisions under the Sherman Anti-trust Act: the Standard Oil Company was to be broken up into thirty-three separate companies. Today, Exxon is governed separately from its many "cousins," including Mobil, Standard Oil of California, Standard Oil of Indiana, Standard Oil of Ohio, Atlantic Richfield, and Marathon Oil. However, the Rockefeller family continues to hold large blocks of stock in each of these corporations.

The ultimate power in Exxon lies with its eighteen directors. Eight of

---

[7]Adolf A. Berle, Jr., *Power Without Property* (New York: Harcourt Brace Jovanovich, 1959), p. 73.

these directors are "inside directors" (officers of the corporation), including Clifton J. Garvin, Jr., chairman and chief executive officer. The ten others are "outside directors" with ties to many other corporations and banks. The Rockefeller family is not directly represented on the board. The "outside" members of the board include some "heavyweights"—individuals holding powerful positions elsewhere in the corporate world. These include Edward G. Harness, chairman of the board of Procter and Gamble, and Harry Jack Gray, chairman of the board of United Technologies (he was also responsible for hiring General Alexander Haig to head United Technologies before his leaving to become Secretary of State). Others are relative "lightweights"—individuals who do not hold powerful positions in the corporate world. These include Martha E. Peterson, president of tiny Beloit College in Wisconsin; Randolph W. Bromery, former chancellor of the University of Massachusetts; and Franklin A. Long, a professor of science and technology at the University of Chicago, who also serves on the board of United Technologies. The board includes two retired board chairmen James K. Jamieson (Exxon) and William H. Franklin (Caterpillar Tractor.) There is no outward evidence that these outsiders could effectively challenge management control.

The members of the management committee really rule Exxon. The board of directors meets once a month to review the company's activities. However, the eight inside directors compose what is officially called the "management committee." They meet, on an average, three mornings a week, and usually only committee members attend. Chairman Garvin presides. The president, Howard C. Kauffmann, is second in command. Other officers of the corporation may be called in from time to time to make presentations (plans, proposals, reports of progress, investigations, and so on) to the management committee. The management committee decides when and where to explore for oil, build refineries and pipelines, and expand or contract retail outlets. It decides whether or not to expand its interests beyond petroleum; it recently decided to enter the business-computer market. It governs relations with all of the foreign countries in which its operations are located.

Exxon has its own system of checks and balances. Exxon is divided into thirteen operating companies, or affiliates. Some of these are geographically based: Esso Eastern, Esso Middle East, Esso Europe, Esso InterAmerican, Imperial Oil (Canada), and Exxon U.S.A. Other affiliates are based on functions: Exxon Chemical, Esso Exploration, Exxon Enterprises (new products), and Reliance Electric. Another layer of authority is concentrated in its New York City headquarters: Seventeen staff departments advise the Exxon directors and the subsidiaries on everything from law, public relations, and international affairs, to production, refining, and marketing.

The *staff executives* and the *operating executives* are frequently at odds over power and policy. The operating executives want more corporation resources for their own operations and greater independence of action. The staff executives are supposed to take a "corporation-wide" point of view. Exxon expects some "creative tension" between the two sets of executives to achieve better overall results for the corporation. However, to reduce corporate infighting, Exxon regularly exchanges top executives from operating companies to central staff and back again. Moreover, the management committee members themselves are simultaneously heads of both operating companies and staff vice-presidents.

Each fall the presidents of the thirteen operating companies bring their plans for the coming year to New York for review at a meeting with staff executives and the Exxon management committee. Major decisions are made at these meetings: to expand or reduce oil production or refining capacity; to commit more or less funds to exploration; to increase or reduce the tanker fleet; to limit or expand operations in one part of the world or another; to raise or lower prices. Each spring the management committee works to evaluate the performance of the affiliated companies. Presidents of affiliated companies can spend about $5 million on their own say-so; from $5 million up to $25 million, they must have the approval of a senior vice-president and director; over $25 million they must have the approval of the management committee. Well before any presentation to the management committee, there are many months of preparation. "Rarely would you open your in-box and find a proposal for a refinery," explains one senior vice-president. "There would have been a lot of discussions with our refining people, for example, and this thing would slowly develop over time."[8] "No surprises" is a favorite phrase at Exxon. A formal proposal by an affiliate must run the gamut of staff examination in New York before it is presented to the management committee. "This doesn't prevent us from making bad investments. But it makes damn sure that we're all in accord."

THE CORPORATE DIRECTORS

Who are the people at the top of the nation's corporate structure? Let us begin with some brief sketches of a few selected corporate leaders. Later in this volume we will examine recruitment patterns, interlocking and specialization, social backgrounds, attitudes and opinions, cohesion and competition, and patterns of interaction. Let us first, however, give a general notion of who the people at the top are.

[8]*New York Times Magazine,* August 3, 1980, p. 25.

David Rockefeller. Former chairman of the board of Chase Manhattan Bank. Youngest of five sons of John D. Rockefeller, Jr.; heir of the Standard Oil Co. (Exxon) fortune; grandson of John D. Rockefeller, Sr., who founded the company that made the Rockefeller family one of the richest families in the world. Attended Lincoln School in New York, Harvard, The London School of Economics, and the University of Chicago (Ph.D. degree in economics). Also a member of the board of directors of the B.F. Goodrich Co., Rockefeller Bros., Inc., and Equitable Life Insurance Co. He is a trustee of Rockefeller Institute of Medical Research, Museum of Modern Art, Rockefeller Center, and Harvard College. He is also chairman of the Council on Foreign Relations, and chairman of the Trilateral Commission.

Henry Ford II. Former chairman and chief executive of the Ford Motor Co. Eldest son of Edsel Bryan Ford (president of the company from 1918 to his death in 1943); grandson of Henry Ford, founder of the company. Attended Hotchkiss School and Yale University. Started in the automobile industry at age twenty-five as vice-president of Ford Motors; took over the presidency one year later. He was director of General Foods Corp., and a trustee of the Ford Foundation. He was chairman of the National Alliance of Businessmen, and the National Center for Voluntary Action. He is personally responsible for Detroit's new downtown Renaissance Center. His brother, Benson Ford, was also a director of Ford Motor Co. and the Ford Foundation before his death in 1978. Another brother, William Clay Ford, is president of the Detroit Lions professional football club and a director of the Girl Scouts of America and the Henry Ford Hospital.

Ellmore C. Patterson. Former chairman of the board of Morgan Guaranty Trust Co. Attended Lake Forest Academy and the University of Chicago. Married to Ann Hude Choate, daughter of a prominent investment banker who was associate of J.P. Morgan & Co. Became vice-president of Morgan Guaranty Trust in 1951, executive vice-president in 1959, president in 1969, and chairman of the board from 1971 to 1977. He is a director of AT&T, General Motors, Bethlehem Steel, Standard Brands, and Comsat. He is a trustee of the Alfred P. Sloan Foundation, Memorial Sloan-Kettering Cancer Center, Carnegie Endowment for International Peace, University of Chicago, and Council on Foreign Relations.

Clifton C. Garvin. Chairman of the board of Exxon Corporation, the world's largest industrial corporation. Attended public school and received a B.S. degree in chemical engineering from Virginia Polytechnic Institute. He began work as an engineer for Standard Oil Co. (now Exxon) in Baton Rouge, Louisiana, in 1947. He climbed the executive ranks of Standard Oil and its subsidiaries for 28 years, becoming chairman of the board in 1975. He is also a director of Citicorp, Pepsico, and Sperry Rand, and is a member of the National Petroleum Council. He is chairperson of the Business Roundtable. He is a trustee of the Committee on Economic Development, the Business Council, and the American Petroleum Institute, Memorial Sloan-Kettering Cancer Center, Alfred P. Sloan Foundation, Vanderbilt University, and the Council on Foreign Relations.

John D. DeButts. Former chairman of the board of American Telephone and Telegraph (AT&T), the world's largest corporation. He attended public schools and received an engineering degree from the Virginia Military Institute. After failing an eye test, he was denied a military commission; so he began work as a telephone traffic controller for the Chesapeake and Potomac Telephone Co., a subsidiary of AT&T. He became chairman of the board in 1972 and served until 1979. He is also a director of Citicorp, U.S. Steel, Kraft, General Motors, and Hospital Corporation of America. He is a trustee of the Duke Endowment Foundation, United Way of America, Duke University, and Loyola University of Chicago. He is also a director of the Business Council, Brookings Institution, and the Business Roundtable.

Alden W. Clausen. Chairman of the board of BankAmerica, the nation's largest commercial bank. He received a public school education and a B.A. degree from tiny Carthage College before obtaining a law degree from the University of Minnesota. He immediately started with BankAmerica in San Francisco under its founder and long-term president, A.P. Gianini. He worked his way up to vice-president, senior vice-president, and executive vice-president, and to president and chairman of the board in 1970. He is a director of the Federal Reserve Bank of San Francisco. He is chairman of the San Francisco Bay Area Council, United Way of the Bay Area, and Japan-U.S. Advisory Council. He is a trustee of the San Francisco Opera, the Stanford Research Institute, and the Harvard Business School.

Robert V. Roosa. Senior partner of Brown Brother, Harriman & Co. (Wall Street investment firm). Chairman of the board of trustees of the Brookings Institution, Washington, D.C. An earned Ph.D. (economics) from the University of Michigan and is a Rhodes Scholar. A director of American Express Co., Owens-Corning Fiberglass, and Texaco. Former Under Secretary of the Treasury. A director of the Council on Foreign Relations and a trustee of the Rockefeller Foundation and Memorial Sloan-Kettering Cancer Center.

Walter Wriston. Chairman of the board of Citicorp, the nation's second largest bank. Attended Wesleyan University; M.A. degree, Tufts University. He joined Citibank as an inspector in 1946. He climbed through various corporate ranks to chairman of the board in 1970. He is a director of General Electric, J.C. Penney, and Clubb Corporation. He is a trustee of the RAND Corporation, Tufts University, and the American Enterprise Institute. He is a member of the Council on Foreign Relations and the Business Council.

Irving Saul Shapiro. Chairman of the board of E.I. duPont de Nemours Co., Inc. University of Minnesota, undergraduate and law school. Began as U.S. Department of Justice attorney. Recruited to duPont in 1951 and climbed the corporation ladder to chairman of the board in 1974. A director of Citicorp, IBM, and Continental American Insurance. A trustee of the Ford Foundation and the University of Delaware. A director of the Business Roundtable and the Business Council.

Peter G. Peterson. Chairman of the board of Lehman Brothers and Kuhn Loeb, Inc. (investments). Attended Northwestern University and University of Chicago, M.B.A. degree. Former Secretary of Commerce under Richard M. Nixon. Former chairman of the board of Bell and Howell Co. A director of RCA, Minnesota Mining and Manufacturing (3M), Black and Decker, General Foods, and Federated Department Stores. A director of the Council on Foreign Relations and the Trilateral Commission, and a trustee of the Museum of Modern Art and the University of Chicago.

J. Paul Austin. Chairman of Coca Cola Company. Attended Harvard College and Harvard Law School. Climbed the ranks at Coca Cola through the legal department. A director of Morgan Guaranty Trust, Federated Department Stores, General Electric, Trust Company of Georgia, Dow Jones & Co., a member of the Council on Foreign Relations and the Trilateral Commission. He supported the Dinning Center in politics through Coca Cola and Harnez.

Frank T. Cary. Chairman of the board of International Business Machines (I.B.M.). Attended U.C.L.A. and Stanford where he earned an M.B.A. Began climbing the ladder at IBM in 1948, became president in 1971, and later became chairman of the board. A director of Morgan Guaranty Trust, American Broadcasting Company (ABC), and Merck & Co. (drugs). A trustee of the Brookings Institution, Museum of Modern Art, Rockefeller University, and M.I.T. He is a member of the Business Council, the Business Roundtable, and the Committee for Economic Development.

It is clear from these brief sketches that some individuals gain corporate power through inheritance, while others come up through the ranks of corporate management. People such as Rockefeller and Ford inherited their position and power. Others, such as Shapiro, Garvin, DeButts, Cary, and Clausen, rose to power through the ranks of management. In fact, we will see that a surprising percentage of top corporate leaders achieved their power that way.

THE MANAGERS:
CLIMBING THE CORPORATE LADDER

The top echelons of American corporate life are occupied primarily by people who have climbed the corporate ladder from relatively obscure and powerless bottom rungs. It is our rough estimate that less than 10 percent of the 1,475 presidents and directors of the top 100 corporations are heirs of wealthy families. The rest—the "managers"—owe their rise to power not to family connections, but to their own success in organizational life. Of course, these managers are overwhelmingly upper middle class and upper class in social origin, and most attended Ivy League colleges and universities. (The social origin and background of top elites is discussed in Chapter 7.) The rise of the manager is a recent phenomenon. As recently as 1950, we estimate that 30 percent of the top corporate elite were heirs of wealthy families, compared to our figure of 10 percent for 1980. (Indeed, even since 1980, Henry Ford II stepped down as chairperson of Ford Motors, and David Rockefeller retired as chairperson of Chase Manhattan.) How can we explain the rise to power of the corporate manager?

Today the requirements of technology and planning have greatly increased the need in industry for specialized talent and skill in organization. Capital is something that a corporation can now supply to itself. There is little need for the old-style "tycoon." Thus, there has been a shift in power in the American economy from capital to organized intelligence. This is reflected in the decline of individual- and family-controlled large corporations and in an increase in the percentage of large corporations controlled by management.

Individual capitalists are no longer essential to the accumulation of capital for investment. Approximately three fifths of industrial capital now comes from retained earnings of corporations rather than from the investments of individual capitalists. Another one fifth of industrial capital is borrowed, chiefly from banks. Even though the remaining one fifth of the capital funds of industry comes from "outside" investments, the bulk of these funds are from large insurance companies, mutual funds, and pension trusts, rather than from individual investors. Indeed, the individual investor who buys stock in corporations provides only about 5 percent of total industrial capital. Thus, investors are no longer in a position of dominance in American capital formation.

American capital is primarily administered and expended by managers of large corporations and financial institutions. Stockholders are supposed to have ultimate power over management, but as we have noted, individual stockholders seldom have any control over the activities of the corporations they own. Usually "management slates" for the board of directors are approved as a matter of course by stockholders. Occasionally, banks and financial institutions and pension trust or mutual fund managers will get together to replace a management-selected board of directors. But more often than not, banks and trust funds sell their stock in corporations when they distrust the management, rather than use the voting power of their stock to replace management. This policy of nonaction by institutional investors means that the directors and management of corporations are becoming increasingly self-appointed and unchallengeable, in effect achieving absolute power within the corporation.

Most of the capital in America is owned not by individuals, but by corporations, banks, insurance companies, mutual funds, investment companies, and pension trusts. Liberal economist John Kenneth Galbraith summarizes the changes in America's economic elite:

> Seventy years ago the corporation was the instrument of its owners and a projection of their personalities. The names of these principals—Carnegie, Rockefeller, Harriman, Mellon, Guggenheim, Ford—were well known across the land. They are still known, but for the art galleries and philanthropic foundations they established and their descendants who are in politics. The men who now head the great corporations are unknown. Not for a generation did people outside Detroit in the automobile industry know the name of the current head of General Motors. In the manner of all men, he must produce identification when paying by check. So with Ford, Standard Oil, and General Dynamics. The men who now run the large corporations own no appreciable share of the enterprise. They are selected not by the stockholders but, in the

common case, by a board of directors which narcissistically they selected themselves.[9]

How do you climb the corporate ladder? It is not easy, and most who begin the climb fall by the wayside at some point in their careers before reaching the top. Howard Morgens, president of Procter & Gamble, is a successful manager. He climbed within his organization to succeed its president, Neil McElroy (who left to be Secretary of Defense), and headed the corporation for over fifteen years. In an interview with this executive, *Forbes* magazine described the qualities of a corporate career riser:

> Just to be in the running, a career riser must discipline himself carefully. He must become a seasoned decision-maker. He must cultivate an aura of success and sustain his upward momentum on the executive ladder. He must be loyal to a fault, tolerably bright, fairly creative, politically agile, always tough, sometimes flexible, unfailingly sociable and, in the minds of his company's directors, seem superior to a dozen men who are almost as good. He must also be lucky.[10]

Over time, the organization person accepts the goals of the organization as his or her own, and the procedures of the bureaucracy as a way of life:

> In staying, however, the career riser must accept the necessarily bureaucratic ways and the shared beliefs of a huge organization. He must be willing to follow prescribed procedures and behavioral norms. He must do things the P & G way or the IBM way or the General Motors way. Moreover, he must find it in himself to believe in the essential goodness of the company, in its traditions and in his co-employees. He must be willing to accept a good deal on faith. He must, in short, conform.[11]

Today, more than ever before, getting to the top requires the skills of a "technocrat"—knowledge of bureaucratic organization, technical skills and information, extensive formal education (including post-graduate degrees), and proven ability to work within legal constraints and governmental regulations. Very few sons and no daughters are taking over the presidencies of large corporations owned by their families. Only 9 percent of the nation's 500 largest corporations in 1976 were headed by men whose families had previously run the corporation.[12] Top corporate management

---

[9]John Kenneth Galbraith, *The New Industrial State* (Boston: Houghton Mifflin, 1967), p. 323.

[10]"Proud to Be An Organization Man," *Forbes*, May 15, 1972, p. 241.

[11]*Ibid.*

[12]Charles G. Burch, "A Group Profile of the Fortune 500 Chief Executives," *Fortune*, May 1976, p. 174.

Who is the corporate director "most respected" by his peers?

A *Wall Street Journal*/Gallup survey in 1980 collected nominations from 306 chief executives of large corporations (including 100 of the Fortune 500 companies) and from 276 heads of medium-sized firms. Their top choice by a wide margin: Reginald Jones, chief executive of General Electric Co. He was mentioned by about a third of all respondents and by more than half of the heads of the largest corporations.

Mentioned most often, in descending order, were the following executives:

1. Reginald Jones, General Electric Corp.
2. Irving Shapiro, DuPont Corp.
3. Thomas Murphy, General Motors Corp.
4. Walter Wriston, Citicorp.
5. John Swearingen, Standard Oil Co. (Indiana).
6. Rawleigh Warner, Mobil Oil Corp.
7. Henry Ford II, Ford Motor Co., (retired).
8. Clifton Garvin, Exxon Corp.
9. Justin Dart, Dart Industries, Inc.
10. Frank Cary, International Business Machines Corp.
11. A.W. Clausen, Bank of America.
12. Henry Singleton, Teledyne Inc.
13. David Roderick, U.S. Steel Corp.
14. Byron Fletcher, Koppers Co.
15. Lee Iacocca, Chrysler Corp.
16. David Rockefeller, Chase Manhattan Bank.
17. E.M. de Windt, Eaton Corp.
18. Mark Shepherd, Texas Instruments Inc.
19. Robert Anderson, Atlantic Richfield Co.
20. Harold Geneen, International Telephone & Telegraph Corp.

Source: *Wall Street Journal*, August 18, 1980.

is drawn from the ranks of upper-middle-class, well-educated, white, and male, management, financial, and legal experts.

Perhaps the most significant change over the years has been the rising number of top corporate and governmental executives who have acquired graduate degrees. Today over half of the corporate presidents of the 500 largest corporations have advanced degrees, including M.B.A.'s (Master's of Business Administration), law degrees, and Ph.D.'s. Less than 3 percent are not college educated.

An increasing number of top corporate leaders are coming out of finance and law, as opposed to production, operations, advertising, sales, engineering, or research. Lawyers and accountants now head two out of every five large corporations.[13] This is further evidence that finance, taxation, and governmental regulation are the chief problems confronting large corporations. The problems of production, sales, engineering, and

[13]*Ibid.*, p. 176.

transportation have faded in relationship to the pressing problems of money and power. Indeed, a *Fortune* survey of the chief executives of the 500 largest corporations in America produced the following listing of "most important problems faced by their companies": government (28.1 percent); inflation (11.7 percent); financing (7.9 percent); employee relations (7.8 percent); rapid change (5.5 percent); profit levels (5.0 percent).[14]

But the "managers" who head the nation's largest corporations are not merely paid administrators. On the contrary, the vast majority of corporate presidents, and other top management personnel, own substantial shareholdings of their company's stock. According to *Fortune* magazine, 30 percent of the presidents of the 500 largest companies personally own $1 million or more in their own company's stock. Fully 45 percent own over one-half million dollars worth; 75 percent own at least $100,000 worth; and only 10 percent own none at all. When G. William Miller, former chief executive officer at Textron, was appointed chairman of the Federal Reserve Board in 1976, he was obliged to reveal that $2.3 million (80 percent) of his $2.8 million in personal assets was in shares of Textron stock. The "managers" have a personal stake in their company's growth and profitability—a stake that extends beyond their jobs to their personal investments as well.

Getting to the top by climbing the ladder of the giant corporation is not only difficult, it is also risky. The percentage chances of any one individual making it to the top are infinitesimal.

> Yet hundreds of thousands of executives willingly devote entire careers to working their way up through these giant corporations. On the lower rungs of the ladder, when they are in their 20's, all of them dream of reaching the top. As they advance into their 30's, and receive more responsibility and more money, the dream flowers brightly. Some time in their 40's and 50's, however, most realize they aren't going to make it. They are sorely disappointed, but it's too late to change. Comfortable and secure, they stay. Then each year there are perhaps a dozen or so—the lucky men who go all the way.[15]

It might be instructive to sketch briefly the careers of some of the "lucky people" who went "all the way."

UP THE ORGANIZATION: THE CEO'S AT AT&T

The chairperson of the board and chief executive officer (CEO) of the world's largest corporation, American Telephone and Telegraph (AT&T), has traditionally been recruited up through the managerial ranks of the

---

[14]*Ibid.*, p. 177.
[15]"Proud to Be An Organization Man," p. 244.

corporation itself. Until 1982 AT&T controled over $100 billion in assets; it had 70 million customers, and one million employees, more than any other private corporation in the world. The chairperson headed AT&T itself, twenty-two subsidiary telephone companies, Western Electric Corporation (which manufactures telephone equipment), and Bell Laboratories. "Ma Bell," as the giant corporation is nicknamed, liked to train and groom its own "technocrats" for top positions. The last three chairpersons of AT&T testify to the importance of organizational loyalty, administrative experience, and technical competency in modern management.

H.I. Romnes. From 1966 to 1972 AT&T was headed by the son of Norwegian immigrant "Hi" Romnes. Romnes had a very modest start in life, working in his father's bakery while attending public schools and the University of Wisconsin. His boyhood hobby was building crystal radios, and he received a B.A. degree in electrical engineering in 1927. Upon graduation he joined Bell Laboratories and never left the warm embrace of "Ma Bell." For many years he was lost in the laboratories of AT&T's giant engineering department, but in 1952 he put his knowledge of electrical circuitry to work by helping to introduce long-distance direct-dialing in the Bell system. Romnes became chief engineer and later won a series of rapid promotions as vice-president of operations, president of Western Electric, vice-chairman of the board, and finally chairman of the board in 1966 at age fifty-nine. Romnes became a director of Chemical Bank of New York, United States Steel, Cities Service, and Mutual Life Insurance, but these directorships came to him *after* his rise in AT&T. Romnes was also active in civic, educational, and charitable organizations: he was a director of the American Cancer Society, the Downtown Lower Manhattan Association (with his friend David Rockefeller), the United Community Campaigns of America, the National Safety Council, and M.I.T. He was a member of the Urban League and the United Negro College Fund.

John D. DeButts. From 1972 to 1979 AT&T was headed by the son of a middle management railroad executive from North Carolina. John DeButts attended public schools and aspired to no more than a career in the military. He attended Virginia Military Academy and graduated with a degree in electrical engineering in 1936. He was class valedictorian, but he failed an eye examination and was rejected for a military commission. He began work for the Chesapeake and Potomac Telephone Co., an AT&T subsidiary, and he never left "Ma Bell." He rose through the ranks to become president of Illinois Bell Telephone and then was transferred to AT&T corporate headquarters in New York as vice-president and later vice-chairman of the board. DeButts was instrumental in defeating a Justice Department attempt to force the separation of Western Electric from AT&T. He used his technical knowledge to convince a federal court that the Bell system had to remain under single corporate control to ensure compatibility of telephone equipment and smoother transferring of calls throughout the country. By 1972 DeButts had spent thirty-six years in twenty-two separate managerial posts in AT&T. When he became chairman at age fifty-eight, he focused a great deal of energy on fending off government attempts to break up parts of AT&T. Later DeButts became a director of Citicorp, United States Steel, Kraft, and General Motors. He has remained active in civic affairs as a trustee of

Brookings Institution and a director of the Business Roundtable and the Business Council.

Charles L. Brown. In 1979, DeButts was replaced by the tall, slim, handsome Charles L. Brown. Brown attended public schools and majored in electrical engineering at the University of Virginia. He began his career with AT&T in 1946 and climbed the corporate ladder over a thirty-three-year time span. Like his predecessor, he was president of Illinois Bell for five years before coming to AT&T headquarters as executive vice-president and later vice-chairperson of the board. The selection of two successive chairpersons from one subsidiary—Illinois Bell—suggests that cliques grow up in large corporations based on personal friendship and loyalties. Brown became chairman at age fifty-eight. He began his tenure by creating a new subsidiary to manufacture electronic business equipment and compete directly with IBM and Xerox. Brown is also a director at E.I. duPont de Nemours, Hart, Shaffner & Marx, and Chemical Bank of New York, and he is a trustee of the University of Chicago.

It was Brown who presided over the most sweeping changes in the corporation's history in 1982. AT&T agreed, in a long-standing anti-trust suit with the U.S. government, to divest itself of 22 local telephone companies in exchange for removal of traditional utility restrictions against competing in telecommunications, computers, and information processing. AT&T gave up two-thirds of its assets—all in local telephone service—but retained its control of long distance telephone facilities, Western Electric (its manufacturing company), and Bell Laboratories (its research and development unit). Brown is gambling that the new AT&T will come to dominate "The Information Age."

It is interesting that all three of these "climbers" in the world's largest corporation began as electrical engineers and acquired a firm, basic knowledge of the technology of their industry. In addition, all three remained with the same corporation for over thirty years, climbing the invisible rings on the corporate ladder of success. All of them reached the top at age fifty-eight and held the reigns of power for about six years. They all sit on several corporate boards, and they are active in civic and educational affairs as well. However, very few people recognize their names. They represent the "technocratic" leadership of corporate America today.

THE INHERITORS: STARTING AT THE TOP

Unquestionably, the Rockefellers, Fords, duPonts, Mellons, and other families still exercise great power over America's corporate resources. The Ford family maintains control of Ford Motor Company, and the Rockefellers continue their dominant interest in Chase Manhattan Bank, Exxon, Mobil, Standard Oil, Equitable Life Assurance Society, Eastern Airlines,

and other key banks and industries. The duPonts continue to control E.I.
duPont de Nemours Corporation through their family holding company,
Christiana Securities. Prior to his death, Richard King Mellon had the final
say in the boardrooms of Alcoa and Gulf Oil.

Research on family holdings in large corporations is not easy. Table
2–8 lists major family holdings of large corporations as revealed in a
variety of sources. It is an even more difficult task to learn whether a family
really "controls" the operations of a corporation, or whether control has
been passed on to the managers. It is possible for families who no longer
hold active management positions in a corporation to exercise "latent"
power—that is, to use their control blocks of stock as a restraint on
management. Sometimes families interfere only when something goes
seriously wrong.

Table 2–8   Family Influence in Corporations

Corporation	Family
E.I. duPont de Nemours	duPont
Remington Arms Co., Inc.	Dodge, Rockefeller
Ford Motor Co.	Ford
Aluminum Co. of America	Mellon
Carborundum Co.	Mellon
Gulf Oil Co.	Mellon, Scaife
Sun Oil Co.	Pew
Pittsburgh Plate Glass	Pitcairn
Exxon	Rockefeller
Standard Oil of Indiana	Rockefeller
Mobil	Rockefeller
Standard Oil of California	Rockefeller
Standard Oil of Ohio	Rockefeller
Sears, Roebuck & Co.	Rosenwald
Reynolds Metals	Reynolds
The Singer Company	Clark
Scott Paper Co.	McCabe
Minnesota Mining & Mfg. Co.	Ordway, McKnight
Polaroid Corp.	Land
IBM	Watson, Fairchild
Dow Chemical Co.	Dow
Corning Glass Works	Houghton
International Paper Co.	Phipps
W.R. Grace & Co.	Grace, Phipps
Weyerhaeuser	Weyerhaeuser
Winn-Dixie, Inc.	Davis
Georgia-Pacific	Cheatharn
General Tire & Rubber Co.	O'Neil
Campbell Soup Company	Dorrance
H.J. Heinz Co.	Heinz
Wm. Wrigley Jr. Co.	Wrigley
Firestone Tire & Rubber	Firestone
National Steel	Hanna
Columbia Broadcasting Co. (CBS)	Paley

Table 2–8   Family Influence in Corporations (continued)

Olin Chemical	Olin
Ralston Purina Co.	Danforth
Crown-Zellerbach Corp.	Zellerbach
Texas Eastern Transmission	Brown
Fairchild Camera	Fairchild
Smith Kline & French Laboratories	Valentine
Merck & Co., Inc.	Rogengarten
American Metal Climax	Hochschild, Dodge
Phelps Dodge	Dodge
W.T. Grant Co.	Grant
E.J. Korvette	Ferkauf
Hilton Hotels	Hilton
Howard Johnson Co.	Johnson
Great Atlantic & Pacific Tea Co. (A&P)	Hartford
K-Mart	Kresge
Woolco	Woolworth
Beech Aircraft Corp.	Beech
McDonnell Douglas Aircraft	McDonnell
General Dynamics Corp.	Crown
Colgate-Palmolive	Colgate
Greyhound	Armour
Kennecott Copper	Guggenheim
Union Pacific	Harriman
R.J. Reynolds	Reynolds
International Harvester	McCormick
Coca Cola	Woodruff
Crown Zellerbach	Zellerbach
Hess Oil & Chemical	Hess
Eli Lilly & Co.	Lilly
Duke Power Co.	Duke
Kaiser Industries	Kaiser
Rockwell Mfg. Co.	Rockwell
Gerber Products Co.	Gerber
Deere & Company	Deere
Jos. Schlitz Brewing Co.	Uihlein
George A. Hormel & Co.	Hormel
Oscar Mayer & Co.	Mayer
Borden Co.	Borden

Sources: Ferdinand Lundberg, *The Rich and the Super-Rich* (New York: Lyle Stuart, 1968); *Fortune,* June 15, 1967; update to *Fortune,* "Directory of the Largest 500 Corporations," June 1981; and Edward S. Herman, *Corporate Control, Corporate Power* (Cambridge: Cambridge University Press, 1981), Table 2–7.

Control of some family corporations has passed on to the managers. Consider the losses of the Kresge family, for example. In 1964, the family owned 37 percent of the stock of the S.S. Kresge Company (retail merchandising chain), and they occupied several top management and directors posts. Like most families of great wealth, the Kresge's consolidated their family wealth in a foundation—the Kresge Foundation. This is usually done to protect family wealth from inheritance taxes each generation, as well as from the division of holdings among family heirs.

However, by 1975 only one family member, Stanley Kresge, remained on the board; his personal holdings amounted to about 1 percent of the company's stock. The Kresge Foundation held about 10 percent of the stock. Ordinarily this would be enough to produce a "control block" sufficient to keep the family dominant in corporate affairs. However, management had been very successful in expanding the S.S. Kresge corporation in the 1960s and 1970s. Their success consolidated their power over the corporation. The family was happy with management until 1977, when management proposed to change the name of the corporation from S.S. Kresge to K-Mart. A battle ensued at the annual stockholders meeting, but management held the proxies and defeated the family. The S. S. Kresge Company became the K-Mart Corporation, and Stanley Kresge retired from the board.

Some members of the corporate elite "start at the top." *Fortune* suggests that 150 of the largest 500 industrial corporations are controlled by one or more members of a single family. True, most of these individual- or family-controlled corporations are ranked *below* the top 100. But if indeed 30 percent of American industrial corporations are controlled by individuals or family groups, then the claimed disappearance of the traditional American capitalist may have been exaggerated. *Fortune* concludes:

> After more than two generations during which ownership has been increasingly divorced from control, it is frequently assumed that all large U.S. corporations are owned by everybody and nobody, and are run and ruled by bland organization men. The individual entrepreneur or family that holds onto the controlling interest and actively manages the affairs of a big company is regarded as a rare anachronism. But a close look at the 500 largest industrial corporations does not substantiate such sweeping generalizations.... The demise of the traditional American proprietor has been slightly exaggerated and the much advertised triumph of the organization is far from total.[16]

Nonetheless, even family-controlled corporations recruit professional managers from the ranks. Indeed, nearly all of the directors of Ford, Alcoa, Gulf, Exxon, Chase Manhattan, DuPont, and other such corporations are professional managers recruited from outside the family.

It really does not matter a great deal whether the "inheritors" or the "managers" really control America's largest corporations; the end policies appear to be the same. Management is motivated by considerations of growth, stability, and profit, and so are prudent family stockholders. Moreover, "managers" themselves usually acquire sizable blocks of stock in their own companies as they move up through the ranks. It is doubtful that

---

[16]Robert Sheehan, "Family Run Corporations: There Are More of Them Than You Think," *Fortune*, June 15, 1967, p. 179.

the decisions of "managers" differ a great deal from those of "inheritors." *Fortune* magazine agrees:

> It was expected that the demise of the owner-manager would markedly affect the conduct and performance of business. Some have predicted that the new managerial brass, as essentially non-owners, would lack the self-interested maximization of profits that inspired proprietors, would be inclined to curb dividends, and would be tempted to provide themselves with disproportionately large salaries and bonuses....
>
> Despite these theories, it is extremely doubtful that ownership or the lack of it motivated the conduct of executives in such a direct way. Very few executives agree that the managers of a widely held company run their business any differently from the proprietors of a closely held company. Competition is a great leveler, and both managers and proprietors respond to its pressures with equal spirit and objectivity.[17]

After carefully comparing the performance of managerial-run corporations with owner-dominated corporations, Wharton Business School professor Edward S. Herman reaches the same conclusion:

> In sum, the triumph of management control in many large corporations has not left them in the hands of neutral technocrats. The control groups of these organizations seem as devoted to profitable growth as are the leaders of entrepreneurial and owner-dominated companies, past and present.[18]

HENRY FORD II: THE INHERITOR AS BOSS

"The first thing you have to understand about the company is that Henry Ford is the boss.... He *is* the boss, he always was the boss since the first day I came in and he always will be the boss." These are the words of Arjay Miller, who spent twenty-three years climbing the rungs of Ford management to become president of the company, only to find that Henry Ford II actually ran things. Miller eventually resigned to become dean of the Graduate School of Business at Stanford University.

Lee Iacocca, who introduced Ford's very profitable "Mustang," also climbed the ladder for twenty-four years to become president of the company, only to be fired by "the chairman." When Iacocca asked, "What did I do wrong?", Ford replied, "I just don't like you."[19] Iacocca subsequently became chairman of the board of the Chrysler Corporation.

[17]*Ibid.*, p. 183.

[18]Herman, *Corporate Control, Corporate Power*, pp. 112–113.

[19]Quotation from Victor Lasky, *Never Complain, Never Explain* (New York: Richard Marek Co., 1981), p. 86.

Henry Ford II grew up in a very narrow society; he was a member of a rich, insulated family that was dominated by his grandfather, known to be an exceedingly suspicious, prejudiced, and willful man. Young Ford attended Hotchkiss School and later Yale University. However, he failed to graduate in 1940 after admitting that he had cheated on a term paper. He enlisted in the Navy and served until his father died in 1943; President Roosevelt directed the Secretary of the Navy to release Ford to return to the family business.

Ford started in the automobile industry at the age of twenty-five as vice-president of Ford Motors, serving under his aged grandfather. A year later he took over the presidency. His initial decisions were to replace the one-person autocratic rule of the company with a modern management structure, recruiting bright, young management types (the famous Ford "Whiz Kids," including Robert S. McNamara, who later resigned as Ford president to become Secretary of Defense; Lee Iacocca; Arjay Miller; and Charles B. Thornton, later to become chairman of Litton Industries). He also initiated a modern labor relations program and ended the company's traditional hostility toward labor unions. As commonplace as these policies appear today, they were considered advanced, enlightened, and liberal for the Ford Motor Company at the time.

Over the years Ford proved himself a capable director of the company, despite some occasional and even colossal mistakes. (The Edsel fiasco cost the company over $300 million.) Ford worked long hours at the company headquarters in Detroit. He personally approved style changes in Ford cars and test-drove them himself. He was active on the board of the Ford Foundation, and conscientiously reviewed research and grant proposals with other board members. His younger brothers, Benson and William Clay, eventually became Ford vice-presidents and board members. (William Clay Ford married the daughter of tire manufacturer Harvey S. Firestone, Jr. and purchased the Detroit Lions professional football team.)

Henry Ford II helped launch the National Urban Coalition and organized the National Alliance of Businessmen to provide more jobs for minorities. He was a prime mover in Detroit's urban renewal and redevelopment program, Renaissance Center. It was Ford himself who convinced his old rival, General Motors, as well as Amoco, K-Mart, Parke-Davis, and Western International Hotels, to invest in the central city project. When cost overruns forced up the price of the project, Ford "arm-twisted" many Ford suppliers—U.S. Steel, Firestone, Budd Company—to come up with the additional funds.

Like many people born to wealth and power, Ford's personal style is far from that of the bland organizational person. He is frequently unpredictable, sometimes abrasive, often profane; he expresses his opinions directly. His public and private actions are often controversial. (He divorced his wife of many years and married a beautiful, young Italian actress in 1965; in 1980, he divorced her to marry an American model.)

The Ford Foundation was created before the death of the elder Henry Ford to protect the family fortune from inheritance taxes. Originally, it supported charities in the Detroit area; its assets were primarily Ford stock. As the company prospered, the value of the Foundation assets increased. In 1951, Henry Ford II asked Robert Hutchins, chancellor of the University of Chicago, to take over the Foundation and make it a national force in civic affairs. Hutchins immediately funded some projects that "the Chairman" did not like; Hutchins was cut loose to become head of the Fund for the Republic, a smaller, Ford-funded foundation. The Ford Foundation supported the moderate black civil rights organization, the Urban League, with Henry Ford II's approval. In 1966, McGeorge Bundy, Presidents Kennedy and Johnson's national security adviser, became the Ford Foundation head.

Bundy gradually sold off the Ford stock from the Foundation assets. Bundy and Henry Ford clashed over the liberal programs of the Foundation. Finally, in 1976, Ford resigned from his directorship of the Ford Foundation. In his resignation letter, he pointedly advised the Foundation to direct more attention to strengthening the capitalist system. "The Foundation is a creature of capitalism.... I'm just suggesting to the trustees and the staff that the system that makes the Foundation possible very probably is worth preserving."[20]

By 1980, Henry Ford II faced many troubles. The Pinto car had to be recalled for a faulty gas tank—the largest recall in auto history. Brother Benson Ford died of a heart attack. The break with Lee Iacocca was troublesome. Henry went through another divorce and remarriage. His nephew, Benson Ford, Jr., sued him over his father's will and demanded a seat on the Ford board, which Henry denied him. And in 1980, the Ford Motor Company lost $1.5 billion—the largest annual loss in the history of any American corporation. (Of course, General Motors lost money that year, and Chrysler would have gone bankrupt without favorable U.S. government loan guarantees.) Henry Ford II resigned as chairperson of the board of Ford Motors and handed over the reign to Phillip Caldwell.

Whether Henry Ford II has *really* stepped down is uncertain. His son, Edsel B. Ford, and his nephew, William Clay Ford, Jr., are both promising Ford Company executives who might make it to the top with Henry's help. Henry says that his son and nephew are still "a good ten years" away from top management. When Henry is reminded that he himself inherited the presidency at age twenty six, he says only that "times have changed."

[20]*Newsweek,* January 24, 1977, p. 69.

CHANGING OF THE GUARD

Top leadership in the corporate world changes slowly over time. A reasonably successful president or chairperson and chief executive officer can expect to run the corporation for eight to ten years. Management "climbers," those who have spent thirty years in the corporation, may become president or chairperson at age fifty eight or sixty and may expect to serve to sixty five or sixty seven. Of course, family "inheritors" may have much longer tenures at the top; Henry Ford II has been the dominant figure at Ford Motors for over forty years.

Nonetheless, there is inevitably a "changing of the guard"—a succession to power—in the corporate world as elsewhere. At the beginning of the 1980s, it seemed as if a generation of powerful corporate leaders was stepping aside: Irving S. Shapiro of DuPont, Thomas A. Murphy of General Motors, Reginald Jones of General Electric, J. Paul Austin of Coca Cola, and Harold Geneen of ITT all announced their retirements. Alden W. Clausen left the board chair of BankAmerica to become president of the World Bank, replacing former Secretary of Defense Robert McNamara in that job. Moreover, David Rockefeller retired as chairman of Chase Manhattan, and Henry Ford II retired as chairman of Ford Motors. However, it is not clear whether these powerful men *really* retired. As the *Wall Street Journal* speculated about the strong-willed Harold Geneen, "He may step aside, but he rarely steps down." Certainly the same could be said about Ford and Rockefeller.

Most chief executives remain as directors after they retire. (Rockefeller announced he would become chairman of Chase Manhattan's International Advisory Committee, which advises the bank on foreign affairs, replacing former Secretary of State Henry Kissinger in that job. Kissinger would remain on the committee and remain as counsel to the bank on foreign affairs.) Often this practice gives rise to the question, "Who's in charge here?" Former chairmen usually have more power on the board than other directors simply because they have more knowledge about the operations of the corporation. Former chairmen have been known to lead movements to oust their successors if their successors fail to meet their expectations.

Chairmen are seldom fired, but it has happened on occasion. Unhappy stockholders with a control block of stock, and perhaps support among inside officers who are not loyal to their chairmen, can unseat a CEO. However, "Things have to get very bad before the board says the CEO has to go. Even his mother has to be against him."[21] A. Robert

---

[21]Quotation from *Newsweek*, July 7, 1980, p. 55.

Abboud, former chairman of the board of First Chicago Corporation (the nation's ninth largest bank), was one of the most powerful CEO's fired in recent years.

Perhaps the most publicized corporate firing was NBC's dismissal of one of the very few female CEO's in the country—Jane Cahill Pfeiffer. As a subsidiary of the Radio Corporation of America (RCA), NBC executives must please the RCA Corporation. Jane Pfeiffer lasted only twenty-six months at NBC. Ironically, she learned of her firing from a television report. Her dismissal was considered "messy." Ousted top executives are supposed to resign quietly or take early retirement. While NBC president Fred Silverman *announced* Jane Pfeiffer's dismissal, the *real* decision came from Edgar H. Griffiths, chairman of RCA and a thirty-two-year veteran of the corporation. Griffiths was displeased with NBC's ratings compared to its rival televison networks, ABC and CBS; two years later he fired President Fred Silverman.

Despite these few highly publicized firings, top corporate directors are well-insulated in their positions. Turnover rates are far lower than in government. The average CEO still controls the directors, having selected most of them in the first place. Only a really disastrous corporate performance can inspire a revolution against management.

PERSONAL WEALTH AND ECONOMIC POWER

It is a mistake to equate *personal* wealth with economic power. Persons with relatively little personal wealth can exercise great power if they occupy positions that give them control of huge institutional resources. A president of a large company who came through the ranks of management may receive an income of only $300,000 or $400,000 a year, and possess a net worth of $2 or 3 million. Yet these amounts are small when you consider that this person may control a corporation with annual revenues of $2 *billion* and assets worth $10 or 20 *billion*. (The contrast is even greater in government where $45,000-a-year bureaucrats manage government expenditures of $50 *billion* a year!) The important point is that personal wealth in America is insignificant in comparison to corporate and governmental wealth.

One must occupy top *positions* in large corporate *institutions* to exercise significant economic power. The mere possession of personal wealth, even $100 million, does not guarantee economic power. Indeed, among America's 150 "centimillionaires"—individuals with personal wealth in excess of $100 million—there are many people such as widows, retired persons, and other inheritors who have never played any role in the family business. There are also many "independent operators" who have acquired great wealth in, say, independent oil operations or land speculation, but who do not occupy high positions in the corporate world. Of course, there are many centimillionaires whose personal wealth has come to them through their personal ownership of corporate shares. Familiar names— Ford, Rockefeller, duPont, Mellon—are liberally sprinkled among the nation's top personal wealth-holders. However, their personal wealth is a *by-product* of their role, or their ancestor's role, in the corporate structure.

Socialist critics of America usually do not comprehend the insignificance of personal wealth in relation to corporate and governmental resources. They direct their rhetoric against inequality in personal income in the nation, when in fact the greatest inequities occur in the comparisons between corporate and government resources and the resources of individuals.

Let us illustrate our point: If the personal wealth of every one of America's 150 centimillionaires were *completely confiscated* by government, the resulting revenue (about $30 billion) would amount to less than 5 *percent* of the federal budget for a *single year!*

The relationship between personal wealth and institutional power is described well by economist Adolf Berle:

> As of now, in the United States and in Western Europe, the rich man has little power merely because he is rich. . . . [He] amounts to little unless he connects himself with effective institutions. He must master past institutions or must create new ones. . . . However large his bank account, he can do nothing with it but consume. He can build or buy palaces, amuse himself at Mediterranean or Caribbean resorts, become a figure in Monte Carlo, Miami, or Las Vegas. He can amuse himself by collecting books or purchasing bonds. He can give libraries or laboratories to universities and have his name put on them. He can receive the pleasant but powerless recognition of decorations, honorary degrees, and even titles of nobility. None of these things entitle him to make decisions affecting other men or to give orders (outside his household) with any likelihood they will be fulfilled. Even when he seeks to give his son a career in business, he must ask the assistance of acquaintances and friends who will give the boy a fair chance—and can give him little more. Beyond that, he can leave his son nothing but the ability to live without work and to waste as long as his wealth holds out. All of this does not add up to power.
>
> So, if he wishes a power position, he must find it outside his bank account. He can, it is true, use the bank account to buy into, or possibly create, an institution. He can buy control of a small corporation. (Few rich men are left who are capable of buying individual control of really large ones.) He can undertake the management of that corporation. Then he can derive power from the institution—if, and only if, he is capable of handling it. Whatever power he has comes from the corporation or other institutions, and from such intellectual or organizing skill as he may have—not from his wealth, which is largely irrelevant. He at once discovers that he is subordinate to the institution. It operates under, and in conditions accepted or laid down or directed by, the paramount political power. Then he is tested, not by the

dollar value of his wealth, but by his performance as director or manager of the institution.[22]

Of course, income inequality is and has always been a significant component of the American social structure. The top fifth of income recipients in America accounts for over 40 percent of all income in the nation, while the bottom fifth accounts for only about 5 percent (see Table 2–9). However, the income share of the top fifth has declined since the pre-World War II years. The income share of the top 5 percent of families has declined dramatically from 30 to 14.4 percent. However, the bottom fifth of the population still receives a very small share of the national income. The significant rise in income shares has occurred among the middle classes in the second, third, and fourth income fifths.

Table 2–9   The Distribution of Family Income in America

(By quintiles and top 5 percent)								
Quintiles	1929	1936	1944	1950	1956	1962	1972	1976	1980
Lowest	3.5	4.1	4.9	4.8	4.8	4.6	5.5	5.4	5.2
Second	9.0	9.2	10.9	10.9	11.3	10.9	12.0	12.0	11.6
Third	13.8	14.1	16.2	16.1	16.3	16.3	17.4	17.6	17.5
Fourth	19.3	20.9	22.2	22.1	22.3	22.7	23.5	24.1	24.1
Highest	54.4	51.7	45.8	46.1	45.3	45.5	41.6	41.0	41.5
Total	100.0	100.0	100.0	100.0	100.0	100.0	100.0	100.0	100.0
Top 5 Percent	30.0	24.0	20.7	21.4	20.2	19.6	14.4	14.2	15.6

Source: U.S. Bureau of the Census, *Current Population Reports,* Series P-60; data for early years from Edward C. Budd, *Inequality and Poverty* (New York: W.W. Norton and Co., 1967).

Any list of top wealth-holders in America today includes at least two categories—old and established Eastern families with wealth derived from corporate ownership; and newly rich, self-made Southern and Western centimillionaires whose wealth is derived from "independent" oil operations, real estate speculations, aerospace industries, or technological inventions. (Further contrasts between new wealth and established wealth are found in Chapter 8.) Representative of new-rich, self-made wealth were J. Paul Getty and H.L. Hunt, both now deceased, whose fabulous fortunes were amassed in independent oil operations; Howard Hughes (also now deceased), whose fortune was made in the aerospace industry and is now invested in Las Vegas real estate; and Edwin H. Land, an inventor whose self-developing "Land" camera was the foundation of the Polaroid Corporation. (America's richest man is Daniel K. Ludwig, sole

[22]From Adolf A. Berle, *Power,* copyright © 1967, 1968, 1969. Reprinted by permission of Harcourt Brace Jovanovich, Inc.

owner of the world's largest fleet of super-tankers and cargo vessels, owner of many luxury resorts in the Caribbean, and builder of an entire city in Brazil, Jari, which is larger than the state of Connecticut.) Representative of established Eastern wealth derived from stable corporate enterprise are the Mellons, duPonts, Fords, Rockefellers, and others whose wealth extends back through several generations.

THE LABYRINTH OF CORPORATE OWNERSHIP

If *individuals* no longer own America's corporations, who does? Other corporations. And who owns the owning corporations? Still other corporations. Tracing corporate ownership in America leads one into an endless labyrinth of holding companies, "street names" (camouflage ownership names), banks, insurance companies, and pension funds.

Various federal regulatory agencies require reporting of corporate ownership. However, many corporations fall between the jurisdiction of different agencies, and the ownership reports actually submitted generally hide more than they reveal about corporate ownership.

The Securities and Exchange Commission, for example, requires a corporation to report all owners of 5 percent or more of its common stock; but simply by buying several blocks under different names, an owner can escape official reporting. The Federal Communications Commission requires that owners of 1 percent or more of broadcasting companies be publicly accounted for; the Interstate Commerce Commission requires complete ownership reports on the largest railroads; and the Federal Power Commission requires complete ownership reports on the largest utilities.

But consider this 1975 report submitted by AT&T, the world's largest corporation, of its ten largest owners:

1. Kabo & Co.
2. AT&T
3. Merrill, Lynch
4. Cudd & Co.
5. Kane & Co.
6. Sior & Co.
7. Pitt & Co.
8. Société de Banque Suisse
9. Crédit Suisse
10. Sigler & Co.[23]

[23]Committee on Government Operations, "Corporate Ownership and Control," 94th Congress, 2nd Session, November 1976, (Washington: Government Printing Office, 1976), p. 340.

Few persons have ever heard of Kabo & Co., Cudd & Co., Sior & Co., or Pitt & Co. (AT&T itself holds its own stock for its shareowner and pension plans; Merrill Lynch is Wall Street's largest investment house). These companies are official owners of record of AT&T, but now we must find out who they are. The addresses given on the official filing forms are worthless—usually only "N.Y., N.Y.," and they cannot be found in the New York City telephone directory. These official owners are "street names," or aliases of major banks and insurance companies. For example, it turns out that Kabo & Co. is really Bankers Trust of New York, the nation's seventh largest bank. Sior & Co. is also Bankers Trust. Cudd & Co. is really Chase Manhattan, and so is Kane & Co. Pitt & Co. is Mellon National Bank, and so on.

The *real* owners of AT&T turn out to be:[24]

1. Bankers Trust
2. AT&T
3. Merrill, Lynch
4. Chase Manhattan
5. Morgan Guaranty Trust
6. Citicorp
7. State Street Bank (Boston)
8. Chemical Bank
9. Manufacturers Hanover
10. Crédit Suisse (Switzerland), which holds stock for anonymous foreign investors

However, it is rare that ownership can be traced even to the extent that we have done so here for AT&T.[25]

---

[24]*Ibid.*, p. 402.

[25]For example, Cede & Co. is a front name for Depository Trust Co. of New York, but Depository refuses to reveal the names of anyone it represents. However, it was learned that Cede & Co. held at least the following corporate ownership shares in 1975:

Ashland Oil	8.1%
Chrysler	15.8
LTV Corp	34.0
Bethlehem Steel	8.6
Greyhound	13.8
TransWorld Airlines	27.4
PanAmerican Airways	23.8
Eastern Airlines	31.9
Braniff	30.0
American Electric Power	13.4
American Natural Gas	11.6
Niagara Mohawk Power	13.5
Western Union	19.6

Nonetheless, despite Cede & Co.'s obvious importance, it has refused to reveal the names of its institutional investors. See Vic Reinemer, "Uniform Reporting Dealing with Corporate Ownership." Paper delivered at the Conference on Government Information Needs, Columbia University Center for Law and Economic Studies, November 1976.

In short, the nation's largest corporations are "owned" by holding companies, street names, banks, insurance companies, pension funds, and other corporations. These "owners" almost always assign their voting rights as shareholders to the officers and directors of the companies they own. Thus, the officers and directors—"management"—control the decisions of the corporation. The institutional owners rarely try to oust management. If the owning institutions do not like the way a corporation is managed, they simply sell their stockholdings in it on the open market.

Stock *voting* power is even more concentrated than stock ownership. Many, if not most, stockholders turn over their voting power, via "proxies," to management, banks, pension funds, and investment firms. A Congressional investigation in 1978 into the question "Who Votes the Big Blocks?" produced convincing evidence of concentration of voting power in the nation's largest industrial, financial, transportation, insurance, and utility companies.[26] For example, Morgan Guaranty Trust was identified as the largest *stockvoter* in 56 of the 122 largest corporations studied. Citibank was the largest stockvoter in 25 of these corporations. Moreover, Morgan Guaranty Trust is the largest stockvoter in Citibank (as well as Bank-America, Manufacturers Hanover, Chemical New York Bank, and Bankers Trust New York). And Citicorp, in turn, is the largest stockvoter in Morgan Guaranty Trust! In short, these banks "direct" each other, in that they have the major voting rights in each others' stocks. The study also confirmed that these banks and other large institutional investors generally vote to support management-backed programs and resolutions. They support management not only by voting the stock they own themselves, but also by voting the "proxies" they receive from other investors.

THE CORPORATE CONSCIENCE

Today those at the top of the corporate world are far more liberal and oriented toward public welfare in their attitudes and decisions than the "robber baron" industrial capitalists of a few decades ago. Radical critics of American business who portray top corporate elites as reactionary, repressive, narrow-minded, or short-sighted vastly underestimate their chosen enemy.

Rugged individualism, laissez-faire, public-be-damned business attitudes are far more characteristic of new-rich, self-made men than of established corporate leaders. The people who head the nation's large corporations—both inheritors and up-from-the-ranks managers—are gen-

---

[26]Subcommittee on Reports, Accounting, and Management, U.S. Senate Committee on Government Operations, "Voting in Major Corporations," January 15, 1978; courtesy of Victor Reinemer, staff director. Also reported in *The New York Times*, January 19, 1978, p. 59.

erally sympathetic to the ideals of social welfare. They are concerned with the public interest and express a devotion to the "corporate conscience." The corporate conscience is, in Adolf Berle's words,

> the existence of a set of ideas, widely held by the community and often by the organization itself and the men who direct it, that certain uses of power are "wrong," that is, contrary to the established interest and value system of the community. Indulgence of these ideas as a limitation on economic power, and regard for them by the managers of great corporations, is sometimes called— and ridiculed as—the "corporate conscience." The ridicule is pragmatically unjustified. The first sanction enforcing limitations imposed by the public consensus is a lively appreciation of that consensus by corporate manage- ments. This is the reality of the "corporate conscience."[27]

These top leaders place a great value on social prestige and popular esteem. Thus, although the public has no direct economic control over management, and government control is more symbolic than real, society does wield a powerful weapon—the deprivation of prestige—to aid in enforcing its values upon individuals and groups. Moreover, most of the values of the prevailing liberal consensus have already been internalized by corporate managers themselves.

Corporate elites are by no means hostile to big government. Indeed, in his popular book, *The New Industrial State,* John K. Galbraith argues effectively that we are experiencing a gradual blurring of the distinction between corporate versus governmental enterprise with the growth of a giant, bureaucratic "techno-structure." Corporate planning and govern- mental planning are replacing market competition in America. Corpora- tions avoid vigorous price competition, and the government also endeavors to fix overall prices. Both corporations and the government seek stable relations with large labor unions. Solid, prosperous growth is the keynote of the planned economy, without undue, disruptive, old-style competition. Wars, depressions, or overheated inflations are to be avoided in the interest of stable growth. Big government, big industry, and big labor organizations share in this consensus. Within it, the big quietly grow bigger and more powerful. Government protects this secure, stable world of corporate giants, unless one of them should abuse the accepted standards of behavior or openly try to improve its position.

Thus, the interests of the government and the corporate world come together on behalf of a consensus for stable planned growth:

> The state is strongly concerned with the stability of the economy. And with its expansion or growth. And with education. And with technical and scientific advance. And, most notably, with the national defense. These are *the* national

---

[27]Berle, *Power Without Property,* pp. 90–91.

goals; they are sufficiently trite so that one has a reassuring sense of the obvious in articulating them. All have their counterpart in the needs and goals of the techno-structure. It requires stability in demand for its planning. Growth brings promotion and prestige. It requires trained manpower. It needs government underwriting of research and development. Military and other technical procurement support its most developed form of planning. At each point the government has goals with which the techno-structure can identify itself.[28]

The new jargon in the board room is "corporate responsibility" and "social consciousness." These notions are more prevalent in larger corporations than in smaller ones, but it is the larger corporations that control the greatest share of America's economic resources. Only a few "classic" economists—most notably, University of Chicago's Milton Friedman— continue to argue that America's corporations best serve the nation by concentrating on business alone, allocating resources on the basis of profit alone, and striving for optimum efficiency and productivity. In contrast, most top corporate elites are advocates of corporate responsibility—they want a larger social role for industry and generally are willing to sacrifice some profits to perform such a role. They believe that business should undertake positive efforts to expand minority opportunities, abate pollution, assist in the renewal and redevelopment of the nation's cities, and, in general, *do good.*

Of course, the profit motive is still important to corporate elites, because profits are the basis of capital formation within the corporation. Increased capital at the disposal of corporate managers means increased power; losses mean a decrease in the capital available to the managers, a decrease in their power, and perhaps eventual extinction for the organization. But a certain portion of profits can be sacrificed for social concerns. The prudent corporate leader views such expenditures as being in the long-run interest of the corporation and self.

SUMMARY

In later chapters, we will examine interlocking, recruitment, conflict, and consensus, as well as corporate involvement in national policy-making, in greater detail. Now, however, let us summarize our initial observations of corporate management as one of the key elites in the institutional structure of American society.

Economic power in America is highly concentrated. For example, a small number of corporations control over half the nation's industrial assets; half of all assets in communications, transportation, and utilities;

[28]Galbraith, *The New Industrial State,* p. 316.

and two thirds of all insurance assets. This concentration of economic power is increasing gradually over time, as the nation's largest corporations gain ever larger shares of total corporate assets.

Power over corporate assets rests in the hands of about 4,500 presidents and directors. These directors, not the stockholders or employees, decide major policy questions, choose the people who will carry out these decisions, and even select their own replacements. However, most of these presidents and directors have climbed the corporate ladder to their posts. These "managers" owe their rise to power to their skill in organizational life, and to their successful coping with the new demands for expertise in management, technology, and planning. Individual capitalists are no longer essential in the formation of capital assets. In fact, four fifths of industrial capital is raised either within the corporation itself or from institutional borrowing.

It is true that the Rockefellers, Fords, duPonts, Mellons, and other great entrepreneurial families still exercise great power over corporate resources. But a majority of the directors of family-dominated firms have been brought in from outside the family; and only about 150 of the 500 largest corporations are family dominated.

Personal wealth is insignificant in relation to corporate (or governmental) wealth. Individuals may own millions, but institutions control billions. Thus, it is necessary for individuals to achieve top corporate positions in order to exercise significant economic power.

Top corporate leaders generally display moderately liberal, socially responsible attitudes and opinions on public issues. They are not necessarily hostile to government, but generally share with government an interest in stable growth, the avoidance of disruption, and planned scientific and technological development. The notion of "corporate responsibility" involves a willingness to sacrifice some profits to exercise a larger role in social policy-making. Profits, however, remain essential to the accumulation of capital and the continued existence of the corporation.

3

The governing circles

If there ever was a time when the powers of government were limited—
when government did no more than secure law and order, protect
individual liberty and property, enforce contracts and protect against
foreign invasion—that time has long passed. Today it is commonplace to
observe that governmental institutions intervene in every aspect of our
lives—from the "cradle to the grave." Government in America has the
primary responsibility for providing insurance against old age, death,
dependency, disability, and unemployment; for providing medical care for
the aged and poor; for providing education at the elementary, secondary,
collegiate, and postgraduate levels; for providing for public highways and
regulating water, rail, and air transportation; for providing police and fire
protection; for providing sanitation services and sewage disposal; for
financing research in medicine, science, and technology; for delivering the
mail; for exploring outer space; for maintaining parks and recreation; for
providing housing and adequate food for the poor; for providing for job
training and manpower programs; for cleaning the air and water; for
rebuilding central cities; for maintaining full employment and a stable
money supply; for regulating business practices and labor relations; for
eliminating racial and sexual discrimination. Indeed, the list of government responsibilities seems endless, yet each year we manage to find
additional tasks for government to do.

THE CONCENTRATION OF GOVERNMENTAL POWER

Governments do many things that cannot be measured in terms of dollars and cents. Nonetheless, government expenditures are the best available measure of the dimensions of government activity. Such expenditures in the United States amount to about 35 percent of the gross national product. This is an increase from about 8 percent of the GNP at the beginning of the century. (Years ago, the German economist Adolph Wagner set forth the "law of increasing state activity"; in effect, this law states that government activity increases faster than economic output in all developing societies.) The largest governmental cost is "income maintenance"—social security, welfare, and related social services. Defense spending is the second largest governmental cost, followed by education.

Of course, the observation that government expenditures now account for over one-third of the nation's GNP actually understates the great power of government over every aspect of our lives. Government regulatory activity cannot be measured in government expenditures alone. Indeed, large segments of the economy come under direct federal regulation, notably transportation and utilities; yet these are officially classified as private industries and are not counted in the governmental proportion of the GNP.

Concentration of governmental resources is also evidenced in the growing proportion of *federal* expenditures in relation to *state* and *local* government expenditures. There are approximately 80,000 separate governmental units operating in the United States today. (U.S. government—1; state governments—50; counties—3,044; municipalities—18,517; townships—16,991; school districts—15,781; special districts—23,885.) But only one of these, the U.S. government, accounts for *two thirds* of all governmental expenditures. This means that approximately 21 percent of the GNP is accounted for by federal expenditures alone. This centralization of governmental activity is a twentieth-century phenomenon: At the turn of the century, the federal government accounted for only one third of all governmental expenditures; local governments carried on the major share of governmental activity.

We have defined our governmental elite as the top executive, congressional, military, and judicial officers of the *federal* government: the President and Vice-President; secretaries, under secretaries, and assistant secretaries of executive departments; senior White House presidential advisers; congressional committee chairmen and ranking minority members; congressional majority and minority party leaders in the House and Senate; Supreme Court Justices; and members of the Federal Reserve Board and the Council of Economic Advisers. In the pages that follow we will try to describe some members of the governmental elite, as well as to discuss the power they exercise, and how they came to power.

THE POLITICIANS: STYLE AND IMAGE

The politician is a professional office-seeker. The politician knows how to run for office—but not necessarily how to run the government. After victory at the polls, the prudent politician turns to "serious men" to run the government. Pulitzer Prize-winning writer David Halberstam reports a revealing conversation between newly elected President John F. Kennedy and Robert A. Lovett in December 1960, a month before Kennedy was to take office:

> On the threshold of great power and great office, the young man seemed to have everything. He was handsome, rich, charming, candid. The candor was part of the charm: he could beguile a visitor by admitting that everything the visitor proposed was right, rational, proper—but he couldn't do it, not this week, this month, this term. Now he was trying to put together a government, and the candor showed again. He was self-deprecating with the older man. He had spent the last five years, he said ruefully, running for office, and he did not know any real public officials, people to run a government, *serious men*. The only ones he knew, he admitted, were politicians.... Politicians *did* need men to serve, to run the government. The implication was obvious. Politicians could run Pennsylvania and Ohio, and if they could not run Chicago they could at least deliver it. But politicians run the world? What did they know about the Germans, the French, the Chinese?[1]

Robert Lovett was "the very embodiment of the Establishment." His father had been chairman of the board of Union Pacific Railroad and a partner of the great railroad tycoon, E.H. Harriman. Lovett attended Hill School and Yale, married the daughter of James Brown, the senior partner of the great banking firm of Brown Brothers, and formed a new and even larger Wall Street investment partnership, Brown Brothers, Harriman, & Co. Lovett urged Kennedy to listen to the advice of his partner and former Governor of New York and ambassador to the Soviet Union, Averell Harriman; to see "Jack McCloy at Chase" (then chairman of the board of Chase Manhattan), and "Doug Dillon too" (to become Kennedy's Secretary of the Treasury); to look up a "young fellow over at Rockefeller, Dean Rusk," (to become Kennedy's Secretary of State); and to get "this young man at Ford, Robert McNamara," (to become Kennedy's Secretary of Defense). Kennedy gratefully accepted the advice: he turned to these "serious men" to run the government.

Of course, not all politicians are shallow, superficial, office-seekers. Some are "serious men" themselves—that is, they would be influential even if they never won elective office. Following are a few examples of such individuals.

[1]David Halberstam, *The Best and the Brightest* (New York: Random House, 1969), pp. 3–4. [Italics added.]

George Herbert Walker Bush. Vice-President of the United States. Son of former U.S. Senator Prescott Bush of Connecticut. Attended Phillips Academy and Yale University. At age 25 began as vice-president of Dresser Industries (oil drilling equipment) of which his father was a director. Founded Zapata Oil at age 29; served as president and chairman of the board of Zapata Petroleum and Zapata Offshore Oil Co. Served as U.S. Congressman from Houston for two terms, 1967 to 1971. Became U.S. ambassador to the United Nations; Chairman of the Republican National Committee; and Director of the Central Intelligence Agency. A director of First Bancorporation of Dallas, Houston, and London; Eli Lilly Corp.; Texasgulf; Purolator. A trustee of Baylor and Phillips Academy.

Charles Percy. U.S. Senator (R. Ill.). Attended University of Chicago. Former president and chairman of the board of Bell & Howell Corporation. Director of Harris Trust and Savings Bank. Outboard Moving Corporation. Former chairman of National Finance Committee of the Republican Party. Trustee of the University of Chicago, Illinois Institute of Technology, California Institute of Technology.

H.J. Heinz III. U.S. Senator (R. Pa.). Attended Phillips Exeter Academy, Yale University, and Harvard Law School. Began work with his father's H.J. Heinz Co. as marketing manager. He left the family business to win a congressional seat from Pittsburgh in 1970. In 1976 he won election to the U.S. Senate in the most expensive campaign in the State's history.

Daniel Patrick Moynihan. U.S. Senator (D.N.Y.). Attended public schools in New York City; received B.A., M.A., and Ph.D. degrees in political science from Fletcher School of Law and Diplomacy. He was professor of education and urban politics at Harvard and director of the Harvard—M.I.T. Joint Center for Urban Studies. Served as Assistant Secretary of Labor under Presidents Kennedy and Johnson, Assistant to the President for Domestic Affairs under President Nixon, ambassador to India, and ambassador to the United Nations under President Ford. He is the author of numerous books and articles, and he is listed as one of the nation's elite intellectuals.

John C. Danforth. U.S. Senator (R. Mo.). Attended Princeton University and Yale Law School. Heir to Danforth of the Ralston Purina Corporation. A trustee of Yale University.

The backgrounds of these men suggest that they can run a government as well as run for office. However, the great majority of politicians— elective officeholders—have had little or no experience in heading major enterprises. Most have devoted their lives to running for public office. They are specialists in vote-getting, public relations, image-making, bargaining and compromise, and coalition-building.

Most politicians in America are lawyers. But they are not usually top professional lawyers. (We will examine these "superlawyers" in Chapter 5.) Instead, the typical politician-lawyer uses his or her law career as a means of support—one that is compatible with political office holding. Woodrow Wilson said, "The profession I chose was politics; the profession I entered was the law. I entered one because I thought it would lead to the other."[2] The legal profession provides the free time, the extensive public contacts, and the occupational prestige required for political campaigning. The lawyer's occupation is the representation of clients, so he or she makes no great change when moving from representing clients in private practice to representing constituents in public office.

A significant number of top politicians have inherited great wealth. The Roosevelts, Rockefellers, Kennedys, Lodges, Harrimans, Bushes, and others have used their wealth and family connections to support their political careers. *But it is important to note that a majority of the nation's top politicians have climbed the ladder from relative obscurity to political success.* Many have acquired some wealth in the process, but most started their climb from very middle-class circumstances. In fact, only one of the last seven Presidents (John F. Kennedy) was born to great wealth. Thus, as in the corporate world, one finds both "inheritors" and "climbers" in the world of politics.

GERALD R. FORD: FROM THE ROSE BOWL
TO THE WHITE HOUSE

Gerald Ford was always a team player—from his days as an All-American lineman at the University of Michigan, through his long service and rise to leadership in the Congress, during his years of service and support for the Republican Party, to his presidency. He projected the image of an open, accessible, and consensus-building presidency. Ford was the nation's only President not selected by popular vote (or by vote of presidential electors). He is a man whose career was built in the Congress of the United States. His former colleagues there have described him as "solid, dependable, and loyal—a man more comfortable carrying out the programs of others than initiating things on his own."[3] As President, he was thrust into the role of leadership, but there is ample evidence that he acted only after extensive consultation with leaders in Congress, the cabinet, industry, finance, labor, and the mass media.

Gerald Ford was born Leslie King, Jr., but his mother divorced and remarried Gerald R. Ford, a Grand Rapids, Michigan, paint store owner. Ford attended public schools in Grand Rapids, and received his B.A. from the University of Michigan and his law degree from Yale University. He was a star lineman on the University of Michigan's national championship

[2]Quoted in Heinz Eulau and John Sprague, *Lawyers in Politics* (Indianapolis: Bobbs-Merrill Co., 1964), p. 5.
[3]*Congressional Quarterly*, October 20, 1973, p. 2762.

and Rose Bowl football teams in 1932 and 1933, and was the team's most valuable player in 1934. He turned down the opportunity to play professional football in order to take a coaching job at Yale that would permit him to attend law school at the same time. Ford graduated in the top third of his Yale Law School class in 1941. Following service with the Navy in World War II in the South Pacific, Ford returned home to Grand Rapids and, capitalizing on his football reputation and war service, won election to the House in 1948.

Ford served 25 years in the House as a loyal Republican, winning recognition for his integrity, sincerity, and common sense, rather than for his intelligence, initiative, or imagination. He was also careful to cultivate his home constituents with minor services, favors, and visits. In 1965, Wisconsin Congressman Melvin Laird, later to become Secretary of Defense, led a movement among House Republicans to replace the aging Charles Halleck as Minority Leader with the younger, likable Gerald Ford. Ford developed into an excellent House Leader through his engaging personality, honesty, and ability to establish close personal relationships with both allies and opponents.

Ford's voting record was moderately conservative. He voted *for* the Civil Rights Act of 1964, the Voting Rights Act of 1965, and the Fair Housing Act of 1968. But he opposed many aspects of the "war on poverty" and other social welfare spending measures. He supported defense spending, and supported both Presidents Johnson and Nixon in their conduct in the Vietnam War.

As the Watergate Affair expanded and Vice-President Spiro Agnew resigned and pleaded guilty to the charge of tax evasion, President Nixon sought to bring into his administration people of recognized personal intergrity who could improve presidential relations with Congress. Nixon's ultimate decision to make Gerald Ford Vice-President under the 26th Amendment was widely applauded in Congress and the news media. But in a sense, Ford was Congress's choice for the vice-presidency, not Richard Nixon's. Nixon personally preferred former Texas Governor John Connally. Ford was quickly confirmed by the Democratic-controlled Congress.

Ford's style was candid, folksy, unpretentious. His long years in the Congress developed in him a tolerance of differing views, a desire to accommodate, and a willingness to compromise differences. In his first speech to the nation as President he said, "I have had lots of adversaries, but no enemies that I can remember."

When Ford spoke at the Harvard Club of Boston, he was asked to comment on the exile of the world-renowned Russian novelist Alexander Solzhenitsyn. Ford simply said: "Well, I've never read anything Solzhenitsyn has written, but I understand he's quite superb."[4] Doubtlessly there

---

[4]Saul Friedman, "In Praise of Honest Ignorance," *Harpers*, August 1974, p. 16.

were many others at the Harvard Club who had never read Solzhenitsyn, but to admit such a fact in these circles is unheard of. Such openness contributed to his rise to the top. After the years of Watergate, and a notable absence of candor in the White House, Ford's most visible quality— open sincerity—appealed to the Congress, and news media, and the general public.

Indeed, despite the Watergate scandal and the split in his own party with the Reagan conservatives, and despite a two-to-one lead in Democratic party registration, Ford nearly won the 1976 Presidential election. The fact that he came so close (49 percent of the two-party vote) under these adverse circumstances is a tribute to his unpretentious style and "good guy" image. Although Ford had spent most of his adult life in politics, he never implied that he personally could run the country. More than most modern politicians, Ford acknowledged the importance of the "serious men" who worked in his administration. Even in the presidency, Ford remained a team player.

JIMMY CARTER: THE SMILE ON THE FACE OF THE ESTABLISHMENT

James Earl Carter, Jr. is usually portrayed as a political "outsider," who was catapulted from a Plains, Georgia, peanut farmer to President of the United States in less than two years. At first glance, Carter's meteoric rise from rustic obscurity to the nation's most powerful office would seem to demolish the elitist notion of selecting leaders from the ranks of seasoned officeholders. But a closer examination of elite concerns in 1976— especially concern over declining public confidence in established elites themselves—together with Carter's establishment connections, provides a better understanding of how and when an "outsider" will be selected for national leadership.

One year before he was elected President, three quarters of the American people had never heard of Jimmy Carter. He had served only one lackluster term as Governor of Georgia. He had never served in Congress and, except for seven years in the Navy, he had never worked for the federal government. He was not even a lawyer. His family's $4 million holdings in Sumter County, Georgia, may have made them *local* influentials, but few *national* leaders had ever heard of Sumter County, Georgia. However, Carter judged correctly in early 1974 that these political disadvantages could be turned to his favor in an era of popular discontent with national leadership over Watergate, inflation and unemployment, and defeat and humiliation in Vietnam.

The national news media paid little attention to Carter's December 12, 1974, announcement that he was a presidential candidate. Media executives, and political observers everywhere, expected that an established leader—Hubert H. Humphrey or Edward M. Kennedy—would win the presidency in 1976. However, Carter knew that the first two presidential primaries were in New Hampshire and Florida. The first was a small state where he had two years to engage in face-to-face campaigning, and the second was a neighboring Southern state. These two early primary victories brought Carter the recognition that he needed. In the spring of 1976, discussion within national elite circles turned to the question of whether Humphrey or Kennedy could dispel public doubts about national leadership, or whether these men had been tarnished by past scandals, errors, and humiliations.

Carter defeated weaker candidates in the early primaries—Udall, Jackson, Wallace, Shriver, Harris, Schapp, Bentson—although he lost to Brown and Church in later primaries. The real question throughout early 1976, however, was whether either of the political heavyweights, Humphrey or Kennedy, would enter the race and take the prize away from Carter. In the end, consultations with other top leaders convinced both men not to run and to allow Carter to become President.

While Carter was obviously a "climber" in the political world, he was not really the "outsider" that he presented himself to be in the election. In fact, Carter had been introduced to the "political and economic elite" several years before he began his race for the presidency. The Coca Cola Company is the largest industrial corporation headquartered in Atlanta. J. Paul Austin, Chairman of the Board of Coca Cola and a friend and supporter of Jimmy Carter, nominated the Georgia Governor to serve as a U.S. representative on the international Trilateral Commission. The Trilateral Commission was established in 1972 by David Rockefeller, with the assistance of the Council on Foreign Relations and the Rockefeller Foundation. The Trilateral Commission is a group of corporate officials of multinational corporations and government officials of several industrialized nations who meet periodically to coordinate economic policy between the United States, Western Europe, and Japan. Carter's appointment was made by Rockefeller himself and came with the support of Coca Cola and Lockheed, both Atlanta-based, multinational corporations. The executive director of the Commission was Columbia University Professor Zbigniew Brzezinski (later Carter's national security adviser). The Commission's membership was a compendium of power and prestige; it included Cal Tech President, Harold Brown (later Secretary of Defense); Coca Cola's J. Paul Austin; *Time Magazine* editor Hedley Donovan; Paul Warnke, partner in Clark Clifford's Washington law firm; Alden Clausen, president of BankAmerica, the nation's largest bank; United Auto Workers president Leonard Woodcock; Bendix Corporation president Werner M. Blumenthal (later Secretary of the Treasury); Cyrus Vance, senior Wall Street lawyer (later Secretary of State); and U.S. Senator Walter Mondale (later

Vice-President of the United States). Thus, after Carter won the Democratic nomination, he sat down comfortably at New York's exclusive "21" Club as a guest of Henry Ford II to meet with the nation's top corporate elite.[5] He successfully reassured top business leaders that his brand of "populism" would not hurt big business.

Carter as an "outsider" provided the new face, the smile, the reassuring manner that a worried establishment perceived as essential in winning back mass confidence in national leadership. At the same time, Carter reinforced established programs and policies; he was welcomed into top elite circles as a man who could restore mass confidence in public institutions and national leadership, and do so without changing things much.

Jimmy Carter's rapid rise to national leadership, and his welcome into top elite circles, represents still another tactic available to an embattled elite—replace old faces associated with past defeats and humiliations with smiling new faces, promising honesty, compassion, and good times. And indeed Carter's subsequent performance as President emphasized style rather than substance. Carter focused the attention of the news media and the general public on presidential visits to small towns, dial-a-President telethons, eliminating limousine service for high officials, selling the presidential yacht, and similar gestures designed to "get close to the people." But on major foreign and defense policy issues—the SALT talks, détente with the USSR, relations with China, a Mideast peace, restoring a strategic nuclear balance—Carter made little substantive progress. (Carter's only success was helping to negotiate the Camp David Accords promising peace between Egypt and Israel.) Likewise on domestic issues—welfare reform, tax rebates, energy policy, tax reform—Carter made little headway with Congress. This is not necessarily a criticism of the Carter Administration, but a recognition of the fact that style (or "image") took precedence over substantive issues. This is true of most politicians; it was particularly true of a President selected for his smile, his self-assurance, his high moral tone.

RONALD REAGAN: THE QUICK-STUDY COWBOY

Ronald Wilson Reagan was always a "quick study"—he learned his acting lines easily and well. He made fifty-four movies over a period of twenty-seven years. He never won an Oscar; he was never even nominated for one. His best role was the legendary Notre Dame halfback, George Gipp ("win one for the Gipper") in the movie *Knute Rockne, All-American,* with Pat O'Brian in the title role. But Ronald Reagan was a steady, hard-working,

[5]*Wall Street Journal,* August 12, 1976, p. 1.

professional. He showed up on time, knew his lines, and took direction easily. He was comfortable—even modest—in front of the camera. The Hollywood crowd thought he was a square—no drugs, booze, or high-living. He was a liberal and a Democrat, and in 1947 he was elected president of the Screen Actors Guild, a post he held through six terms.

Reagan's boyhood in small towns of the midwest—Tampico, Dixon, and Eureka, Illinois—was far removed from the glitter of Hollywood or the power of Washington. Reagan "climbed" the ladder of success: He was the child of a failed, alcoholic shoe salesperson; he washed dishes at tiny, threadbare Eureka college; he won a partial athletic scholarship (football and swimming); he graduated in 1932 in the middle of the Great Depression; and he struggled for five years as sports announcer (beginning at five dollars per game) for radio station WHO in Des Moines, Iowa. Later, when WHO sent "Dutch" Reagan to California to cover spring training for the Chicago Cubs, Reagan contacted an agent who arranged a screen test for him. The test was shown to Jack Warner, resident tycoon at Warner Brothers, and "a star was born"—or more accurately, another grade-B movie actor was signed to a studio contract.

Reagan was never Humphrey Bogart, or James Cagney, or Errol Flynn. He served in the Army Air Corps in World War II making training films, and his acting career faded after the war. His marriage to actress Jane Wyman (who won best-actress Oscar for her work in "Johnny Belinda") also faded. The good acting roles went to other actors, and new stars—Brando, Newman, Holden—replaced the old. By 1957, Reagan was playing opposite a chimpanzee in *Bedtime for Bonzo*. He met and married another aspiring young actress, Nancy Davis, who was to stick by him in the lean years, all the way to the presidency. He also remained active and well-liked in Hollywood as president of the Screen Actors Guild.

Turning 50, Reagan was rescued from obscurity by Ralph J. Cordiner, president of General Electric. G.E. was putting together a weekly network television show, *G.E. Theatre*, and Reagan was offered the job as host. Reagan realized that a television show would be the end of his Hollywood career, but he had little choice. Fortunately, *G.E. Theatre* turned out to be an Emmy Award winning venture; it held a prime Sunday evening spot for seven years before being replaced by one of Reagan's own favorites, *Bonanza*.

More importantly, Reagan began making public appearances and probusiness speeches across the country on behalf of General Electric. Hollywood receded into the background as Reagan collected a vast array of three-by-five index cards filled with examples of federal bureaucracy run amok, social welfare programs wasting money and ruining lives, and the ever-increasing threat of socialism to America's free enterprise system. Reagan's early liberalism gave way to staunch conservatism, which occasionally even embarrassed General Electric. (Some observers believe that

Reagan's fight to keep the Screen Actors Guild free from communist influence in the 1940's started him on the road to conservatism.) Yet Reagan polished his style—his warm wit, his down-home "aw shucks" mannerisms, and his studied sincerity.

Several new-money Southern California millionaires decided that Reagan had a more promising future than merely speaking at Chamber of Commerce meetings. When *G.E. Theatre* was finally cancelled, and Reagan was hosting *Death Valley Days* at a lower salary, his wealthy admirers came to his rescue. In 1964, Reagan was in debt; he had failed to invest his money when he was in Hollywood, and he owed back income taxes to the U.S. government. A group headed by Justin Dart (Dart Industries; Rexall Drugs; Kraft Foods), Holmes Tutle (a Los Angeles Ford dealer), William French Smith (a wealthy Los Angeles attorney), and A.C. (Cy) Rubel (chairman of Union Oil Co.) formed the Ronald Reagan Trust Fund to take over his personal finances and free him to concentrate on a political career. His first political venture was the production of a film to assist Republican presidential candidate Barry Goldwater in 1964. Reagan made the perfect pitch; the money rolled in, but Goldwater was overwhelmingly rejected at the polls. Nonetheless, Reagan won the hearts of conservatives throughout the country, who recognized a new and highly gifted media politician.

Two years later, Ronald Reagan took on the incumbent governor of California, Edmund G. "Pat" Brown (the father of Governor Jerry Brown), who had defeated Richard Nixon for the post in 1962. It was Reagan's first try for public office. Like so many other politicians, Brown underestimated Reagan's appeal. Reagan buried him with nearly a million-vote margin.

In his campaign for governor of California, Reagan had promised a conservative government: cracking down on campus rioting; cleaning up the welfare mess; halting the growth of government spending. He did not succeed. California's spending doubled during his eight years in office; welfare administration was improved only slightly; and campus rioting remained common. Yet Reagan won the admiration of many in government: he was willing to compromise; he was never angry or bitter; if he could not reduce the size of government, he was satisfied to slow its growth. He was described as a pleasant, charming, amicable "closet moderate" whose hard-line conservative speeches did not reflect his pragmatic approach to administration. He delegated responsibility and relied on his staff. He did not read books; he wanted one-page summaries of major issues. He worked in a relaxed manner, frequently ending his workday in the early afternoon. He built his Rancho del Cielo on weekends. He assembled an excellent staff, including many who would later come with him to the White House—Ed Mease, Michael Deaver, Lyn Nofzinger. Paul Laxalt, then governor of neighboring Nevada, became his close friend. Reagan was re-elected in 1970 by another million-vote margin.

In the meantime, the Ronald Reagan Trust Fund turned a $65,000 investment in Malibu Canyon into $1.9 million by selling the land to Twentieth Century Fox Studios. The Fund also purchased Rancho California for $347,000 and sold it for $856,000. Reagan bought his Pacific Palisades residence for less than $50,000 and placed it on sale in 1981 for $1.9 million. By 1980, Reagan was worth over $2 million and had an annual income of over $500,000.

It is considered politically foolish, if not suicidal, to challenge an incumbent president of one's own party for the presidential nomination. In 1976, Gerald Ford was the Republican president, and it appeared unlikely that the Republican Party would deny him renomination. However, Reagan decided to make a run for Ford's job (some say because Ford had bypassed Reagan for a "liberal," Nelson Rockefeller, as Vice-President). Reagan hired a media consultant, John Sears, who mistakenly tried to keep Reagan under wraps, fearing his old conservative instincts would result in verbal miscues. But Reagan almost defeated Ford in the 1976 Republican convention. Reagan left the convention believing his political days were over; he would be nearly seventy by the next election. However, Ford lost to Carter, and conservatives throughout the country turned to Reagan for leadership in 1980.

The camera is a tool of both of Ronald Reagan's trades—actor and politician. Newspaper journalists could never understand Reagan's success. Reporters wrote up his commonplace phrases and time-worn slogans—the simple messages on the old and yellowed three-by-five cards. The printed words were lifeless and uninspiring. Journalists missed Reagan's true appeal as a comfortable, pleasant, reassuring man of traditional American values. Even John Sears, the professional PR adviser, underestimated his candidate's personal appeal. Sears believed Reagan could only win by staying above the political fray and avoiding blunders in speeches, debates, and press conferences. But just before the crucial New Hampshire primary, Sears was fired, and Reagan set out on his own with his index cards to battle Bush, Baker, Connolly, Dole, Crane, and Anderson (and to scare Ford out of the race). In a New Hampshire debate, Reagan won over the state's Republican voters by spontaneously defending the rights of the other candidates (besides the invited George Bush) to be there. Before the GOP convention met in July, 1980, Ronald Reagan had tied up the nomination with the support of the party's conservative stalwarts.

The political landscape is littered with candidates who underestimated Reagan—the supposedly lightweight, "too-old" actor. President Carter hoped Reagan would win the Republican nomination in 1980, because Carter's aides thought Reagan would be the easiest person to beat. In the general election, however, Reagan skillfully turned his age from a liability to an asset. In 1980, the "good old days" never looked better. Reagan spoke of traditional values; he knew that America could be "great again." Carter mistakenly tried to portray Reagan as an unstable warmonger. But Reagan's polished style and charm—his appearance as a kindly, older, soft-spoken, western rancher—deflected Carter's attack. In the presidential debate, Carter was clearly the master of the substance: he talked about programs, figures, budgets. He talked rapidly and seriously. But during the ninety minutes of debate, Reagan was the master of the stage: he was relaxed, smiling, even joking. He never raised his voice or hyped the tempo. He never said anything of great importance. He merely asked, "Are you better off now than you were five years ago?" Simple, yet highly effective.

In the final few days before the election, the media decided to publicize the first anniversary of the Iranian hostage-taking. This decision sealed Carter's fate. By reminding Americans of international humiliations, military weaknesses, and administration blunders during the Carter years, the media set the stage for a Reagan landslide. In the end, NBC announced the winner on national television before the polls closed, and Jimmy Carter immediately conceded defeat.

Just as Reagan's opponents underestimated his abilities as a campaigner, they also underestimated his skills as President. Upon taking office, Reagan did not turn to conservative ideologists to run the government, but instead he called upon a mature, educated, and experienced team (see "The Reaganauts" later in this chapter). When he called for substantial reductions in the Carter budget for 1982, the Washington correspondents said he could not succeed. (Reagan had helped to elect a Republican-controlled Senate, but the House was still under Democratic control.) Yet with skillful personal appeals to Democratic and Republican Congresspersons, and very successful national television appeals, Reagan rolled over his congressional opponents. He reduced proposed government spending and later pushed through the largest tax cut in the nation's history. He was more successful in changing the course of government than any President since Franklin D. Roosevelt.

THE REAGANAUTS

The top posts in the Reagan Administration are filled with individuals with extensive experience in industry, finance, government, law, and university-level education. Indeed, Reagan's far-right supporters have complained bitterly that Reagan turned to so many establishment figures to fill top government posts. But like Presidents before him, Reagan relies upon "serious men," not conservative ideologists, to run the government.

Consider the impressive credentials of the nineteen Cabinet-level officials in the Reagan Administration: thirteen Secretaries together with the Vice-President, UN Ambassador, CIA Director, OMB Director, National Security Advisor, and Council of Economic Advisors Chairman. Ten Cabinet officers have "Ivy League" educations, and two others (Secretary of State Haig and Secretary of Agriculture Block) are West Point graduates—a total of 63 percent. Thirteen Cabinet officers (68 percent) have advanced degrees: three have Ph.D.'s, five have law degrees, and five have master's degrees. Harvard alumni are most numerous (5), followed by Yale (2) and West Point (2). Eleven cabinet officers (58 percent) have served as officers or directors of corporations. Eight cabinet officers (42 percent) are members of the Council on Foreign Relations, including the Vice-President, Secretary of State, Secretary of Defense, Secretary of the Treasury, and Attorney General. In short, Reagan himself may be a small town, Eureka College, radio announcer, movie actor, but his administration is composed of highly educated, well-connected, eastern establishment types.

No one better represents the eastern establishment than Reagan's choice for Vice-President, George Bush. Bush is a Phillips (Andover) Academy "preppy" and Yale University graduate, whose father was a U.S. Senator from Connecticut. Bush went to Houston at age twenty-five as vice-president of Dresser Industries, an oil drilling equipment firm of which his father was a director. Later Bush formed his own oil company, Zapata Petroleum, and he became a multimillionaire. He served as a director of the First International Bank of Houston and London as well as Eli Lilly, Texas Gulf, and Purolator. Having conquered the business world, Bush ran for Congress as a Republican from a wealthy, suburban Houston district. He won in 1966 and served two terms. However, he lost to the Democratic conservative Lloyd Bentsen in a bid for the Senate in 1970. He was named by Nixon to the post of ambassador to the United Nations (serving from 1971 to 1973), and later he was chairman of the Republican National Committee (from 1973 to 1974). Bush headed the GOP during the Watergate crisis, but avoided any bad publicity himself. Ford sent him off as U.S. envoy to the Peoples Republic of China and then called him back to head the C.I.A. Bush was a member of all of the right clubs and organizations (Bohemian Club, Council on Foreign Relations, Trilateral Commission). In his primary campaign for the presidency, Bush tried to portray Reagan as an ultraconservative "cowboy" whose supply-side notions were "voodoo economics." However, Bush has been a team player in the Reagan Administration.

Treasury Secretary Donald T. Regan relinquished the chair of Wall Street's largest brokerage firm, Merrill Lynch, and gave up a salary estimated to be above $500,000 a year, to take his $67,000 Cabinet post. Secretary of State Alexander Haig gave up the prestigious position of president of United Technologies, the twenty-eighth largest industrial corporation in America in 1980, and a salary in excess of $500,000, to take his $67,000 job with the Reagan Administration. Defense Secretary Caspar

Weinberger gave up the position of vice-president of the world's largest construction company, the Bechtel Corporation. *Time* magazine estimated that the average Reagan Cabinet official earned $285,000 before entering the government.[6]

The Reagan team is mature; their average age was fifty five when they took office in 1981. Reagan himself is the nation's oldest President; he turned seventy two weeks after taking office. *Washington Post* columnist David Broder was demonstrably wrong when he predicted in 1980 that the new decade would see a transfer of power to a "new generation of young leaders sharply different from their predecessors of the Great Depression—World War II generation."[7] The average Reagan Cabinet member was born in 1926, grew up in the Great Depression, and served in the military during World War II. Rather than bringing "new values" to the nation, the Reagan team represents a reaffirmation of traditional American values.

The Reagan Cabinet includes one black member, Secretary of Housing and Urban Development Samuel R. Pierce. Pierce was one of the first blacks to become a senior partner in a large New York law firm. He had been a director of General Electric, Prudential First National Boston Corp., International Paper, and U.S. Industries, and he had held several high government posts in the Eisenhower and Nixon administrations. The only woman with Cabinet rank is Jeane Kirkpatrick, ambassador to the United Nations (she is also the only Democrat). Kirkpatrick was a professor of political science at Georgetown University who had written an article in *Commentary* critical of Carter's handling of his "human rights" policy. Reagan read the article and contacted her for help during his campaign. The only person in the higher echelons of the Reagan Administration who is under forty years of age is David Stockman, director of the Office of Management and Budget. Despite his relative youth (he was thirty-four in 1980), Stockman served two terms as a Republican Congressman from Michigan (from 1976 to 1980). He graduated from Michigan State in 1968 and attended Harvard Divinity School; he worked as an aide to Republican Representative John Anderson (from 1970 to 1972). He gave up his seat in the House of Representatives to become Office of Management and Budget director.

Reagan's senior White House aides are also well-educated and experienced. White House Counselor, Edwin Meese, is a Yale graduate with a law degree from Berkeley. He was Reagan's chief of staff when Reagan was governor of California. He served as chief of staff during the Reagan campaign. When Reagan was out of office, Meese was a professor of law at the University of San Diego. White House Chief of Staff, James A.

---

[6]*Time*, January 5, 1981, p. 64.

[7]David S. Broder, *Changing of the Guard* (New York: Simon and Schuster, 1980).

Table 3–1   The Reaganauts

Name (Year of birth)	Government Posts	Professional and Corporate Posts	Education	Memberships
George Bush Vice-President (1924)	Director C.I.A. (76–77); U.S. envoy Peking (74–75); Ch. Republican Party (73–74); Amb. U.N. (71–72); Congress (67–71).	Ch. Zapata Off-Shore Co.; founder Zapata Oil; dir. First National Bank Houston, Eli Lilly, Texas Gulf, Purolator.	Phillips (Andover) Academy; Yale University.	Council on Foreign Relations; Trilateral Commission; American Enterprise Institute; Trustee of Baylor, Trinity, and Phillips Academy; Bohemian Club.
Alexander M. Haig Secretary of State (1924)	Supreme Allied Commander NATO (74–79); White House Chief of Staff (73–74); Vice-Chief of Staff U.S. Army (73); Deputy Nat'l Security Advisor (69–73); Asst. to Secretary of the Army (65); Deputy Asst. Sect. of Defense (64–65).	Pres. United Technologies (79–81); Dir. Chase Manhattan, Crown Cork.	U.S. Military Academy at West Point; M.A. Georgetown.	Council on Foreign Relations.
Donald T. Regan Secretary of Treasury (1918)	None	Ch. Merrill Lynch & Co. (71–80); Vice-Ch. New York Stock Exchange (72–75); Pres. Merrill Lynch & Co. (68–71).	Harvard	Council on Foreign Relations; Business Roundtable; Committee on Economic Development.
Caspar Weinberger Secretary of Defense (1917)	Secretary HEW (73–75); Dir. OMB (72–73); Dep. Dir. OMB (70–72); Ch. Federal Trade Commission (70); California Finance Dir. (68–70); California State Legislator (52–58).	Vice-President Bechtel Corp. (75–80); Dir. Pepsico, Quaker Oats.	Harvard; Harvard Law School.	Council on Foreign Relations—Trilateral Commission; American Enterprise Institute; Bohemian Club.

Name				
William French Smith Attorney General (1917)	Board of Regents Univ. of California (68–81).	Los Angeles attorney; Dir. Crocker Nat'l Bank, Pacific Telephone, Pacific Lighting, Pacific Mutual Life, Jorgensen Steel, Pullman Co.	UCLA; Harvard Law School.	Council on Foreign Relations; Los Angeles World Affairs Council; California Chamber of Commerce; Trustee of Clarmont College and Cate School; Trustee of JFK School at Harvard and Center for Strategic and International Studies at Georgetown; Bohemian Club.
Malcolm Baldridge Secretary of Commerce (1922)	Republican Finance Committee	Ch. Scoville Corp.; Dir. Bendix, AMF, Uniroyal, Connecticut Mutual Life Insurance, Northeast Utilities, Waterbury Savings Bank, Colonial Bank & Trust, Lewis Engine Co., American Chain and Cable Co.	Yale.	Council on Foreign Relations; Business Council; International Chamber of Commerce.
Richard S. Schweiker Secretary of Health and Human Services (1926)	U.S. Senator, R. Pa., (68–80); U.S. Representative, R. (61–68).	None	Penn State.	None
Drew Lewis Secretary of Transportation (1931)	Republican National Committee (76–81).	Pres. Lewis & Associates; Pres. Snelling & Snelling; Chief Exec. Officer Simplex Wire and Cable; Vice-Pres. National Gypsum Co.	Haverford; M.B.A. Harvard	Philadelphia World Affairs Council; Trustee of Temple Univ. and Haverford College.

77

Table 3–1 The Reaganauts (continued)

Name		Education	Other
James G. Watt Secretary of Interior (1938)	Federal Power Commissioner (75–77); Bureau Dir. Dept. of Interior (72–75); Deputy Asst. Sect. of Interior (69–72); Asst. to U.S. Senator, Wyoming (62–66).	Pres. and Chief Counsel Mountain States Legal Foundation (77–81) (prodevelopment lobby group).	Wyoming; Wyoming Law School	None
James B. Edwards Secretary of Energy (1927)	Governor of South Carolina (75–79); Ch. Southern Governors Conference Assn. (77–78); South Carolina State Legislature (72–75).	Dentist; Dir. First National Bank of South Carolina, Burris Chemicals, AMVEST Corp., Edwards & Brook (real estate).	College of Charleston; Univ. of Pennsylvania Dental School	Trustee of Guggenheim Foundation.
Raymond J. Donovan Secretary of Labor (1930)	None	Vice-Pres. Schiavone Construction Co.	Notre Dame of New Orleans	None
John R. Block Secretary of Agriculture (1935)	Illinois Secretary of Agriculture (77–81)	"Farmer" (3,000 acres in Illinois)	U.S. Mil. Acad. at West Point.	None
Samuel R. Pierce Secretary of Housing and Urban Development (1922)	General Counsel, Dept. of Treasury (70–73); New York City Court Judge (59–60); Asst. to Under sect of Labor (54–56); Asst. U.S. Attorney (52–54); Asst. District Attorney N.Y. (49–52).	Sr. Partner, Fowler, Jaffin, Pierce & Kheel; Governor, American Stock Exchange; Professor N.Y.U. Law School; Dir. General Electric, Prudential, IBEE, First National Boston Corp., International Paper, U.S. Industries.	Cornell; Cornell Law School.	Trustee of NAACP, Cornell University, Mt. Holyoke College, Hampton Institute, Rand Corp., and Boy Scouts of America.

Name/Position	Career Positions	Other Positions	Education	Memberships
Terrell H. Bell Secretary of Education (1921)	Utah Commissioner of Education (76–81); U.S. Commissioner of Education, HEW (74–76); Asst. Commissioner, U.S. Office of Education HEW (70–71); Utah Superintendent of Public Instruction (63–70).	Utah school superintendent; high school chemistry teacher	Southern Idaho College; M.S. Univ. of Idaho; Ed.D. Univ. of Utah.	None
William J. Casey Director Central Intelligence Agency (1913)	Small Business Adm. Task Force (76–81); Foreign Intelligence Advisory Board (76–77); Pres. Export-Import Bank (74–75); Under Sect. of State, Economic Affairs (73–74); Ch. Securities and Exchange Commission (71–73); Arms Control & Disarmament Agency Advisor (69–71); Chief of Secret Intelligence, European Theatre, OSS (44–45).	Sr. Partner, Rogers & Wells; Dir. Capital Cities Broadcasting Co., Advancement Devices, Kalver Co., Multiphonics Co.	Fordham; St. John's Law School	Council on Foreign Relations; National Intelligence Study Center; National Strategic Information Center; Trustee of Fordham University
Jeanne D. Kirkpatrick United Nations Ambassador (1926)	Democratic National Committee Convention Staff (72); Democratic National Convention Credentials Comm. (76); research analyst, State Dept. (51–53).	Professor of political science, Georgetown University.	Barnard College; M.A. and Ph.D. Columbia Univ.	American Enterprise Institute; Committee on the Present Danger; Robert A. Taft Institute of Gov't.
Richard V. Allen National Security Advisor (1936)	Dep. Asst to Pres. Intn'l Affairs (71–72); Dep. Com. Intn'l Trade (69–71); Dep. National Security Advisor (69).	Pres. Potomac Int'l Corp.; staff Hoover Institute; staff Center for Strategic and Intn'l Studies, Georgetown.	Notre Dame; M.S. Notre Dame.	Council on Foreign Relations; Committee on the Present Danger.

Table 3–1 The Reaganauts (continued)

David A. Stockman Director, Office of Management and Budget (1946)	U.S. Representative R. Mich. (76–80); Dir. Staff, House Rep. Conference (72–75); aide, Rep. John B. Anderson R. Mich. (70–72).	None	Michigan State; Harvard Divinity School	American Enterprise Institute.
Murray L. Weidenbaum Chairman, Council of Economic Advisers (1927)	Asst. Sect. of Treas. (69–71).	Professor of economics, Washington Univ., St. Louis; economist, Stanford Research Institute; economist Boeing Aircraft.	C.C.N.Y.; M.A. Columbia; Ph.D. Princeton	Council on Foreign Relations; American Enterprise Institute (Editor of *Regulation*) *Time* Board of Economists.

Baker, is a Princeton graduate with a law degree from the University of Texas. Baker was Under Secretary of Commerce in the Ford Administration and presidential campaign manager for George Bush. Prior to entering politics, Baker was a successful Houston attorney. Domestic Policy Advisor, Martin C. Anderson, is a Dartmouth graduate with a Ph.D. in economics from M.I.T. He was a professor of business at Columbia University and a fellow of the Hoover Institute, a conservative think tank.

TED KENNEDY: CROWN PRINCE

John F. Kennedy once said of his brothers, "Just as I went into politics because Joe [the oldest Kennedy brother, killed in World War II] died, if anything happened to me tomorrow Bobby would run for my seat in the Senate. And if Bobby died, our young brother Ted would take over for him."

Edward M. "Ted" Kennedy's major qualifications for public office are his style, appearance, accent, and name. He is the image of his late brothers, John and Robert. Their deaths by assassins' bullets make the youngest Kennedy brother the sentimental favorite of millions of Americans—the last guardian of the Camelot legend. The Kennedy charisma attaches to Ted despite tragedy, scandal, and defeat at the hands of fellow Democratic senators (Kennedy was unceremoniously ousted as Senate Democratic Whip in 1971). The Kennedy wealth is another major political asset. Ted Kennedy's public tax returns reveal an income of $.5 million per year from interest on his inheritance, suggesting a personal net worth of about $10 million. Total family wealth probably exceeds $100 million.

The Kennedy dynasty began with the flamboyant career of Joseph P. Kennedy, son of a prosperous Irish saloon-keeper and ward boss in Boston. Joseph Kennedy attended Boston Latin School and Harvard, receiving his B.A. in 1912. He started his career in banking, moved into stock market operations, dabbled in shipbuilding, formed a movie-making company (RKO and later Paramount), and married the daughter of the mayor of Boston. "Old Joe" made the major part of his fortune in stock market manipulations. With his associate, William Randolph Hearst, Kennedy provided key financial backing for the 1932 presidential campaign of Franklin D. Roosevelt. FDR later made Kennedy head of the Securities and Exchange Commission. But making a market speculator head of a commission that was designed to protect investors caused such public outcry that he was forced to resign after one year. FDR then appointed Kennedy head of the Maritime Commission, but rumors of extravagant subsidies to shipbuilding friends forced his resignation after only two months on the job. In 1937, FDR appointed him ambassador to England. His diplomatic career lasted three years and ended over differences with FDR regarding U.S. assistance to the Allies. Old Joe is said to have advised FDR of the likelihood of German victory and the advantages of placating Hitler.

Joseph P. Kennedy, Sr., was a family man, a prominent Catholic, and the father of nine children. (Joseph P., Jr., was killed as a World War II Navy Pilot; President John F. Kennedy was assassinated; Senator Robert F. Kennedy was assassinated: Kathleen died in a plane crash; Rosemary is living in an institution for the mentally retarded; Eunice is married to Sargent Shriver, former director of the Peace Corps and the War on Poverty and replacement for Senator Thomas Eagleton as the Democratic vice-presidential nominee in 1972; Patricia, formerly married to actor Peter Lawford; Jean, wife of Stephen Smith; and the youngest, Edward M. "Ted" Kennedy.)

Although born to great wealth and accustomed to an upper-class style of living (he received his first communion from Pope Pius XII), Ted Kennedy acquired the sense of competition fostered in the large Kennedy household. In 1951, suspended from Harvard for cheating on a Spanish examination, he joined the Army and served two years in Germany. He was readmitted to Harvard, where he played on the Harvard football team and graduated in 1956.

Despite his family background, Harvard Law School rejected Ted Kennedy's application for admission. He enrolled instead in the University of Virginia Law School and completed his law degree in 1959. Following graduation and work on his brother's 1960 presidential campaign, he was appointed assistant district attorney for Suffolk County, Massachusetts.

In 1962, when he was just thirty years old, the minimum age for a U.S. senator, he announced his candidacy for the Massachusetts Senate seat formerly held by his brother, who was then President. In the Democratic primary he faced Edward J. McCormack, nephew of the then Speaker of the House, John W. McCormack. During a televised debate, McCormack said to Kennedy, "You never worked for a living. You never held elective office. You lack the qualifications and maturity of judgment. . . . If your name were not Kennedy, your candidacy would be a joke." But Kennedy won overwhelmingly and went on to defeat the Republican candidate, George Cabot Lodge. (George Cabot Lodge was the son of U.S. Ambassador to South Vietnam and former U.S. Senator Henry Cabot Lodge, Jr. In 1916, Kennedy's grandfather, Boston Mayor John F. Fitzgerald, had been defeated in a race for the same Senate seat by Lodge's great-grandfather, Senator Henry Cabot Lodge.)

Kennedy performed better in the Senate than many had expected. He cultivated Senate friends, appeared at fund-raising dinners, and informed himself about several important policy fields. He worked hard learning about national health problems and eventually became chairman of the Subcommittee on Health of the Senate Labor and Public Welfare

Committee. He also devoted considerable attention to problems of the elderly and to the activities of the National Science Foundation. In 1969 he was elected Senate Democratic Whip by his colleagues.

His personal life, however, was marred by accident, tragedy, and scandal. He nearly died in a 1964 plane crash in which he suffered a broken back. An athletic and handsome six foot two inches, Kennedy was frequently the object of romantic gossip at Washington cocktail parties. On July 19, 1969, a young woman, Mary Jo Kopechne, died when the car Kennedy was driving plunged off a narrow bridge on Chappaquiddick Island after a late-night party. Missing for ten hours after the accident, Kennedy later made a dramatic national television appearance, saying that the tragedy had been an accident, that he had tried unsuccessfully to save Miss Kopechne, and that he had been too confused to report the tragedy until the next day. The official inquest has been kept secret, and many feel that there are still unresolved discrepancies in Kennedy's story.[8] Kennedy pled guilty to the minor charge of leaving the scene of an accident. Senate Democrats removed Kennedy from his position as majority Whip. But the national news media never pressed the Chappaquiddick incident and continued favorable reporting of the still charismatic senator. He recovered quickly in public opinion polls and generally led all other Democrats in presidential preference polling.

Kennedy deliberately avoided the Democratic presidential nomination in both 1972 and 1976. His advisers argued that the public's memory of Chappaquiddick was still too fresh for Kennedy to enter a campaign battle in which the issue of his personal life would certainly be raised. However, in late 1979, with Carter standing at an all-time low for Presidents in the opinion polls, Kennedy announced his presidential candidacy. Most observers thought that Kennedy was unbeatable, despite Carter's pledge "I'll whip his ass." But Carter was temporarily saved by the Iranian seizure of American embassy employees in Iran as hostages. Shortly thereafter, Soviet troops invaded neighboring Afghanistan. Support for the President was equated with support for America. Carter's approval ratings in the polls leaped upward, even though he failed to obtain both early release of the hostages and Soviet withdrawal from Afghanistan. Nonetheless, these events provided a "rally round the flag" effect. Carter was temporarily transformed from a lackluster politician to commander-in-chief of all of the people. He defeated Kennedy in the Democratic primaries from the White House Rose Garden without even campaigning. The media focus was on the President, and the news from Iran simply obliterated the Kennedy campaign.

Clearly, Ted Kennedy is an "inheritor," rather than a "climber," in the world of politics. Yet, like other successful politicians, his success rests

[8]See Robert Sherrill, "Chappaquiddick + 5," *New York Times Magazine,* July 14, 1974.

upon his image and style more than upon his substantive contributions to public policy. He was elected to the Senate solely because he was a Kennedy—an inheritor of a famous political image. The image survived tragedy and scandal, although his fellow senators seem less impressed with his mystique than the general public. Kennedy still leads the liberal wing of the Democratic party. He is relatively young (forty eight in the 1980 campaign). He quietly divorced his long-suffering wife, Joan, and his personal problems now seem distant. His power today stems not from what he knows about government, but from the realization that he may someday convert his popular image into a successful presidential candidate.

THE ASPIRING POLITICOS

For people of great ambition in American politics, there is only one goal— President of the United States. Aspiring political leaders will cultivate a style and image which encourages others to think of them as "presidential timber", and they will prepare themselves to seize the opportunity when it arises. Edward M. Kennedy and George Bush are among these ambitious people. Both Kennedy and Bush are "inheritors" in a world of politics; they were blessed with personal wealth, Ivy League educations, and family connections to help establish their careers. Still others are "climbers" in the political world—men of relatively modest backgrounds who have devoted themselves to the quest for the presidency. Among these men are Walter F. Mondale, Gary Hart, and Jack Kemp.

Walter F. Mondale

"Fritz" Mondale relies on his clean-cut, boyish, good looks, his liberal voting record, and his thirty years of Washington experience, to help him remain a contender for the presidency. Mondale projects the image of a preacher's son—which he is. He was raised in small towns in Minnesota, attended Macalester College in St. Paul, and graduated from the University of Minnesota in 1951. He temporarily dropped out of college in 1948–49 to help Hubert Humphrey win his U.S. Senate seat. Mondale spent two years in the Army and then returned to complete a law degree at the University of Minnesota in 1956. Mondale managed the campaign of Governor Orville Freeman and was rewarded by appointment as assistant attorney general for the state in 1958. In 1960, Mondale won his first electoral race—for Attorney General of Minnesota. When his old mentor, Hubert Humphrey, left the U.S. Senate to become Lyndon Johnson's vice-president in 1964, Mondale was appointed by the governor of Minnesota to take Humphrey's seat. In 1966, Mondale won election to the Senate by a comfortable margin. In the Senate, Mondale upheld the liberal traditions of his predecessor Hubert Humphrey; he led Senate battles for the "Great Society" programs, for the poor and the elderly, for children, for migrant workers, for blacks and other minorities. In 1972, it was rumored that Mondale turned down George McGovern's offer to join the Democratic ticket as the vice presidential candidate. Instead, Mondale won re-election to the Senate.

Mondale was an early entry into the 1976 Democratic presidential race, with the open support of the *New York Times*. But Mondale pulled out of the race: "I do not have the overwhelming desire to be President, which is essential for the kind of campaign that is required." He never gave any convincing reason for his withdrawal. With Humphrey dying of cancer, and Kennedy still vulnerable from Chappaquiddick, and Mondale withdrawn, the left-liberal wing of the Democratic Party had no champion. The way was clear for Carter to capture the nomination.

Carter wisely chose Mondale as his running mate in order to solidify liberal support behind the Democratic ticket. But Fritz Mondale turned out to be an excellent campaigner and major contributor to Carter's 1976 victory. Mondale's clean and earnest looks and simple and honest responses won the TV debate with a witty but sometimes sarcastic Robert Dole.

Although Mondale had excellent access to the Carter White House, the failures of the Carter Administration were never publically attributed to Mondale. Indeed, even though the Carter-Mondale ticket went down to defeat in 1980, the defeat is universally credited to Carter, not Mondale. Fritz Mondale managed to escape the crash of the Carter presidency, and Mondale remains a key Democratic leader.

Gary Hart

When Democrat Gary Hart was re-elected to the Senate in 1980, despite a heavy Reagan vote in Colorado, his supporters started to chant "Eighty-four! Eighty-four!" Hart avoids direct attacks on Kennedy or Mondale, but he enjoys talking about a "new generation" of Democratic politicians who are ready to pick up the banner if the established leaders fall. And certainly the youthful Gary Hart (44 in 1980) thinks of himself as the leader of the "new generation."

Hart is the son of a prosperous Colorado farm equipment dealer. Early in his life Hart planned for a career in the ministry: He graduated from Bethany Nazarene College and went on to earn a degree from the Yale Divinity School. But after a taste of political campaigning for John F. Kennedy in 1960, he went back to Yale and completed a law degree. He began his legal career as an attorney in the Justice Department and later moved to the Interior Department. In 1967 he returned to Colorado to teach at the University of Colorado Law School. Hart campaigned in the

Western states for Robert F. Kennedy in 1968, and he was recruited very early by George McGovern to manage his presidential campaign in 1972.

The McGovern campaign was a disaster. "Don't ask me what happened" said Hart, after McGovern lost 49 of the 50 states to Richard Nixon. Yet, Hart was determined to pursue a political career. At the height of the Watergate scandal, he perceived his opportunity. He ran for the U.S. Senate seat held by Peter H. Dominick, a conservative Nixon supporter. The 1974 election was a disaster for Republicans everywhere; Watergate swept many new Democrats into Congress, including Gary Hart.

Shortly after arriving in Washington, Hart sensed that the national mood was no longer "McGovern liberal." He slowly began a shift toward the middle of the political spectrum. He continued to voice concern for the poor, the aged, the black, and other minorities, but he also joined the chorus of voices attacking big government and bureaucratic waste, and calling for deregulation of business. Instead of opposing *all* defense spending, Hart has pushed for more reliable, more numerous, and simpler battlefield weapons; he argues that a conventional non-nuclear conflict is a more likely prospect than a nuclear war and that the U.S. military is too preoccupied with highly-sophisticated, very expensive weapons.

In 1980, Democrat Hart survived the Reagan Republican landslide in Colorado to retain his Senate seat. The media were impressed with his victory and began talking about him as a national candidate for the future. Hart immediately formed "a national issues" staff to begin preparation for a future race for the presidency.

Hart's major assets are his good looks—he is tall, slender, and young (43 in 1980), with modishly long hair. His looks and personality are perfectly matched to television. Following the 1980 defeat of Carter and many other Democrats, Hart announced that "traditional liberalism is near bankruptcy" and he called for "fresh" ideas for the Democratic Party. It is clear that he was also calling for a "fresh" face—his own.

Jack Kemp

Jack Kemp's "game plan" for politics is to "get first downs, and the touchdowns will come up and hit you in the face." The former quarterback for the Buffalo Bills and AFL Most Valuable Player in 1965 has made a great many political "first downs" since winning election to the Congress in 1970. The boyishly handsome, square-jawed, athletic Jack Kemp is the Republican Party's brightest young star (Kemp was 45 in 1980).

Kemp grew up in Los Angeles, where his father owned a small trucking firm. Kemp admits to being "totally tunnel-visioned" about his early goal in life—"to play football." Kemp chose smaller Occidental College, rather than USC or UCLA, to insure that he would get a lot of playing time. He was only an average student, majoring in physical education. But he was an outstanding quarterback and he was drafted by the Detroit Lions. He spent thirteen years with various professional teams, but his best years were with the Buffalo Bills in 1963, '64, and '65, when he led the team to three consecutive Eastern division titles and two AFL championships. Kemp compiled a number of AFL records and served as co-founder and president of the AFL Players Association. But by 1970, he had accumulated two broken ankles, two broken shoulders, a broken knee, and eleven concussions. When he quit, the Buffalo Bills permanently retired his number 15 jersey.

Kemp moved directly from the playing field to the political arena. Buffalo Republicans urged him to run for a suburban congressional seat held by the Democrats. Kemp's high name recognition and his success as the hometeam quarterback helped him win a narrow victory over the incumbent. In later elections, his margin of victory soared to 70, 73, and 78 percent of the vote; in 1978 the Democrats did not even run a candidate against him.

In his first years in Washington, Kemp was regarded as an "ex-jock" and a "lightweight." Kemp took advantage of these years by informing himself about a wide range of social, economic, military, and foreign policy issues. Kemp was especially impressed with the ideas of Arthur B. Laffer, an economist at the University of Southern California. Laffer argued that high federal tax rates have reached a point of diminishing returns: taxes are so high that they are undermining incentives to produce and save; lowering tax rates might actually increase federal revenues if more people were encouraged to work and save.

Kemp became the leading Congressional spokesman for the new "supply-side" economics. "If you tax something, you get less of it. If you subsidize something, you get more of it. In America we tax work, growth, investment, employment, savings, and productivity. We subsidize non-working, consumption, welfare, and debt." In 1978, Kemp, together with Republican Senator William V. Roth of Delaware, proposed an across-the-board slash in income taxes by 30 percent in three years. This "Kemp-Roth" tax bill was at first ridiculed in Establishment circles. (The Brookings Institution called it "the most irresponsible financial policy ever suggested in U.S. history.") But in 1980 it was incorporated into the Republican platform. When Ronald Reagan captured the White House, his first priority was economic recovery, and Jack Kemp's tax plan became a key part of the President's program. The 1981 Reagan tax cuts included a 25 percent reduction in personal income taxes over three years, only a slight modification of Kemp's original plan. Jack Kemp became a recognized leader in the Congress.

Kemp's political future may depend upon the success of Reagan's economic recovery plan. If "supply-side" economics, and taxing and spending cuts, fail to halt inflation, Kemp will be especially hurt, since

Kemp is so closely identified with these proposals. On the other hand, if Reagan's economic program succeeds, Jack Kemp may become a choice for president or vice-president.

**EXECUTIVE DECISION MAKERS:
THE SERIOUS PEOPLE**

Politicians deal in style and image. However, the responsibility for the initiation of national programs and policies falls primarily upon the top White House staff and the heads of executive departments. Generally, Congress merely responds to policy proposals initiated by the executive branch. The President and his key advisers and administrators have a strong incentive to fulfill their responsibility for decision-making: In the eyes of the American public, they are responsible for everything that happens in the nation regardless of whether or not they have the authority or capacity to do anything about it. There is a general expectation that every administration, even one committed to a "caretaker" role, will put forth some sort of policy program.

The President and Vice-President, White House presidential advisers and ambassadors-at-large, Cabinet secretaries, under secretaries, and assistant secretaries constitute our executive elite. Let us take a brief look at the careers of some of the people who have served in key Cabinet positions in recent presidential administrations.

Defense

Charles E. Wilson. Secretary of Defense, 1953-57; president and member of the board of directors of General Motors.

Neil H. McElroy. Secretary of Defense, 1957–59; former president and member of the board of directors of Procter & Gamble; member of the board of directors of General Electric, of Chrysler Corp., and of Equitable Life Assurance Co.; member of the board of trustees of Harvard University, of the National Safety Council, and the National Industrial Conference.

Thomas S. Gates. Secretary of Defense, 1959–60, and Secretary of the Navy, 1957–59; chairman of the board and chief executive officer, Morgan Guaranty Trust Co.; member of the board of directors of General Electric, Bethlehem Steel, Scott Paper Co., Campbell Soup Co., Insurance Co. of North America, Cities Service, Smith Kline and French (pharmaceuticals), and the University of Pennsylvania.

Robert S. McNamara. Secretary of Defense, 1961–67; president and member of the board of directors of the Ford Motor Co.; member of the board of directors of Scott Paper Co.; president of the World Bank, 1967 to 1981.

Clark Clifford. Secretary of Defense, 1967–69; senior partner of Clifford & Miller (Washington law firm); member of board of directors of the National

Bank of Washington and of the Sheridan Hotel Corp.; special counsel to the President, 1949–50; member of board of trustees of Washington University in St. Louis.

Melvin Laird. Secretary of Defense, 1969–73; former Wisconsin Republican Congressman and chairman of Republican Conference in the House of Representatives.

James R. Schlesinger. Secretary of Defense, 1973–77; former director, Central Intelligence Agency; former chairman of Atomic Energy Commission; formerly assistant director of Office of Management and Budget, economics professor, and research associate of the RAND Corp.

Harold Brown. Secretary of Defense, 1977–81; former president of the California Institute of Technology. A member of the board of directors of International Business Machines (IBM) and the Times-Mirror Corp. Former Secretary of the Air Force under President Lyndon Johnson, and U.S. representative to the SALT I talks under President Richard Nixon.

Caspar W. Weinberger. Secretary of Defense, 1981 to date. Former vice-president and director of the Bechtel Corporation, the world's largest privately owned corporation. A member of the board of directors of Pepsico and Quaker Oats Co. Former secretary of Health, Education, and Welfare under President Richard M. Nixon; former director of the Office of Management and Budget; former chairman of the Federal Trade Commission. A former San Francisco attorney and California State legislator.

State

John Foster Dulles. Secretary of State, 1953–60; partner of Sullivan & Cromwell (one of 20 largest law firms on Wall Street); member of the board of directors of the Bank of New York, Fifth Avenue Bank, American Bank Note Co., International Nickel Co. of Canada, Babcock and Wilson Corp., Shenandoah Corp., United Cigar Stores, American Cotton Oil Co., United Railroad of St. Louis, and European Textile Corp. He was a trustee of New York Public Library, Union Theological Seminary, Rockefeller Foundation, and the Carnegie Endowment for International Peace; also a delegate to the World Council of Churches.

Dean Rusk. Secretary of State, 1961–68; former president of Rockefeller Foundation.

William P. Rodgers. Secretary of State, 1969–73; U.S. attorney general during Eisenhower Administration; senior partner in Royall, Koegal, Rogers, and Wells (one of the 20 largest Wall Street law firms).

Henry Kissinger. Secretary of State, 1973–77; former special assistant to the President for National Security Affairs; former Harvard Professor of International Affairs, and project director for Rockefeller Brothers Fund and for the Council on Foreign Relations.

Cyrus Vance. Secretary of State, 1977–80; senior partner in the New York law firm of Simpson, Thacher and Bartlett. A member of the board of directors of International Business Machines (IBM) and Pan American World Airways; a trustee of Yale University, the Rockefeller Foundation, and the Council on

Foreign Relations, Former Secretary of the Army under President Lyndon Johnson.

Alexander M. Haig, Jr. Secretary of State, 1981 to date; president of United Technologies Corporation, and former four-star general, U.S. Army. He was former Supreme Allied Commander, NATO forces in Europe; former assistant to the President under Richard M. Nixon; former deputy assistant to the President for National Security under Henry Kissinger; former deputy commandant, U.S. Military Academy at West Point; former deputy Secretary of Defense.

Treasury

George M. Humphrey. Secretary of the Treasury, 1953–57; former chairman of the board of directors of the M.A. Hanna Co.; member of board of directors of National Steel Corp.; Consolidated Coal Co. of Canada and Dominion Sugar Co.; trustee of M.I.T.

Robert B. Anderson. Secretary of the Treasury, 1957–61; Secretary of the Navy, 1953–54; deputy Secretary of Defense, 1945–55; member of board of directors of Goodyear Tire and Rubber Co. and Pan-American Airways; member of the executive board of the Boy Scouts of America.

Douglas Dillon. Secretary of the Treasury, 1961–63; chairman of the board of Dillon, Reed, and Co., Inc. (one of Wall Street's largest investment firms); member of New York Stock Exchange; director of U.S. and Foreign Securities Corp. and U.S. International Securities Corp.; member of board of governors of New York Hospital and Metropolitan Museum.

David Kennedy. Secretary of the Treasury, 1969–71; president and chairman of the board of Continental Illinois Bank and Trust Co.; director of International Harvester Co., Commonwealth Edison, Pullman Co., Abbott Laboratories, Swift and Co., U.S. Gypsum, and Communications Satellite Corp.; trustee of the University of Chicago, the Brookings Institution, the Committee for Economic Development, and George Washington University.

John B. Connally. Secretary of the Treasury, 1971–72; former Secretary of the Navy, governor of Texas, administrative assistant to Lyndon B. Johnson; attorney for Murcheson Brothers Investment (Dallas); former director of New York Central Railroad.

George P. Schultz. Secretary of the Treasury, 1972–74; former Secretary of Labor and director of the Office of Management and Budget; former dean of the University of Chicago Graduate School of Business; former director of Borg-Warner Corp., General American Transportation Co., and Stein, Roe & Farnham (investments).

William E. Simon. Secretary of the Treasury, 1974–77; former director, Federal Energy Office, and former Deputy Secretary of the Treasury; formerly a senior partner of Salomon Brothers (one of Wall Street's largest investment firms specializing in municipal bond trading).

Warner Michael Blumenthal. Secretary of the Treasury, 1977–79; former president of the Bendix Corporation; former vice-president of Crown Cork Co.; trustee of Princeton University and the Council on Foreign Relations.

G. William Miller. Secretary of the Treasury, 1979–81; chairman and chief executive officer of Textron Corporation. Former partner in Crarath, Swaine, and Moore (one of the nation's twenty-five largest and most prestigious law firms); a former director of Allied Chemical and Federated Department Stores; former chairman of the Federal Reserve Board.

Donald T. Regan. Secretary of the Treasury, 1981 to date; chairman of the board and chief executive officer of Merrill Lynch & Co. Inc., the nation's largest investment firm; former vice-chairman of the New York Stock Exchange; a trustee of the University of Pennsylvania and the Committee for Economic Development, and a member of the policy committee of the Business Roundtable.

It makes relatively little difference whether a President is a Democrat or a Republican. The same type of "serious men" must be called upon to run the government.

THE PROFESSIONAL BUREAUCRATS

The federal bureaucracy has grown to nearly three million civilian employees. The professional federal executives who supervise this giant institution occupy a uniquely influential position in American society. They advise the President on decisions he must make; they present and defend legislative recommendations before the Congress; and they supervise the day-to-day decisions of the hundreds of departments, agencies, commissions, and boards that influence the lives of every American. These federal executives comprise a powerful bureaucratic elite—particularly the secretaries, assistant secretaries, and under secretaries of the thirteen federal departments (State, Treasury, Defense, Justice, Health and Human Services, Education, Interior, Agriculture, Commerce, Labor, Housing and Urban Development, Energy, and Transportation); the same officials for the Army, Navy, and Air Force departments; administrators of important independent agencies in the executive office of the President (including the Office of Management and Budget, the National Security Council, and the Council of Economic Advisers); and members of key regulatory commissions and boards (Federal Reserve Board, Civil Aeronautics Board, Federal Communications Commission, Federal Power Commission, Federal Trade Commission, Interstate Commerce Commission, National Labor Relations Board, and Securities and Exchange Commission). Most of these top federal executive positions are filled by presidential appointment with Senate confirmation.

What kind of people head the federal bureaucracy? In an interesting study[9] of over 1,000 persons who occupied the positions listed above

[9]David T. Stanley, Dean E. Mann, and Jameson W. Doig, *Men Who Govern* (Washington: Brookings Institution, 1967).

during the presidential administrations of Roosevelt, Truman, Eisenhower, Kennedy and Johnson, the Brookings Institution reports that 36 percent of these top federal executives came up through the ranks of the government itself, 26 percent were recruited from law, 24 percent from business, 7 percent from education, and 7 percent from a variety of other fields. A plurality of top federal executives are *career bureaucrats.* Moreover, most of these people have served in only one government agency,[10] slowly acquiring seniority and promotion in the agency in which they eventually became chief executives. A total of 63 percent of the top federal executives were federal bureaucrats at the time of their appointment to a top post; only 37 percent had no prior experience as federal bureaucrats.[11] (If experience in *state* bureaucracies is counted, a total of 69 percent of the top federal executives can be said to have been government bureaucrats at the time of their appointment.)

Thus, a majority of top federal executives are themselves career bureaucrats. The federal bureaucracy itself is producing its own leadership, with some limited recruitment from business and law. (Later in this volume, see Table 7–4, we will compare our own data for the 1970s on governmental and military elites with the earlier Brookings Institution's data, but we can say now that our figures are roughly comparable.) The federal bureaucracy, then, is an independent channel of recruitment to positions of governmental power in America. Consider, for example, the careers of the following individuals.

Joseph A. Califano, Jr.

The grandson of an Italian immigrant who owned a fruit store in Brooklyn, New York, and the son of a middle echelon administrator of IBM. Califano attended Catholic schools in New York and graduated from Holy Cross College in 1952. He went on to Harvard Law School and graduated in 1955 with honors, and with the prestige of having edited the *Harvard Law Review.* After serving as a legal officer in the Navy, Califano was recruited by the prestigious Wall Street Law firm of Dewey, Ballantine, Bushby, Palmer, and Wood. After two years on Wall Street and the election of John F. Kennedy as President, Califano wrote to the new administration seeking a job. He said he was "bored with splitting stocks."[12] His letter was answered by another former Wall Street lawyer and establishment figure, Cyrus Vance, who was then general counsel for the Department of Defense. Califano became Vance's assistant. Like many bureaucrats who aspire to climb the rungs of the Washington ladder, Califano's success was based in part upon the success of his mentor, Cyrus Vance.

[10]*Ibid.*, p. 8.

[11]*Ibid.*, p. 45.

[12]*Current Biography*, June 1977. p. 14.

When Vance became Secretary of the Army, Califano became general counsel for the Department of the Army and later special assistant to the Secretary of Defense. His work for the Defense Department included liaison with the White House, and he was brought into close contact with top White House staff and President Lyndon Johnson. (Another lesson for aspiring bureaucrats, besides finding a highly placed mentor, is to establish contact with the White House as soon as possible.) In 1965, President Johnson chose Califano as special assistant to the president for domestic affairs. In this capacity, Califano shepherded much of the Great Society legislation through Congress. Thus, Califano helped to create the giant bureaucracy at HEW that he later administered. As President Johnson became preoccupied with the war in Vietnam, Califano came to exercise a great deal of independent power over domestic affairs in the White House. When Republicans captured the White House in 1968, Califano joined the prestigious Washington law firm of Arnold and Fortas (which included Abe Fortas, Lyndon Johnson's close personal friend and unsuccessful nominee to the Supreme Court). Later Califano worked with the well-known criminal lawyer Edward Bennett Williams. His years in the Washington bureaucracy brought him wealthy clients including Washington Post-Newsweek, Inc. His 1976 income was reported at $560,000. He toured the world on Ford Foundation money and wrote two lackluster books. He kept a hand in politics by serving as general counsel for the Democratic National Committee, and he joined the Carter campaign as an adviser in early 1976. He was named Secretary of Health, Education, and Welfare in January 1977. Thus, while Califano was associated with two of the nation's top law firms (see Chapter 5), his rise to the top was achieved primarily through his mastery of the Washington bureaucracy. Califano was dumped from the Carter Cabinet in 1979 when it became apparent that his close friend, Ted Kennedy, was going to oppose Jimmy Carter in the race for the 1980 Democratic presidential nomination. However, Califano's knowledge of the many corridors of power in Washington immediately made him one of Washington's most prestigious and sought-after lawyers.

Phillip Habib

The Brooklyn-born son of Lebanese immigrants, he received a B.A. from the University of Idaho and a Ph.D. from the University of California-Berkeley. Habib joined the U.S. foreign service even before his Ph.D. dissertation was completed. He spent his entire career in the foreign service, including his efforts at Arab-Israeli peace-keeping in 1981 as Special Presidential Envoy to the Mideast. Habib worked his way up through the foreign service slowly: he began as a third secretary to the U.S. Embassy in Ottawa, Canada; moved to New Zealand; came back home to the State Department bureaucracy in Washington; went to Trinidad; then went on to a more important rank, political officer, at the U.S. Embassy in Seoul, Korea. At the beginning of the Vietnam War, Habib was posted to the U.S. Embassy in Saigon and was later made deputy assistant secretary of state for East Asian and Pacific Affairs. Habib was a member of the U.S. delegation to the Paris Peace talks which fashioned an end to U.S. involvement in Vietnam. Later he was made ambassador to South Korea. He returned in 1974 as assistant Secretary of State and later Under Secretary of State. In 1981, with war between Israel and Syria appearing eminent, Reagan appointed Habib as Special Presidential Envoy to find a solution to the Syrian occupation of Lebanon and Israeli strikes against Palestinian and Syrian military targets in Lebanon. Habib began the "shuttle diplomacy"—flying from capital to capital in peace negotiation—which Henry Kissinger had done so successfully in the Mideast a few years earlier.

Of course, top federal bureaucrats are recruited primarily from the middle- and upper-middle-class segments of the population, as are leaders in other sectors of society. The Brookings Institution reports that the percentage of college-educated top executive bureaucrats rose from 88 percent in the Roosevelt Administration to 99 percent in the Johnson Administration. Moreover, 68 percent had advanced degrees—44 percent in law, 17 percent with earned master's degrees, and 11 percent with earned doctorates. However, the class composition of the top bureaucrats is better reflected in information on *which* schools and colleges were attended. The Brookings Institution reports that the Ivy League schools plus Stanford, Chicago, Michigan, and Berkeley educated over 40 percent of the top federal executives, with Yale, Harvard, and Princeton leading the list.[13] Moreover, this tendency has increased over time; there were larger proportions of Ivy Leaguers in top posts in 1965 than in 1945. Perhaps more importantly, the Brookings study reports that 39 percent of the top federal executives attended *private* schools (compared to only 6 percent of the U.S. population); and 17 percent went to one of only 18 "name" prep schools.[14] The Brookings Institution study also reports that most top federal executives come from large Eastern cities.

There is little difference between Republican and Democratic administrations in the kind of men who are appointed to top executive posts. It is true, of course, that Republican Presidents tend to appoint Republicans to top posts, and Democratic Presidents tend to appoint Democrats; only about 8 percent of the top appointments cross party lines. However, the Brookings study reports few discernible differences in the class back-

[13]Stanley, Mann, and Doig, *Men Who Govern*, p. 21.

[14]Avon Old Farms, Choate, Deerfield, Groton, Hill, Hotchkiss, Kent, Lawrenceville, Loomis, Middlesex, Milton, Phillips Andover, Phillips Exeter, St. George's, St. Mary's, St. Paul's, Taft, Thatcher.

65, and Litton as 81 in the top 100 industries in Table 2–1. The others do not appear in the top 100 at all.) Other companies among the corporate giants also accept defense contracts (AT&T, Chrysler, GM, IBM, and so on), but their military sales are only a small proportion of total sales. Yet there is enough military business to make it a real concern of certain companies, the people who work for them, the communities in which they are located, and the congresspeople and other public officials who represent these communities.

American business in general, however, is not interested in promoting war or international instability. The defense industry is considered an unstable enterprise—a feast or famine business for industrial companies. The price-earnings ratios for military-oriented companies are substantially lower than for civilian-oriented companies. More importantly, corporate America seeks planned stable growth, secure investments, and guaranteed returns. These conditions are disrupted by war. The stock market, reflecting the aspirations of businesspeople, goes *up* when peace is announced, not *down*.

A frequent criticism of the military-industrial complex is that defense-oriented industries have become dependent on military hardware orders. Any reduction in military spending would result in a severe economic setback for these industries, so they apply great pressure to keep defense spending high. This is particularly true of the industries that are almost totally dependent upon defense contracts. The military, always pleased to receive new weapons, joins with defense industries in recommending to the government that it purchase new weapons. Finally, congresspeople from constituencies with large defense industries and giant military bases can usually be counted on to join with the armed forces and defense industries in support of increased defense spending for new weapons.

For many years, however, the military-industrial complex was notably *unsuccessful* in influencing the federal budget. Federal spending for defense *declined* from 49.8 percent of the budget in 1960, to 40.8 percent in 1970, and down to 25 percent of the budget in 1978. Federal spending for social security and welfare surpassed defense spending long ago. Only after 1978, when Soviet superiority in both conventional and nuclear weapons was very clear and threatening, did U.S. defense spending begin to increase very slowly. First Jimmy Carter, and later Ronald Reagan, proposed increased defense budgets for the 1980s. But the long neglect of U.S. defenses suggests that the American military-industrial complex is *not* a very powerful conspiracy.

How many top federal executives come to Washington from employment by large defense contractors? The Brookings Institution reports that of 1,000 top federal executives studied from 1954 through 1965, *only 4 percent* had been employed by major defense contractors before their employment by the federal government.[18] Of course, there were slightly more people with defense industry backgrounds in the Defense Department itself, but even here, the Brookings study reports that only 12 percent of all top executives in the Defense Department and the Departments of the Army, Navy, and Air Force had had previous employment with defense contractors.

It seems clear in retrospect that C. Wright Mills placed too much importance on the military in his work, *The Power Elite*.[19] Mills was writing in the early 1950s when military prestige was high following victory in World War II. After the war, a few high-level military men were recruited to top corporate positions: General Douglas MacArthur became chairman of the board of Remington-Rand (now Sperry-Rand corporation); General Lucius D. Clay, who commanded American troops in Germany after the war, became board chairman of Continental Can Company; General James H. Doolittle, head of the Air Force in World War II, became vice-president of Shell Oil; General Omar M. Bradley, Commander of the 12th Army Group in Europe in World War II, became board chairman of Bulova Research Laboratories; General Leslie R. Groves, head of the Manhattan Project, which developed the atomic bomb, became vice-president of Remington-Rand; General Walter Bedell Smith, Eisenhower's Chief of Staff, became vice-president of the board of directors of American Machine and Foundry Company; General Matthew B. Ridgeway, Army Chief of Staff during the Korean War, became chairman of the board of the Mellon Institute of Industrial Research.

The selection of *General Alexander M. Haig, Jr.* as Secretary of State tends to overstate the influence of the military in the nation's power elite. The really interesting aspect of Haig's career is that he was *not* highly rated as a military commander. His success can be directly attributed to his political skills. Haig graduated from West Point in the bottom one third of his class, but his first post provided an excellent opportunity for launching a military career: Haig was assigned to the staff of General Douglas MacArthur in 1949. Haig served MacArthur in Japan and later during the Korean War. After MacArthur's career ended, Haig held a variety of lackluster jobs. He tried to refuel his ambitions by studying international relations at Georgetown University, earning an M.A. in 1961. It worked; he was assigned to the Pentagon and later to the staff of Cyrus R. Vance. It was in Washington that Haig met Joseph A. Califano, who was then general counsel for the Army. Although Vance and Califano were powerful mentors, Haig realized that he had no combat command experience, so he volunteered for a six-month hitch as a brigade commander in Vietnam in

[18]*Ibid.*, p. 38.
[19]C. Wright Mills, *The Power Elite* (New York: Oxford, 1956).

1967. Haig was then a colonel. When Henry Kissinger was forming his National Security Council staff in late 1968, Califano and Vance recommended Haig. Haig was taken on as military assistant to Kissinger and was promoted quickly to major general. Apparently, Haig served Kissinger and Nixon very well. In 1972, Nixon skipped over 240 other top-ranking generals with more seniority and promoted Haig from a two-star major general to a four-star general. Nixon appointed Haig Army Vice-Chief of Staff (second in command of the Army). When, in 1973, the Watergate affair forced the resignations of Nixon's senior White House aides, Nixon selected Haig to be White House Chief of Staff. Haig remained calm despite the turmoil around him, and many observers credit him with holding the White House together during Nixon's final days. Indeed, Haig helped Nixon to recognize the injuries to the nation which might occur if an impeachment trial were held, and thus helped Nixon to make his decision to resign. President Ford rewarded Haig by naming him Supreme Allied Commander of NATO, a post which he held from 1974 to 1978. Haig was generally given good marks by European governments in this highly political position. When Haig returned from Europe, he wanted to run for the Republican nomination for President, but he failed to generate much money or enthusiasm for his campaign. Haig retired from the Army in 1979 and accepted the board chair of United Technologies, a top 100 corporation. United Technologies wanted him as an active chief executive officer with worldwide connections in government and industry, but Haig succumbed to a serious heart attack and bypass surgery. He never had a real opportunity to take charge at United Technologies. When Ronald Reagan was organizing his Cabinet, he knew that nominating Haig for Secretary of State might create trouble among conservatives (who distrusted his early associations with Kissinger and Vance) and among liberals (who distrusted his association with Nixon). But Haig reflected Reagan's own view that the Soviet Union is the greatest threat to world peace. Haig overwhelmed his critics at his Senate confirmation hearings with his military bearing and tough authoritative replies to questioners.

However, as sociologist Morris Janowitz points out, "The practice of appointing military personnel to politically responsible posts, although it continues, has declined sharply since 1950. Much of the political debate about military personnel in government policy positions centers on a few conspicuous cases where civilian leadership sought to make use of prestigious military officers to deal with difficult political problems."[20] Indeed, the contrast between the political prestige of the military in the 1950s and the 1970s is striking: the Supreme Allied Commander in Europe in World War II, Dwight D. Eisenhower, was elected President of

---

[20]Morris Janowitz, *The Professional Soldier* (New York: Free Press, 1960), p. 378.

the United States; the U.S. Commander in Vietnam, William Westmoreland, was defeated in his bid to become governor of South Carolina!

Moreover, in contrast with corporate and governmental elites, military officers do *not* come from the "upper classes" of society. Janowitz reports that a general infusion of persons from lower- and lower-middle-class backgrounds has occurred in all branches of the Armed Services (particularly the Air Force). He also reports that military leaders are more likely to have rural and Southern backgrounds than corporate or governmental elites.

INTELLECTUALS IN POWER

No president wants to be isolated from the intellectual community—scholars from the universities, research institutes, and policy-planning organizations. Even presidents deeply suspicious of intellectuals have relied on them to fill key posts in government and in the White House staff.

Consider, for example, the position of Assistant to the President for National Security Affairs. This is the only person to meet *daily* with the President to discuss questions of war and peace. This senior White House adviser also heads the staff of the National Security Council and develops and presents alternative policies for the President's selection. Interestingly, over the last twenty-five years this post has been filled by intellectuals. McGeorge Bundy, dean of arts and sciences at Harvard University, held the job under Presidents Kennedy and Johnson; Henry Kissinger, professor of government at Harvard, had the post under President Nixon; Zbigniew Brzezinski, professor of government at Columbia University, held the position in the Carter Administration; and Richard Allen, once a staff member of the Georgetown University Center for Strategic and International Studies, held the post under President Reagan. (Another Georgetown University professor of government, Jeane Kirkpatrick, is Reagan's ambassador to the United Nations.)

Henry Kissinger

Heinz Alfred Kissinger (he changed his name to Henry after coming to the United States) was born in Furth in Bavaria, Germany. His father was a teacher in the local *Gymnasium*, or prep school. The Kissingers were an educated, middle-class German Jewish family. When the Nazis came to power in the early 1930s, the Kissingers were subjected to increasing persecution. Young Henry was denied entrance to the *Gymnasium* and was forced to attend an all-Jewish school. He and his fellow Jewish students were frequently beaten up on their way to and from school. His father was humiliated and then dismissed from his teaching post. At Henry's mother's urging, the family emigrated to New York City in 1938. His father found work as a clerk and bookkeeper, and his mother worked as a cook. Henry attended public school in New York; he was a straight-A student, but his heavy accent and unhappy experiences in Germany caused him to be withdrawn.

After graduation, Kissinger took a job in a shaving-brush factory and took evening courses at the City University of New York in hopes of becoming an accountant. He was drafted in 1943, and as a private in the 84th Infantry Division, he saw action in France and Germany. Kissinger once observed about his own early career: "Living as a Jew under the Nazis, then as a refugee in America, and then as a private in the Army, isn't exactly an experience that builds confidence." But it was in the Army that Kissinger first made his mark. When his division moved into Germany, he was made interpreter for the division's commanding general. Later he was placed in charge of the military government of the small German town of Drefeld and was promoted to staff sergeant. One of his officers urged him to return home after his service to complete his college education. He also advised him that "gentlemen do not go to the College of the City of New York." Kissinger took the advice, returned home, won a New York State scholarship, and was admitted to Harvard University.

Kissinger graduated as a Phi Beta Kappa, summa cum laude government major in 1950 and continued his studies at the Harvard Graduate School. He received his M.S. in 1952 and his Ph.D. in 1954. Shortly thereafter, he was appointed to head an important study by the Council on Foreign Relations to develop methods short of all-out war for coping with the perceived Soviet challenge to Western Europe. Key members of this influential council had become disenchanted with the "massive retaliation" doctrine of then Secretary of State John Foster Dulles. In 1957 Kissinger produced his major work, *Nuclear Weapons and Foreign Policy*,[21] which argued persuasively that strategy must determine weapons rather than vice versa, and that the U.S. should strive for greater flexibility in weapons development, including tactical nuclear weapons.

The book established Kissinger as a leading "defense intellectual." He was named associate professor (1959), and professor (1962), in Harvard's Government Department and director of Harvard's Defense Studies Program. He became a consultant to the Joint Chiefs of Staff, the National Security Council, Arms Control and Disarmament Agency, and the State Department, as well as the RAND Corporation. His close association with the Rockefellers began when Nelson A. Rockefeller asked him to direct a Rockefeller Brothers Foundation special study of foreign policy. Later Kissinger became foreign policy adviser to Nelson Rockefeller and drafted

---

[21]Henry Kissinger, *Nuclear Weapons and Foreign Policy* (New York: Council on Foreign Relations, 1957). Published also as an Anchor Book by Doubleday, 1958.

his key statements on world affairs during the New York governor's unsuccessful bid for the presidency in 1968.

Although Nixon viewed himself as an expert on world affairs, one of his earliest moves after assuming the presidency in 1968 was to ask the Rockefellers, the Council of Foreign Affairs, and the Harvard University intellectuals for their choice of a foreign affairs specialist. They recommended Kissinger and, even though Nixon had only met him once, Kissinger was appointed Special Assistant to the President for National Security Affairs.

Kissinger's performance as the President's national security adviser and special emissary can only be described as spectacular. He met secretly with North Vietnamese representatives over a prolonged period of negotiations which eventually ended the Vietnam War. He undertook his now-celebrated clandestine trip to Peking to arrange the President's historic visit to that nation. In trips to Moscow he paved the way for the President's visit and the establishment of a new Soviet-American détente. He played the major role in the Strategic Arms Limitation Talks (SALT), which resulted in the world's first agreement to limit strategic nuclear weapons. His performance overshadowed that of Secretary of State William P. Rodgers. In 1974, upon the resignation of Rodgers, Kissinger was appointed Secretary of State.

Kissinger's power and reputation generally survived the demise of the Nixon presidency. The new President, Gerald Ford, with little experience in foreign policy, relied on Kissinger as much or more than had Nixon.

One final note: Kissinger's rise to power depended more upon his affiliation with Nelson Rockefeller, the Rockefeller Foundation, and the Council on Foreign Affairs than his intellectual achievements.

Zbigniew Brzezinski

Brzezinski is the son of an upper-class Polish diplomat who was consul in Montreal, Canada, when the Nazis overran his country in 1939. Brzezinski was educated in private schools in Canada and received his B.A. from McGill University. He went to Harvard for his Ph.D. in Eastern European studies. He married the niece of the last democratic President of Czechoslovakia, Edward Benes. Brzezinski was well-known among upper-class emigrant families from Eastern Europe. He was an assistant professor at Harvard and later professor of government at Columbia.

Although Brzezinski produced eight books and scores of articles on world politics, his work was never accorded the scholarly praise of Kissinger's books. The result was a distinct feeling of academic competitiveness between the two men. Brzezinski was noted for his quick summaries of complicated questions, his development of balanced approaches to world problems, and his ability to come up with useful slogans to describe national policies. This latter ability is greatly appreciated by political leaders. Brzezinski served for two years on the State Department's policy planning staff in the Johnson Administration where he gained a reputation as a "hawk." As late as February 1968, he was quoted as saying, "We must make it clear to the enemy [North Vietnam] that we have the staying power—we're willing to continue for 30 years and we happen to be richer and more powerful."[22] But when Nixon became President, Brzezinski returned to Columbia and became a "dove."

At Columbia, Brzezinski became a close confidant of David Rockefeller. (Brzezinski's Northeast Harbor, Maine, summer home is near Rockefeller's Seal Harbor, Maine, estate.) When Rockefeller became chairman of the Council on Foreign Relations, he turned principally to Brzezinski for assistance. When top bankers and businesspeople in the United States, Western Europe, and Japan decided in 1972 to form a group to study their mutual problems, it was Brzezinski who coined the term "trilateralism." The resulting Trilateral Commission was formed with elite representatives from the advanced industrial world, funded by David Rockefeller, and directed by Zbigniew Brzezinski. At the request of J. Paul Austin, the head of the Atlanta-based Coca Cola Company, Rockefeller named the then little-known governor of Georgia, Jimmy Carter, to the new, prestigious Commission.

Carter never missed a meeting of the Trilateral Commission. He relied heavily on Brzezinski's counsel on world affairs; Carter himself had no experience in international diplomacy. As the Carter presidential campaign rolled into high gear, the word went out to the campaign staff: "Clear it with Zbig." All of Carter's foreign and defense policy statements were either written by or approved by Brzezinski. Carter's competent performance on the television debate with President Ford on foreign policy is generally attributed to Brzezinski's coaching.

Brzezinski became Special Assistant to the President for National Security Affairs immediately upon Carter's taking office in 1977. In contrast to Kissinger's spectacular style of personal diplomacy and his renown as an international celebrity, Brzezinski maintained strict personal privacy, shunned social gatherings, and did not engage in personal diplomacy. (Indeed, he declines to provide biographical material for *Who's Who, Current Biography,* and other standard reference works.) While Kissinger overshadowed all those around him, one insider reports, "I was shocked to see how much Zbig defers to Jimmy. He seems to be telling Jimmy what he wants to hear. He comes on as sort of a brilliant yes man. But no doubt Jimmy trusts and relies on him in foreign policy more than anyone else."[23] Yet despite their differences in social background and

[22]*U.S. News and World Report,* February 1968.
[23]*Los Angeles Times,* January 23, 1977, p. 3.

personal style, Brzezinski and Kissinger shared the view that U.S. power has waned in the world and that America must seek a new world order. This includes detente with the Soviet Union, normalization of relations with China, and greater interdependence with the industrialized nations of Western Europe and Japan. It is difficult to identify any basic policy differences between the two men.

Both Kissinger and Brzezinski owe their rise to power to their relationships with the Rockefellers: Kissinger with Nelson Rockefeller; Brzezinski with David Rockefeller. But the upper-class Brzezinski resents comparisons between his and Kissinger's relationship to the Rockefellers: "Henry Kissinger worked closely but also for Nelson Rockefeller. I worked closely but *with* David Rockefeller. I didn't work *for* David Rockefeller. He is not my employer."[24] Nonetheless, despite these personal differences, both intellectuals rose to power through their establishment connections.

Richard Allen

Allen's credentials as an "intellectual" are less impressive than those of his predecessors. He was a private prep-schooler who went on to Notre Dame for a B.A. and an M.A. in international affairs (although Notre Dame is not particularly distinguished in this field of study). He worked on a doctorate at the Universities of Freiberg and Munich in Germany, but his dissertation was rejected for what Allen said were "political" reasons—he was too anticommunist. He became an assistant professor of international studies at Georgia Tech in 1961–62 and then came to Washington as a staff member of the Georgetown University Center for Strategic and International Studies. He left Georgetown in 1966 for the Hoover Institute on War, Revolution, and Peace at Stanford University. Both the Georgetown Center and the Hoover Institute are generally considered "conservative" think tanks. Before the Reagan Administration came to power, neither were considered very influential.

Allen worked for Nixon during the 1968 presidential campaign, and he was disappointed when Kissinger was named National Security Advisor, instead of him. Allen became Kissinger's deputy, but they soon clashed, and Allen was out after only ten months. Allen served briefly as Deputy Assistant to the President for International Economic Affairs. However, he soon left government and academics behind to form his own consulting firm, Potomac International Corporation.

Allen's income as a consultant greatly exceeded what he would have made if he had returned to academic life, but his work later raised questions about potential conflicts of interest. The *Wall Street Journal* charged that he used his insider connections in the Nixon Administration to win lobbying fees from Nissan Motors, makers of Datsun automobiles. It

---

[24]*Los Angeles Times,* January 24, 1977, p. 13.

was also charged that Allen was paid as a consultant by the famous fugitive financier, Robert Vesco. Allen worked hard for Reagan in both the 1976 and 1980 campaigns, writing speeches and position papers on international affairs. Allen resigned from the Reagan staff briefly as a result of the conflict of interest charges, but he re-emerged as National Security Advisor in 1981.

The Washington Press Corps remained suspicious of Allen's international business dealings. Allen never did acquire any real influence with his boss- President Reagan. When interviewers for a Japanese magazine gave $1,000 to Allen for helping to arrange a meeting with Nancy Reagan, Allen put the money in a White House safe but failed to report it. He was cleared of any wrongdoing, but the Reagan team used the incident to ease Allen out of office.

Clearly Allen is *not* a distinguished intellectual with Ivy League academic contacts. He is not a Kissinger, Brzezinski, nor Bundy. He made it to the top through loyalty to Ronald Reagan and years of work in conservative think tanks. In his conservatism Allen is *un*representative of most of the nation's intellectual elite.

Allen's replacement, William P. Clark, is the least qualified person ever to hold the office of National Security Advisor. Clark dropped out of both college and law school but passed the California bar examination on his second attempt. He served as Reagan's executive secretary for two years when Reagan was governor of California; Reagan then named him to the state's supreme court. In 1981 Reagan named him assistant secretary of state, apparently to keep an eye on Haig, who was not a part of Reagan's inner circle. At his Senate confirmation hearings, Clark did not know the prime minister of South Africa (P. Botha) or Zimbabwe (R. Mugabe), nor could he describe the British party system. He has scant knowledge of foreign and defense policy, but he apparently has the friendship of the president.

THE CONGRESSIONAL ESTABLISHMENT

While national policies are developed outside Congress, Congress is no mere "rubber stamp." Key congresspersons do play an independent role in national decision-making; thus, key congressional leaders must be included in any operational definition of a national elite.

But Congress does *not* initiate policy; instead, it responds to the policy initiatives of others. Congress accepts, modifies, or rejects the policies and programs developed by the President and White House staff, executive departments, influential interest groups, and the mass media.

Many important government decisions, particularly in foreign and military affairs, are made without any direct participation by Congress. The President, with the support of top people in the administration, the mass media, the foundations, and civic associations, can commit the nation to foreign policies and military actions that Congress can neither foresee, prevent, nor reverse. Congress had little or no role in the Korean War and the Vietnam War, other than to appropriate the necessary funds. Détente with the Soviet Union, new relationships with Communist China, the U.S. role in the Middle East, and similarly important policy directions are decided with little congressional participation. Often congressional leaders are told of major foreign policy decisions or military actions only a few minutes before they are announced on national television.

Congress is more influential in domestic affairs than in foreign or military policy. It is much freer to reject presidential initiatives in education, welfare, health, urban affairs, civil rights, agriculture, labor, business, or taxing and spending. Executive agencies must go to Congress for needed legislation and appropriations. Congressional committees can exercise power in domestic affairs by giving or withholding the appropriations and the legislation wanted by these executive agencies.

Finally, congressional committees are an important communication link between governmental and nongovernmental elites; they serve as a bridge between the executive and military bureaucracies and the major nongovernmental elites in American society. Congressional committees bring department and agency heads together with leading industrial representatives—bankers, cotton producers, labor leaders, citrus growers, government contractors.

Political scientists have commented extensively on the structure of power *within* the Congress. They generally describe a hierarchical structure in both houses of the Congress—a "congressional establishment" which largely determines what the Congress will do. This "establishment" is composed of the Speaker of the House and President Pro Tempore of the Senate; House and Senate Majority and Minority Leaders and Whips; and committee chairpersons and ranking minority members of House and Senate standing committees. Party leadership roles in the House and Senate are major sources of power in Washington. The Speaker of the House and the Majority and Minority Leaders of the House and Senate direct the business of Congress. Although they share this task with the standing committee chairpersons, these leaders are generally "first among equals" in their relationships with committee chairpersons. But the committee system also creates powerful congressional figures, the chairpersons of the most powerful standing committees—particularly the Senate Foreign Relations, Appropriations, and Finance Committees, and the House Rules, Appropriations, and Ways and Means Committees.

"Policy clusters"—alliances of leaders from executive agencies, congressional committees, and private business and industry—tend to emerge in Washington. Committee chairpersons, owing to their control over legislation in Congress, are key members of these policy clusters. One policy cluster might include the chairpersons of the House and Senate committees on agriculture, the Secretary of Agriculture, and the leaders of the American Farm Bureau Federation. Another vital policy cluster would include the chairpersons of the House and Senate Armed Services Committees; the Secretary and Under Secretaries of Defense; key military leaders, including the Joint Chiefs of Staff; and the leadership of defense industries such as Lockheed and General Dynamics. These alliances of congressional, executive, and private elites determine most public policy within their area of concern.

Senators and prominent reporters have described a Senate "establishment" and an "inner club" where power in the Senate and in Washington is concentrated (see Table 3-2). Ralph K. Huitt describes the Senate "establishment" type as

> a prudent man, who serves a long apprenticeship before trying to assert himself, and talks infrequently even then. He is courteous to a fault in his relations with his colleagues, not allowing political disagreements to affect his personal feelings. He is always ready to help another Senator when he can, and he expects to be repaid in kind. More than anything else he is a Senate man, proud of the institution and ready to defend its traditions and prerequisites against all outsiders. He is a legislative workhorse who specializes in one or two policy areas. . . . He is a man of accommodation who knows that "you have to go along to get along"; he is a conservative, institutional man, slow to change what he has mastered at the expense of so much time and patience.[25]

But viewed within the broader context of a *national elite*, congressional leaders appear "folksy," parochial, and localistic. Because of the local constituency of a congressperson, he or she is predisposed to concern himself or herself with local interests. Congresspersons are part of local elite structures "back home"; they retain their local businesses and law practices, club memberships, and religious affiliations. Congresspersons represent many small segments of the nation rather than the nation as a whole. Even top congressional leaders from safe districts, with many years of seniority, cannot completely shed their local interests. Their claim to *national* leadership must be safely hedged by attention to their local constituents. Consider, for example, the parochial backgrounds of these top congressional leaders.

Howard H. Baker, Jr. (R. Tenn.). Senate Majority Leader. Born in 1925 into a political family. Baker's father was a congressman from Tennessee from 1950 until his death in 1964; Baker's mother completed his father's term in the Congress. Baker attended a private academy, and then went on to Tulane

[25]Ralph K. Huitt, "The Outsider in the U.S. Senate: An Alternative Role," *American Political Science Review*, 65 (June 1961), 568.

Table 3–2   The Congressional Establishment 1981–1982

Senate Leadership

President Pro Tempore	Strom Thurmond (R. S.C.)
Majority Leader	Howard H. Baker (R. Tenn.)
Majority Whip	Ted Stevens (R. Alaska)
Minority Leader	Robert C. Byrd (D. W.Va.)
Minority Whip	Alan Cranston (D. Cal.)

House Leadership

Speaker	Thomas P. O'Neill, Jr. (D. Mass.)
Majority Leader	Jim Wright (D. Tex.)
Majority Whip	Thomas S. Foley (D. Wash.)
Minority Leader	Robert H. Michael (R. Ill.)
Minority Whip	Trent Lott (R. Miss.)

Senate Committees

Appropriations	Mark O. Hatfield (R. Or.)
	William Proxmire (D. Wis.)
Armed Services	John Tower (R. Tex.)
	John C. Stennis (D. Miss.)
Labor and Human Resources	Orin G. Hatch (R. Utah)
	Edward M. Kennedy (D. Mass.)
Banking, Housing, and Urban Affairs	Jake Garn (R. Utah)
	Harrison A. Williams (D. N.J.)
Foreign Relations	Charles H. Percy (R. Ill.)
	Claiborne Pell (D. R.I.)
Government Affairs	William R. Roth (R. Del.)
	Thomas F. Eagleton (D. Mo.)
Judiciary	Strom Thurmond (R. S.C.)
	Joseph R. Biden (R. Del.)
Finance	Robert Dole (R. Kan.)
	Russell B. Long (D. La.)
Agriculture	Jesse Helms (R. N.C.)
	Walter Huddleston (D. Ky.)
Budget	Pete V. Domenici (R. N.M.)
	Earnest F. Holling (D. S.C.)

House Committees

Rules	Richard Bolling (D. Mo.)
	James H. Quillen (R. Tex.)
Ways and Means	Dan Rostenkowski (D. Ill.)
	Barber B. Conoble, Jr. (R. N.Y.)
Appropriations	Jamie L. Whitten (D. Miss.)
	Silvio O. Conte (R. Mass.)
Armed Services	Melvin Price (D. Ill.)
	William L. Dickinson (R. Ala.)
Banking and Finance	Fernand J. St. Germain (D. R.I.)
	J. William Stauton (R. Ohio)
Foreign Affairs	Clement J. Zablocki (D. Wis.)
	William S. Broomfield (R. Mi.)
Government Operation	Jack Brooks (D. Tex.)
	Frank Horton (R. N.Y.)
Judiciary	Peter W. Rodino, Jr. (D. N.J.)
	Robert McClory (R. Ill.)
Budget	James R. Jones (D. Ok.)
	Delbert L. Latta (R. Ohio)

University, and the University of Tennessee, where he earned his law degree. He served in the Navy in World War II. He married the daughter of U.S. Senator Everett M. Dirkson (R. Ill.), former Republican leader of the Senate. He is a former chairman of the First National Bank of Oneida, Tennessee, and former president of Colonial Gas Co. of Wytheville, Virginia. Baker passed up the opportunity to win his father's congressional seat in order to run for the U.S. Senate in 1964. He lost this first bid in a close vote, but he succeeded in winning his Senate seat (and first public office) in 1966. As son-in-law of the Senate Minority Leader, he received a great deal of public attention and good committee assignments—Foreign Relations, Public Works, and later the Select Committee on Intelligence. However, he was defeated by Hugh Scott (R. Pa.) in an attempt to become Minority Leader, after the death of his father-in-law. His Senate colleagues resented his efforts to move up too quickly in the Senate hierarchy. His career in the Senate was resuscitated, however, by his brilliant performance as co-chairman of the Senate Select Committee on Campaign Practices (the Watergate investigation committee). Baker received national television prominence by pressing the question: "What did the President know, and when did he know it?" When Hugh Scott, who had defended President Nixon until almost the end of the investigation, retired, Senator Robert P. Griffin (R. Mich.), as Minority Whip, was next in line to succeed Scott. But when President Ford lost to Jimmy Carter in 1976, Griffin lost an important ally in the White House, and many Republicans believed the party should turn to a younger "new face" for leadership. Baker was elected Minority Leader in a close vote over Griffin in January 1977. To Baker's surprise and delight, Reagan's 1980 victory helped Republican Senate candidates throughout the nation, and for the first time in twenty-eight years, the GOP captured control of the Senate. Howard Baker became *majority* leader.

Robert C. Byrd (D. W.Va.) Senate Minority Leader. Former Senate Majority Leader and Whip and chairman of the Judiciary Committee. Born in 1918, and then adopted and raised by relatives in West Virginia. Attended small Beckeley College and later Marshall College in West Virginia for three years. Elected to the West Virginia legislature in 1946, and to the U.S. House of Representatives in 1952. Earned a law degree from American University in 1963 after ten years of night school while serving in Congress. He won his U.S. Senate seat in 1958. For many years he served quietly on the Rules, Administration, and Judiciary committees, mastering parliamentary knowledge and performing small favors for his colleagues. His voting record was conservative: he voted against the Civil Rights Act of 1964, the Voting Rights Act of 1965, and the confirmation of Thurgood Marshall as Supreme Court Justice. In 1967, with the support of then Majority Leader Mike Mansfield, Byrd was made secretary to the Senate Democratic Caucus. Edward M. Kennedy was Majority Whip, but Kennedy was too busy with his national aspirations to tend to his job of lining up votes for the leadership. Byrd, by contrast, put in long hours and devoted much hard work to his Senate assignments. After Kennedy's involvement in the Chappaquiddick scandal, Byrd decided to challenge the Massachusetts senator for the Whip's job. To the surprise of many, Byrd won. Apparently, Kennedy's disregard of the unwritten rules of senatorial behavior, combined with Byrd's intense devotion to the work of the Senate, gave the little-known West Virginian an impressive victory over the nation's leading Democratic political figure. As Whip, Byrd continued to work quietly behind the scenes to consolidate his position with his Senate colleagues. In 1977, when Mansfield retired from the Senate, Byrd confronted the challenge of another leading national Democrat, Hubert H. Humphrey. Again, Byrd's "insider" accomplishments in the Senate brought him victory over Humphrey in the race for Majority Leader. Thus, the little-known West Virginian defeated the two most popular Democratic politicians in the nation in his climb to top of the Senate. When the Republicans captured the Senate in the Reagan landslide in 1980, Byrd was reduced to Minority Leader.

Thomas P. "Tip" O'Neill (D. Mass.) Speaker of the House, former House Majority Leader. O'Neill has been a politician and Democratic party loyalist all of his life. Immediately after graduation from Boston College in 1936, he ran for the Massachusetts state legislature and won. He served there as a party organization loyalist, becoming Democratic leader of the state general assembly in 1947. When Democrats captured control of the legislature in 1948, O'Neill became Speaker of the Massachusetts House. When John F. Kennedy vacated his Boston seat in the U.S. House of Representatives in 1952 to run for U.S. Senate, O'Neill cashed in on his own party alliances and state house prestige to win that seat for himself. Upon arriving in Washington, O'Neill quickly aligned himself with John McCormack, another Boston Irish politician who had risen to Majority Leader and later served as Speaker of the House. McCormack gave O'Neill key committee memberships, and the tall, burly Irishman began his slow rise through the ranks of the House. O'Neill was never known for initiating important new laws, but rather he was known for party loyalty, service to constituents, and political "flexibility" (changing sides when it seemed expedient to do so). O'Neill served many years on the important Rules Committee and moved up from Whip to Majority Leader when Boggs died in a plane crash in 1972. O'Neill was the unanimous choice for Speaker of the House, following the retirement of Carl Albert in 1977. Following Reagan's victory in 1980, O'Neill became the highest ranking Democrat in Washington and a symbol of the liberal crusades of the past. He tried to hold on to the social programs of the past, but the Reagan White House appeared to out-maneuver him at every turn. Despite a Democratic majority, Reagan defeated O'Neill on many key votes by winning over disenchanted Democrats.

Robert H. Michel (R. Ill.). House Minority Leader. The son of a French immigrant factory worker, Michel attended tiny Bradley University. He began his career in politics, fresh out of college, as an administrative assistant to Congressman Harold H. Velde. When Velde decided to retire in 1956, Michel, with several years experience as a Congressional aide, decided to run for the office himself. He won in a close race, and he has represented the city of Peoria in Congress since 1957. One of his constituents was the Senate Republican Leader, Everett Dirkson, who helped him on Capitol Hill. Dirkson's son-in-law Howard H. Baker, the current Senate Republican leader, also became a close friend. The wives of Baker and Michel attended college together. Early in his career, Michel was appointed to a seat on the powerful House Appropriations Committee. Over the years, Michel was described as "a party man and a conservative." He almost always voted with the Republican majority and with the conservative coalition. He was described as "a plodder rather than a thinker." The *Congressional Quarterly* described him as in the "Mr. Nice Guy" tradition—"unpretentious, self-effacing, Rotary Club glad hander with a gee-whiz vocabulary and a rambling speaking style." In 1980, the long-time Republican House Leader John Rodes (R. Ariz.)

voluntarily stepped down. Michel, the conservative party workhorse, found himself in a struggle for Republican leadership with Guy Vander Jagt (R. Mich.), a moderate with an impressive speaking style. Michel won, even though Vander Jagt was better known throughout the nation. Michel immediately set to work to win over his conservative friends in the Democratic party. Michel may officially be the "minority" leader, but with solid Republican backing plus the support of a few conservative Democrats, Michel can put together an ideological majority and win many crucial House votes.

Robert J. Dole (R. Kan.). Chairman of the Senate Finance Committee. Dole left the family farm in Kansas to join the Army during World War II, but he suffered serious wounds in Italy. He was nearly blown apart by mortar and machine gun fire and was left for dead on the battlefield for twenty-four hours. Later he was paralyzed from the neck down; he spent three years in hospitals recovering from his wounds, and even today he cannot use his right arm. He married his physical therapist and completed a law degree at tiny Washburn Municipal University in Topeka in 1952. But even before he finished law school, Dole won a seat in 1950 in the Kansas legislature at the age of twenty-six. He has never been out of public office since then. He was Russell County Kansas district attorney for four terms, and then a Kansas congressman for four terms. In 1968 he was elected to the U.S. Senate; he was re-elected in 1974 and 1980. In 1976 he was Gerald Ford's vice-presidential running mate on the unsuccessful Republican ticket. It was in that vice-presidential campaign that Dole appeared to be a "hatchet man" compared to the boy scout image of his opponent Walter Mondale. Dole is perhaps one of the wittiest elected officials in Washington, but on television quips seem bitter and caustic. Dole is generally conservative on policy issues; he supports programs for his farm constituents as well as for veterans and handicapped persons. He divorced his first wife in 1972 and married Elizabeth Hanford Dole, a member of the Federal Trade Commission, in 1975. As Chairman of the Senate Finance Committee, Dole has had a great deal to say about federal tax cuts.

Henry M. Jackson (D. Wash.). U.S. Senator, a member of the Senate Internal Affairs Committee, the Senate Government Operations Committee, and the Armed Services Committee. Son of Norwegian immigrants in Everett, Washington. Attended the University of Washington and received law degree in 1935. Jackson was popularly elected Snohomish County Prosecuting Attorney, and four years later (1940) he was elected to the House of Representatives. He served in the House until election to the Senate in 1952. He never lost an election, and has been re-elected to the Senate by record margins of over 80 percent. He is the leading spokesman in the Senate on national defense. Boeing Aircraft, a major defense contractor, is a major employer in his district; however, a fellow congressman once remarked: "If the State of Washington did not have a single defense contract or a single military base, Jackson would still be strong for defense." Jackson is co-author of the Environmental Protection Act and a leading advocate of environmental protection. He belongs to the Everett, Washington, American Legion, Elks, Eagles, Masons, and Sons of Norway.

Russell B. Long (D. La.). U.S. Senator, ranking Democrat and former chairman, Senate Finance Committee. The son of Huey Long, Louisiana's most famous politician and a national figure in the 1930s. Russell Long received his bachelor's and law degrees from Louisiana State University, which his father had been instrumental in building. He served in the Navy in World War II and returned to practice law in the capital at Baton Rouge. At age thirty three, he was elected to the U.S. Senate without having held previous office, clearly on the popularity of his family name. But Long applied himself to the work of the Senate under the tutelage of Harry F. Byrd (D. Va.), the long-time chairman of the Senate Finance Committee. Long became a Senate "insider" with close connections to Lyndon Johnson. When Byrd retired in 1965, Long succeeded him in the chair of the Senate Finance Committee. (Long then had fourteen years of seniority). For many years, Long's position as chairman assured him of control over all bills affecting taxation—including jurisdiction over tax reform, energy, welfare, social security, national health insurance, revenue sharing, and anything else that costs money. (At one time, Long's preeminence was shared with Wilbur Mills of the House Ways and Means Committee; however, Mills' downfall after acknowledged alcoholism problems left Long the leading figure on Capitol Hill in tax matters.) In conference committees with House Ways and Means Committee, Long usually wins his battles.

THE JUDGES

Nine people—none of whom is elected and all of whom serve for life—possess ultimate authority over all the other institutions of government. The Supreme Court of the United States has the authority to void the acts of popularly elected Presidents and Congresses. There is no appeal from their decision about what is the "supreme law of the land," except perhaps to undertake the difficult task of amending the Constitution itself. Only the good judgement of the Justices themselves—their sense of "judicial self-restraint"—limits their power over government elites. It was the Supreme Court, rather than the President or the Congress, that took the lead in important issues such as eliminating segregation from public life, ensuring voter equality in representation, limiting the powers of police, and declaring abortion to be a fundamental right of women.

Social scientists have commented on the class bias of Supreme Court Justices. John R. Schmidhauser reports that over 90 percent of the Supreme Court Justices serving on the Court between 1789 and 1962 were from socially prominent, politically influential, upper-class families.[26] Over two thirds of the Supreme Court Justices ever serving on the Court attended well-known or Ivy League law schools (most notably, Harvard, Yale, Columbia, Pennsylvania, N.Y.U., Michigan, Virginia). No blacks served on the Supreme Court until the appointment of Associate Justice Thurgood Marshall in 1967. No women served until the appointment of Sandra Day O'Connor in 1981. Henry Abraham depicts the typical

[26]John R. Schmidhauser, *The Supreme Court* (New York: Holt, Rinehart and Winston, 1960), p. 59.

Supreme Court Justice: "White; generally Protestant...; fifty to fifty-five years of age at the time of his appointment; Anglo-Saxon ethnic stock...; high social status; reared in an urban environment; member of a civic-minded, politically active, economically comfortable family; legal training; some type of public office; generally well educated."[27] Of course, social background does not necessarily determine judicial philosophy. But as Schmidhauser observes; "If...the Supreme Court is the keeper of the American conscience, it is essentially the conscience of the American upper-middle class sharpened by the imperative of individual social responsibility and political activism, and conditioned by the conservative impact of legal training and professional legal attitudes and associations."[28]

Not all Justices, however, conform to this upper-class portrait. Indeed, several current Justices of the Supreme Court are middle-class rather than upper-class in social origin. Their appointments to the Supreme Court have been more closely related to their political activities than either their social backgrounds or their accomplishments in the law.

Warren E. Burger. Chief Justice, U.S. Supreme Court. Son of a successful Swiss-German farmer near St. Paul, Minnesota. Worked his way through the University of Minnesota and St. Paul College of Law, receiving law degree in 1931. Developed a successful twenty-two-year private practice in Minneapolis–St. Paul with a wide range of civil and criminal cases. An early political associate of Minnesota Republican Governor Harold E. Stassen, he brought himself to the attention of eastern Republicans in national GOP conventions in 1940 and 1952. President Eisenhower appointed him Assistant Attorney General in 1953, then to U.S. Court of Appeals in 1956. He served on the Court of Appeals until he was appointed Chief Justice by President Nixon in 1969 on the resignation of Earl Warren.

Byron R. White. U.S. Supreme Court Justice. Son of the mayor of Wellington, Colorado. Attended public schools and the University of Colorado. At Colorado, he was Phi Beta Kappa, a Rhodes Scholar, and an All-American halfback. Attended Yale Law School while playing halfback for the Pittsburgh Steelers and Detroit Lions; was the NFL leading ground gainer in 1938. In World War II he served in the Navy in the Pacific, where he met John F. Kennedy. After the war, White completed his law degree at Yale, served legal clerkship under U.S. Supreme Court Chief Justice Fred M. Vinson, and opened a law practice in Denver, Colorado. His law practice was undistinguished, but in 1960 the Kennedys called on him to organize Colorado for JFK's presidential campaign. White was credited with delivering Colorado's convention votes to Kennedy. He was JFK's only appointment to the Supreme Court.

Thurgood Marshall. U.S. Supreme Court Justice. Son of a Pullman car steward. Educated at Lincoln University and Howard University Law School. Shortly

---

[27]Henry Abraham, *The Judicial Process* (New York: Oxford University Press, 1962), p. 58.

[28]Schmidhauser, *The Supreme Court,* p. 59.

after graduation in 1933, Marshall became counsel for the Baltimore chapter of the NAACP. From 1940 to 1961, he served as director and chief counsel of NAACP's semi-autonomous Legal Defense and Educational Fund. During that period, he argued thirty-two cases before the Supreme Court, winning twenty-nine. His notable victory (indeed, perhaps the black man's most notable judicial victory) came in *Brown v. Board of Education of Topeka* in 1954. President Kennedy chose Marshall as a judge for the U.S. Circuit Court of Appeals in 1961; President Johnson appointed him U.S. Solicitor General in 1965. As the latter, Marshall argued nineteen more cases before the U.S. Supreme Court. When President Johnson announced Marshall's appointment to the Supreme Court in 1967, he accurately noted that "probably only one or two other living men have argued as many cases before the court—and perhaps less than half a dozen in all the history of the nation."

THE POLITICAL CONTRIBUTORS

Political campaigns cost money—usually a great deal more than candidates themselves are willing or able to spend. In 1980, Reagan and Carter each spent $30 million on the general election; Reagan and Carter spent an additional $30 million winning in the many primaries leading to their parties' nominations. Most of these funds came from the Federal Elections Commission from the $1 checkoff provision in the individual income tax. However, all of the candidates had to produce some "matching funds" from private individuals. Indeed, few candidates can even begin a political career in state or local office without first securing financial support from wealthy "angels." Far-sighted persons of wealth may choose to back a promising young politician early in his or her career and continue this support for many years.[29] There are few congresspersons or senators who do *not* have wealthy financial sponsors.

Prior to 1976, the spiraling costs of political campaigns (particularly the high costs of television advertising) placed extreme pressure on candidates and potential candidates to secure the backing of wealthy financial contributors. For example, in 1972 Richard Nixon spent $60 million on his re-election campaign, and his "poorer" opponent, George McGovern, spent $30 million. All of these funds came from private contributors. Nixon's top financial backers were W. Clement Stone, centimillionaire chairman of Combined Insurance Company of America,

[29]Richard Nixon was long supported by Chicago insurance tycoon W. Clement Stone. George McGovern was backed for many years by Stewart Mott, heir to the General Motors fortune. Jimmy Carter was backed in his early races in Georgia by J. Paul Austin, chairman of the board of Coca Cola, Charles Kirbo, Atlanta attorney, and Thomas B. (Bert) Lance, former president of the National Bank of Georgia and director of the Office of Management and Budget. Ronald Reagan was supported in his early years by A.C. Rubel, chairman of Union Oil, Justin Dart of Dart Industries, and William French Smith.

($2 million); Richard Mellon Scaife, director of Mellon National Bank and Trust and Gulf Oil Corporation, and centimillionaire heir to the Mellon fortune ($1 million); Arthur K. Watson, former chairman of the board of IBM; John duPont (Dupont Corp.); Harvey Firestone (Firestone Tire and Rubber); Henry Ford II; Howard Hughes; J. Willard Marriott (motels); Henry J. Heinz II (ketchup); Bob Hope; and Frank Sinatra.

Democrats do not usually receive as much money from the corporate world as Republicans, commonly deriving about half of their funds from this source. The Xerox Corporation, for example, has been a major source of support for Democratic candidates. Traditionally, Democrats have turned to big labor for support, notably the Committee on Political Education (COPE) of the AFL-CIO and the larger international unions, among them the United Automobile Workers and the United Steel Workers. Liberal Democrats have also been supported by upper-class liberal philanthropists. These "limousine liberals" provided much of the financial support for the civil rights movement, the peace movement, and other liberal causes. For example, in 1972, Senator George McGovern's campaign was supported by wealth-holders such as Stewart Mott (heir to the General Motors fortune), Max Palevsky (former chairman of the board of the Xerox Corporation), Nicholas and Daniel Noyes (wealthy students who are heirs to the Eli Lilly Pharmaceutical fortune), and Richard Saloman (president of Charles of the Ritz, Inc.).

Yet over the years the Democratic deficit in campaign finances has provided a stimulus to "reform" of campaign funding, especially when Democrats controlled both houses of Congress by overwhelming margins and a close presidential election was on the horizon. In 1974, Congress passed a comprehensive campaign spending law, with the following provisions:

1. A Presidential Election Campaign Fund was created from the voluntary one dollar per person check-offs from individual income taxes.
2. A Federal Election Commission was created to oversee federal election spending.
3. The Commission would distribute campaign monies from the fund (a) to candidates in the primaries; (b) to the Democratic and Republican parties for their national conventions; (c) and to the Republican and Democratic candidates in the general election.
4. Individuals are limited to a $1,000 contribution in any single election, and organizations are limited to $5,000. All contributions must be reported to the Federal Elections Commission.

The Supreme Court modified these provisions by declaring that individuals, as an exercise of their First Amendment rights, can spend as much of their *own* money on their *own* election as they wish. Moreover, as an exercise of First Amendment rights, any individual may *independently* spend any amount of money to advertise their own political views. As long as these independent expenditures are not tied directly to a political campaign, they are not to be counted against the maximum limits set by the law. While the campaign spending law, as modified by the Supreme Court, reduces the role of the large financial "angels," it permits persons of wealth to spend large amounts on their own campaigns.

With individual contributions limited to $1,000, much of the financial burden of politics has been assumed by political action committees (PACs) which represent corporations, trade associations, professions, labor unions, and other organized interest groups. PACs can contribute up to $5,000 to candidates they decide to support. PACs are very important in congressional elections. PACs provide a direct link between the corporate world and the world of politics. PAC money tends to flow to congressional incumbents who are party leaders or chairpersons or ranking members of powerful congressional committees.However, rarely do PACs buy votes outright. "The most anybody figures they can get in this business is access. You can't buy a vote. What you can do is say 'Listen, I've helped you. Now let me make my case.' "[30]

What do contributors get for their money? Perhaps the most important payoff is simply *access* to the political officeholder—in the presidency, Senate, Congress, or state government. The big contributor can expect to see and talk with the officeholder to discuss general issues confronting the nation as well as the contributor's specific problems with the government. This access assures that the views of top contributors will at least be heard. Another payoff is *assistance* with government-related problems. Large contributions generally ensure speedy consideration of requests, applications, contracts, bids, and so forth, by government bureaucracies. Assistance does not necessarily mean favoritism, but it does mean a reduction of standard red tape, bureaucratic delays, and cumbersome and time-consuming administrative reviews. Of course, *favoritism* itself is a frequent motive for large contributions by individuals and corporations who are dependent upon government contracts, licenses, or regulatory decisions. But despite occasional sensational cases, blatant favoritism is a politically dangerous game avoided by most officeholders.[31]

---

[30]*Congressional Quarterly*, May 17, 1980, p. 1341.

[31]For example, the jury found in the trial of former Attorney General John Mitchell and former Republican Campaign Chairman Maurice Stans that the contribution of financier Robert Vesco merely bought the assistance of John Mitchell in presenting Vesco's argument to the Security and Exchange Commission. The SEC actually decided *against* Vesco, despite his secret $100,000 contribution to President Nixon's re-election. It was Vesco himself who expected White House intervention on his behalf and when he did not get it, threatened to "blow the lid" on his secret contribution. Vesco's top lieutenant attempted to implicate Mitchell and Stans by charging their complicity in bribery, but the jury decided their actions did not constitute illegal acts.

Generally it is only when the contributor's contract, bid, or license application is substantially equal to that of the noncontributor that favoritism plays a decisive role. Another motive of contributors is the *status* a large contribution provides—the opportunity to rub shoulders with the great and near-great in American politics, to be invited to the President's inaugural ball, to visit the White House for dinner and tell one's friends about it, and even to boast of the size of one's contribution at cocktail parties.

Perhaps the most important motive in campaign contributions, however, is *political ideology*. Most of the top contributors, including conservatives W. Clement Stone, Richard Mellon Scaife, Arthur K. Watson, Joseph Coors, and Bob Hope, and liberals Stewart Mott, Max Palevsky, Averell Harriman, and Alan Alda, expect no direct personal gain from their contributions. They believe their contributions are helping to guide the nation's government in the proper direction.

SUMMARY

Governmental power may be even more concentrated than corporate power in America. One indicator of its growing concentration is the increasing proportion of the gross national product produced by government. All governmental expenditures now account for one third of the GNP, and *federal* expenditures account for nearly two thirds of all government expenditures.

Running for office is not the same as running a government. Presidents must depend upon "serious men" to run government. Skill in campaigning does not necessarily prepare individuals for the responsibility of governing. Key government executives must be recruited from industry, finance, the law, the universities, and the bureaucracy itself. These "serious men" do not appear to differ much in background or experience from one administration to another.

The federal bureaucracy, an independent channel of recruitment to positions of power, is now producing its own leadership. The small percentage of federal expenditures devoted to the military and the small percentage of corporate sales devoted to arms suggest that the military-industrial has been notably unsuccessful in recent years. There has been a decline since the 1950s in the exchange of military and corporate personnel and a sharp decline in the power and prestige of the military in general.

Congress seldom initiates programs, but rather it responds to the initiatives of the President, the executive departments, influential interest groups, and the mass media. Power *within* Congress is concentrated in the House and Senate leadership and in the chairperson and ranking minority members of the standing committees. Compared to other national elites, congressional leaders appear localistic. Their claim to national leadership must be safely hedged by attention to their local constituencies. Congresspersons are frequently recruited from very modest, middle-class backgrounds.

The Supreme Court is the most elitist branch of government. Its nine members are not elected, and they serve life terms. They have the authority to void the acts of popularly elected Presidents and Congresses. It was the Supreme Court, rather than the President or Congress, which took the lead in eliminating segregation from public life, ensuring voter equality in representation, limiting the powers of police, and declaring abortion to be a fundamental right of women. Although most Justices have been upper-class in social origin, their appointment has generally been related to their political activities rather than to their experience in the law.

Political contributions are important links between corporate wealth and the political system. Political action committees (PACs) represent a direct link between the corporate world and the world of politics. Contributions are usually given to achieve access or to advance ideological views rather than for direct personal gain.

4

The newsmakers

Television is the major source of information for the vast majority of Americans, and the people who control this flow of information are among the most powerful in the nation. Indeed, today the leadership of the mass media has successfully established itself as equal in power to the nation's corporate and governmental leadership.

The rise of the mass media to a position of preeminence among institutions of power is a relatively recent phenomenon. It is a direct product of technological change: the development of a national television communication network extending to nearly every home in America. (In 1952, only 19.9 percent of all American homes had television sets, compared to 99.8 percent in 1972).[1] Newspapers had always reported wars, riots, scandals, and disasters, just as they do today. But the masses of Americans did not read them—and fewer still read their editorials. But today, television reaches the masses: it is really the first form of *mass* communication devised. It also presents a *visual* image, not merely a printed word.

As children, Americans spend more time in front of television sets than in school. As adults, Americans spend half of their leisure time

[1]*Statistical Abstract of the United States, 1973*, p. 693.

watching television. In the average home, the television set is on seven hours a day. Over two thirds of Americans report that they get all or most of their "news" from television. More importantly, television is the "most trusted" media of communication.[2]

Network television news not only reaches a larger audience than newspapers, but perhaps more importantly, it reaches children, functional illiterates, the poor, and the uneducated. The television viewer *must* see the news or else turn off the set; the newspaper reader can turn quickly to the sports and comics without confronting the political news. But the greatest asset of television is its *visual* quality—the emotional impact that is conveyed in pictures. Scenes of burning and looting in cities, dead American GIs being loaded on helicopters, and terrorists holding frightened hostages, all convey *emotions* as well as *information*.

CONCENTRATION OF POWER IN THE MASS MEDIA

The power to determine what the American people will see and hear about their world is vested in three private corporations—the American Broadcasting Company (ABC), the National Broadcasting Corporation (NBC), a subsidiary of Radio Corporation of America, and the Columbia Broadcasting System, Inc. (CBS). These networks determine what will be seen by the mass viewing audience; there is *no* public regulation whatsoever of network broadcasting. Individual television stations are privately owned and licensed to use public broadcast channels by the Federal Communications Commission. But these stations are forced to receive news and programming from the networks because of the high costs involved in *producing* news or entertainment at the local station level. The top officials of these corporate networks, particularly the people in charge of the news, are indeed "a tiny, enclosed fraternity of privileged men."[3] Nicholas Johnson, a member of the Federal Communications Commission and a self-professed liberal, has said:

> The networks, in particular... are probably now beyond the check of any institution in our society. The President, the Congress of the United States, the FCC, the foundations, and universities are reluctant even to get involved. I think they may now be so powerful that they're beyond the check of anyone.[4]

[2]The Roper Organization, *What People Think of Television and Other Mass Media: 1959–1972* (New York: Television Information Office, 1973), p. 2.

[3]The phraseology is courtesy of former Vice-President Spiro Agnew, who also used the more colorful description of the network top brass—"super-sensitive, self-anointed, supercilious electronic barons of opinion." See *Newsweek*, November 9, 1970, p. 22.

[4]Quoted by Edward Jay Epstein, *News from Nowhere* (New York: Random House, 1973), p. 6.

Top executives in the news media do not doubt their own power. They generally credit themselves with the success of the civil rights movement: the dramatic televised images of the nonviolent civil rights demonstrators of the early 1960s being attacked by police with night-sticks, cattle prods, and vicious dogs helped to awaken the nation and its political leadership to the injustices of segregation. These leaders also credit TV with "decisively changing America's opinion of the Vietnam War," and forcing Lyndon Johnson out of the presidency. The director of CBS News in Washington proudly claims:

> When television covered its "first war" in Vietnam, it showed a terrible truth of war in a manner new to mass audiences. A case can be made, and certainly should be examined, that this was cardinal to the disillusionment of Americans with this war, the cynicism of many young people towards America, and the destruction of Lyndon Johnson's tenure of office.[5]

Television news, together with the Washington press corps, also lays claim, of course, to the expulsion of Richard Nixon from the presidency. The *Washington Post* conducted the "investigative reporting" that produced a continuous flow of embarrassing and incriminating information about the President and his chief advisers. But it was the television networks that maintained the continuous nightly attack on the White House for nearly two years and kept Watergate in the public eye. Richard Nixon's approval rating in public opinion polls dropped from an all-time high of 68 percent in January 1973 following the Vietnam Peace Agreement to a low of 24 percent less than one year later.

Yet the leadership of the mass media frequently claim that they do no more than "mirror" reality. Although the "mirror" argument contradicts many of their more candid claims to having righted many of America's wrongs (segregation, Vietnam, Watergate), the leadership of the three television networks claim that television "is a mirror of society." Frank Stanton, president of CBS, told a House committee: "What the media does is hold a mirror up to society and try to report it as factually as possible." When confronted with charges that television helped to spread urban rioting in the late 1960s, Julian Goodman, president of NBC, told the National Commission on the Cause and Prevention of Violence that "the medium is being blamed for the message."[6]

Of course, the mirror analogy is nonsense. Newspeople decide what the news will be, how it will be presented, and how it will be interpreted. As David Brinkley explained, "News is what I say it is. It's something worth knowing by my standards."[7] Newspeople have the power to create some

[5]*Ibid.*, p. 9.
[6]*Ibid.*
[7]*TV Guide*, April 11, 1964.

national issues and ignore others; elevate obscure people to national prominence reward politicians they favor and punish those they disfavor. The best description of the newsmaking power of television is found in a book significantly entitled *News from Nowhere* by Edward Jay Epstein, who explains:

> The mirror analogy further tends to neglect the components of "will," or decisions made in advance to cover or not to cover certain types of events. A mirror makes no decisions, it simply reflects what occurs in front of it; television coverage can, however, be controlled by predecisions or "policy." . . .
>
> Policy can determine not only whether or not a subject is seen on television but also how it is depicted. . . .
>
> Intervention by the producer or assistant producers in decisions on how to play the news is the rule rather than the exception.[8]

Ninety percent of the national news that reaches the American television public arrives from ABC, NBC, and CBS.[9] Local television stations do not have the resources to produce their own national news, and consequently largely restrict themselves to local news coverage. The three networks "feed" approximately 700 local affiliated stations, with "The Evening News." These stations generally videotape network programs for rebroadcast later in the evening, usually in truncated form, on the local news program. Moreover, the networks also *own* key television stations in the nation's largest cities. While the Federal Communications Commission limits station ownership by the networks to no more than five stations, these network-owned stations are concentrated in the largest "market" cities.[10] The twelve largest "market" cities contain 38 percent of all "TV households" in the nation, and these cities have network-owned stations.[11]

The nation's 1,748 daily newspapers get most of their national news from the Associated Press (AP) and United Press International (UPI) wire services, although the larger newspapers and newspaper chains also disseminate their own national news. Radio stations also rely heavily on AP and UPI. One large radio station admitted to filling its newscasts "90

---

[8]Epstein, *News from Nowhere*, pp. 16–17.

[9]See Lewis H. Lapham, "The Temptation of a Sacred Cow," *Harpers* (August 1973), pp. 43–54.

[10]CBS owns WCBS (New York), WBBM (Chicago), WCAV (Philadelphia), KMOX (St. Louis), and KNXT (Los Angeles). ABC owns WABC (New York), WLS (Chicago), KGO (San Francisco), KABC (Los Angeles), and WXYZ (Detroit). NBC owns WNBC (New York), WKYC (Cleveland), KWBC (Los Angeles), WMAQ (Chicago), and WRC (Washington).

[11]Ben H. Bagdikian, *The Information Machines* (New York: Harper & Row, 1971), pp. 171–172.

percent with verbatim items from UPI teletype."[12] Of course, local newspapers can "rewrite" national news stories to fit their own editorial slant, and they usually write their own headlines on the national news. But the news itself is generated from an extremely small cadre of people at the top of the media industry.

Concentration of newspaper ownership is increasing, as more and more local papers are being taken over by the major newspaper chains. Nine newspaper chains account for one third of the total newspaper circulation in the United States. These chains, in order of their total daily circulation, are: Tribune Company, Newhouse, Scripps-Howard, Knight-Ridder Newspapers, Hearst Corporation, Gannett Newspapers, Times Mirror Company, Dow Jones, and Cox Enterprises.[13]

Our operational definition of leaders in positions of power in the mass media include the presidents and directors of:

Columbia Broadcasting System, Inc. (CBS owns five TV stations, fourteen radio stations, twenty-two magazines, Columbia Records, and more.)

American Broadcasting Company (ABC television, five TV stations, six publishing companies, and various recreational attractions including Weeki Wachee, Silver Springs, and Wild Waters in Florida.)

National Broadcasting Company (NBC television is a subsidiary of RCA with five TV stations and four publishing companies.)

New York Times Company (*New York Times,* plus fourteen daily newspapers in the south, as well as radio and television stations.)

Washington Post Company (*Washington Post–Newsweek* plus five TV stations.)

Time, Inc. (*Time, Sports Illustrated, Fortune,* and *People* magazines, plus five TV stations, HBO (Home Box Office), Little, Brown & Co., publishers, and Book-of-the-Month Club, Inc.)

Associated Press

United Press International

Newhouse (*Denver Post, Cleveland Plain Dealer,* etc.)

Hearst Corporations (Los Angeles, San Francisco, Baltimore, Boston, Albany, Seattle, San Antonio, etc.)

Scripps-Howard

Tribune Company (*Chicago Tribune, New York Daily News, Orlando Sentinel,* etc.)

Field Enterprises (*Chicago Sun-Times, Chicago Daily News,* etc.)

Dow Jones (*Wall Street Journal* and twelve daily newspapers.)

Times Mirror (*Los Angeles Times, Dallas Times Herald,* and seven TV stations.)

---

[12]Edwin Emery, *The Press in America* (Englewood Cliffs, N.J.: Prentice-Hall, Inc., 1972), p. 481.
[13]Raymond B. Nixon, "Nation's Dailies in Group Ownership," *Editor & Publisher,* July 17, 1971, pp. 7, 32.

Knight-Ridder Newspapers, Inc. (*Detroit Free Press, Miami Herald, Philadelphia Inquirer,* etc.)

Cox Enterprises (Merged with General Electric in 1979; includes five television stations, twelve radio stations, and forty-four cable systems in seventeen states.)

THE NEWSMAKERS

Who are the people who govern the flow of information to the nation? The network executives—presidents, chairpersons, producers, editors—decide what Americans will see and hear about their world. The recognized reporters—Dan Rather, Roger Mudd, John Chancellor, David Brinkley, Tom Brokaw, Barbara Walters—simply read scripts that are placed in front of them. The network executives exchange news with the *New York Times,* the *Washington Post, Newsweek, Time,* and a few of the largest newspaper chains. Let us examine a few brief sketches of those in the top leadership positions in the major media institutions.

William S. Paley. Chairman of the board of Columbia Broadcasting System Inc. Attended Western Military Academy, University of Pennsylvania. Began work in father's cigar company, but in 1928 at age twenty seven he purchased CBS for $400,000. Recruited Edward R. Murrow to develop a news policy for CBS, and supported Murrow's successful efforts to make television news an independent political force in America. Paley actively opposed creation of the Federal Communications Commission and over the years helped to prevent its intrusion into network broadcasting. He established the first regular schedule of television broadcasting in the U.S. in 1941. A trustee of the Museum of Modern Art, Columbia University, Resources for the Future, Inc., Bedford-Stuyvesant Restoration Corp. Past chairman of United Jewish Appeal.

Arthur Ochs Sulzberger. Publisher and president of the *New York Times.* Son of the *Times* board chairman and grandson of the newspaper's founder. Attended Loomis School and Columbia University. A corporal in World War II, but was assigned as headquarters aide to General Douglas MacArthur. He began as a reporter with the *Times* in 1953 and became president in 1963. A director of the New York Times Co., the Chattanooga Publishing Co., the Spruce Falls Power and Paper Co. of Toronto, and the Gaspesia Pulp and Paper Company of Canada. A trustee of the Boy Scouts of America, American Association of Indian Affairs, Columbia University, and the Metropolitan Museum of Art.

Thorton Bradshaw. Chairman of the board of Radio Corporation of America. Attended Phillips Exeter Academy, Harvard, and has a Harvard M.B.A. After a few years of teaching at the Harvard Business School, Bradshaw joined the Atlantic Richfield Oil Company and rose to president in 1964. Later he was named an outside director of RCA, and its subsidiary NBC. In 1981, after several years in which NBC ranked lowest in network viewing ratings, Bradshaw took over the reigns of the parent company, RCA, and fired NBC president Fred Silverman. Bradshaw is also director of Security Pacific National Bank, Los Angeles Philharmonic, and the American Petroleum Institute.

Leonard H. Godenson. President, ABC. Attended Harvard College and Harvard Law School. Began as an attorney for Paramount Pictures in Hollywood and became president of Paramount Pictures and United Paramount Theatres. In 1953, he merged Paramount and ABC and became president of ABC. Also invested in Walt Disney Productions and started the popular *Mickey Mouse Club* TV show. Hired top ABC news commentators himself. He is also director of Allied Stores, United Cerebral Palsy Association, John F. Kennedy Library, Lincoln Center for Performing Arts, Will Rogers Memorial Hospital, and United Jewish Appeal.

Hedley Donovan. Editor-in-chief, Time, Inc. Attended the University of Minnesota, Rhodes scholar, Oxford. Began as a reporter for the *Washington Post,* and later for *Fortune* magazine. Became Time, Inc. editor in chief in 1964. Trustee of New York University, Mt. Holyoke College, Carnegie Foundation, Ford Foundation. Member of the Council on Foreign Relations.

THE PROGRAMMERS: FRED SILVERMAN

Prime-time entertainment programming suggests to Americans how they ought to live and what values they ought to hold. Network television entertainment is the most widely shared experience in the country. The network executives who decide what will be shown as entertainment on television have tremendous impact on the values, aspirations, and life-styles of Americans.

Throughout the 1970s no one had a more direct effect on television entertainment than Fred Silverman. Silverman was vice-president for programming at CBS from 1970 to 1975; president of ABC entertainment from 1975 to 1978; and president of NBC from 1978 to 1981. It was Silverman who championed liberal programming with *M.A.S.H.* (antiwar), *All in the Family* (antiracist), and later *Roots* (black experience). He favored producer Norman Lear, whose work—*All in the Family, Maude, The Jeffersons, One Day At A Time, Mary Hartman*—emphasized different and often controversial life-styles. When Silverman moved to ABC, he boldly predicted that he would make a lackluster network into "Number 1" in viewing audience. He did just that. It was Silverman, more than anyone else, who introduced the sex-oriented "jiggles" to prime-time television— *Charlie's Angels,* and *Three's Company.* He also went after younger audiences—*Happy Days,* and *Laverne and Shirley*—with the notion that children in the family really controlled the TV dial. Silverman was never accused of overestimating the intelligence of TV audiences.

When he shifted to NBC, he faced the problem of beating his own program lineups on CBS and ABC. By 1978, NBC had dropped to third in audience ratings. Its biggest success was *The Tonight Show,* starring Johnny

Carson, and the star of that show was demanding a reduction in his workload and threatening to move to another network. Silverman held on to Carson. He made massive changes in program lineups to try to restore NBC audience ratings, but he failed to do so. He spent millions on poor shows (*Supertrain*), and in 1981 NBC was still in the network cellar. It lost the Moscow Olympics when the U.S. boycotted them. Its only long-run, top-ten show—*Little House on the Prairie*—predated Silverman's tenure and emphasized traditional family values. When a new chairperson, Thorton Bradshaw, took over the reigns of NBC's parent company, RCA, Fred Silverman was encouraged to resign. Silverman's replacement was Grant Tinker, whose MTM Enterprises (which he founded with his ex-wife, Mary Tyler Moore) had produced shows generally considered superior to those of Silverman. (*The Mary Tyler Moore Show, Phyllis, Rhoda, Lou Grant.*) These shows emphasized feminism, liberalism, and crusading journalism.

Silverman, Tinker, and other top network executives and producers are generally "coast oriented" in their values and life-styles—that is, they reflect the popular culture in New York and California. They may be genuinely perplexed when it is charged that their programming does not reflect the values of a majority of Americans. It is noteworthy that the few shows that reflect traditional American values (family, work, community) are placed by these programmers in an historical setting (*Little House on the Prairie*, 1890s; *The Waltons*, 1930s; and even *Happy Days*, early 1960s). The implied message is that these values are quaint and interesting as history, but not relevant today.

Occasionally, voices are raised against sex and violence on prime-time television. In 1981, fundamentalist religious groups threatened to boycott the products of companies that advertised on shows that included sex, violence, or profanity, as seen by religious viewers. The networks promptly labeled the proposed boycott as an infringement of their freedom of the press. But the advertisers listened. Procter and Gamble, the nation's single, largest advertiser, announced it would withdraw its ads from shows with "gratuitous sex, violence, and profanity." Religious groups claimed a temporary victory and dropped their proposed boycott. Network television may "clean up its act" for a season, but in the long run it can be expected to broadcast whatever it believes can attract viewing audiences.

KATHERINE GRAHAM: THE MOST POWERFUL WOMAN IN AMERICA

Katherine Graham, the owner and publisher of the *Washington Post* and *Newsweek* magazine, was probably the most powerful woman in America even *before* Watergate. But certainly her leadership of the *Post*, which did more than any other publication to force the resignation of the President of the United States, established Graham as one of the most powerful figures in Washington. The *Washington Post* is the capital's most influential newspaper, and it vies with the *New York Times* as the world's most influential newspaper. These are the papers read by all segments of the nation's elite; and both papers feed stories to the television networks and wire services.

Graham inherited her position from her father and husband, but since 1963, when she became president of the Washington Post Company, she has demonstrated her own capacity to manage great institutional power. She is the daughter of a wealthy New York banker, Eugene Meyer. Like many elites, her education was in the fashionable private preparatory schools; she also attended Vassar College and the University of Chicago. In 1933 her father bought the *Washington Post* for less than $1 million. Katherine Meyer worked summers on her father's paper, and then took a job as a reporter with the *San Francisco News*. After one year as a reporter, she joined the editorial staff of the *Washington Post*. "Father was very strong. There was a great deal of emphasis on not behaving rich and a lot of emphasis on having to *do* something. It never occurred to me that I didn't have to work."[14]

In 1940, she married Philip L. Graham, a Harvard Law School graduate with a clerkship under Supreme Court Justice Felix Frankfurter. After service in World War II, Philip Graham was made publisher of the *Washington Post* by his father-in-law. Meyer later sold the paper to the Grahams for one dollar. The Washington Post Company proceeded to purchase other competitive papers in the nation's capital; it also bought *Newsweek* magazine from the Vincent Astor Foundation, as well as five television stations and several pulp and paper companies.

In 1963, Philip Graham committed suicide, and Katherine Graham took control of the *Washington Post—Newsweek* enterprises. By the early 1970s the *Washington Post* was challenging the *New York Times* as the nation's most powerful newspaper.

Both the *Washington Post* and the *New York Times* published the *Pentagon Papers,* stolen from the files of the Defense and State Departments by Daniel Ellsberg, and led the fight against the Vietnam War. But it was the *Washington Post* that developed the Watergate story and brought about Richard Nixon's humiliation and resignation.

Indeed, the Washington Post Company's domination of the Washington scene gives it great power over federal officials and agencies. As conservative columnist Kevin Phillips observes:

> We might note the quasi-governmental role played by the Washington Post Company. The Post Company has a five-level presence in Washington—a

[14]*Current Biography* (1971), p. 170.

newspaper (the *Washington Post*), a radio station (WTOP), a television station (WTOP-TV), a news magazine (*Newsweek*), and a major news service (L.A. Times—Washington Post). Not only does the Washington Post Company play an unmatched role as a federal government information system—from the White House to Congress to the bureaucracy and back—it serves as a cue card for the network news, and it plays a huge role in determining how the American government communicates to the American people.[15]

Graham is a director of Bowaters Mersey Paper Company, the John F. Kennedy School of Government of Harvard University, and a member of the Committee for Economic Development. She is a trustee of George Washington University, the American Assembly, the University of Chicago, and the Urban Institute.

LIBERAL BIAS IN THE NEWS

When TV newscasters insist that they are impartial, objective, and unbiased, they may sincerely believe that they are, because in the world in which they live—the New York—Washington world of newspeople, writers, intellectuals, artists—the established liberal point of view has been so uniformly voiced. TV news executives can be genuinely shocked and affronted when they are charged with slanting the news toward the prevailing established liberal values.

Network entertainment programming, newscasts, and news specials are designed to communicate established liberal values to the masses. These are the values of the elite; they include a concern for liberal reform and social welfare, an interest in problems confronting the poor and blacks, a desire to educate the ignorant and cure the sick, and a willingness to employ governmental power to accomplish these ends.

There is very little diversity in television news. All three networks— ABC, CBS, and NBC—present nearly identical "packages" each evening. They are "rivals in conformity."[16] Liberal and conservative views can be found in newspapers and magazines—for example, the *New York Times* versus the *Wall Street Journal, Newsweek* versus *U.S. News and World Report, Harpers* versus the *National Review*. But a standard liberal position is presented on all three television networks in both news and entertainment programming.

However, the primary source of bias in the news is *not* the liberal politics of the newsmakers, but rather the need to "hype" the news—to capture and hold audience attention with drama, action, and confrontation. Television must entertain. To capture the attention of jaded audi-

[15]Kevin Phillips, "Busting the Media Trusts," *Harpers* (July 1977), p. 30.
[16]Doris Graber, *Mass Media and American Politics* (Washington: Congressional Quarterly Inc., 1980), p. 68.

ences, news must be selected which includes emotional rhetoric, shocking incidents, dramatic conflict, overdrawn stereotypes. Race, sex, violence, and corruption in government are favorite topics because of popular interest. More complex problems—inflation, government spending, foreign policy—must be simplified and dramatized or ignored. To dramatize an issue, the newsmakers must find or create a dramatic incident; film it; transport, process, and edit the film; and write a script for the introduction, the "voice-over," and the "recapitulation." All this means that "news" must be created well in advance of scheduled broadcasting.

Television, however, has made some serious tactical mistakes in its efforts to advance liberal values. For example, for several years the national networks decided that incidents of violence, disruption, and civil disorder in American cities were to be treated as "news." Generally, the media chiefs believed that the civil rights movement had to be carried to northern black ghettos, that urban conditions had to be improved, that ghetto blacks deserved greater public attention to their plight. Televised riots and disorders dramatized black discontent, and "voice-overs" generally gave legitimacy to such discontent by citing various social evils as causes of the riots—poverty, racism, poor housing, police brutality. The purpose was to pave the way for mass acceptance of urban renewal programs, especially with a view to improving the plight of minority groups.

But the strategy backfired. Whites saw the visual image of black violence and ignored the social message attached to it by the commentators. Images of black violence remained in their minds, while words of explanation were ignored. White mass hostilities and prejudices were actually *reinforced* by the urban violence shown on the media. The liberal network executives had created exactly what they did *not* want: a strong "law and order" movement and a surge of support for George C. Wallace as a presidential candidate.[17]

In an especially candid interview with *Playboy* magazine, Walter Cronkite commented on both the power and the bias of the television networks:[18]

Playboy: A great deal of economic and social power is concentrated in the networks. CBS, for example, does research and development in military and space technology, owns two publishing houses, and has phonograph-record, record club, and film communications divisions.

Cronkite: That's right. We're big. And we're powerful enough to thumb our nose at threats and intimidation from Government. I hope it stays that way.

[17]Byron Shafer and Richard Larson, "Did TV Create the Social Issue?" *Columbia Journal Review,* September/October 1972, p. 10. Also see Richard Scammon and Ben Wattenberg, *The Real Majority* (New York: Coward, McCann, Geoghegan, 1970), p. 162.
[18]"Playboy Interview: Walter Cronkite," *Playboy,* June 1973, pp. 68–90.

Playboy: Implicit in the Administration's attempts to force the networks to "balance" the news is a conviction that most newscasters are biased against conservatism. Is there some truth in the view that television newsmen tend to be left of center?

Cronkite: Well, certainly liberal, and possibly left of center as well. I would have to accept that.... But I don't think there are many who are *far* left. I think a little left of center probably is correct.

The federal government has made only a very feeble attempt to ensure pluralism in television coverage of public affairs. The Federal Communications Commission has developed a Fairness Doctrine that requires all licensed broadcasters of public affairs messages to provide equal air time to present "all sides of controversial issues." The Fairness Doctrine does not restrict reporting or editorializing on television in any way, but it tries to guarantee access to airings of views not shared by the stations. However, the Doctrine has proven impossible to enforce in newscasts, and no station has ever lost its license for violation of the Fairness Doctrine. Yet it is bitterly opposed by the broadcasting corporations. Their argument is that the First Amendment gives them the right to be biased, just as it protects the right of individuals or newspapers to be biased.

AGENDA-SETTING: HOW NEWSMAKERS CREATE ISSUES

The power to decide what will be decided—agenda-setting—is crucial to politics. Indeed, deciding what will be the nation's "problems" is even more important than deciding what will be the solutions. Many civics textbooks imply that agenda-setting just "happens," that in a pluralist democracy any issue can be discussed and placed on the agenda of government decision-makers by anyone. It is true, of course, that we can say whatever we want to say about our society. But will anyone *listen*? Not if we do not have access to the mass media.

In reality, political issues do not just "happen." Creating an issue, dramatizing it, calling attention to it, and pressuring government to do something about it are important political tactics. These are the tactics of agenda-setting. These tactics are employed by influential individuals, organized interest groups, political candidates, government leaders, and, most of all, by the mass media.

Topics for television "news" must be selected weeks or even months in advance of scheduled broadcasting. Network crews must be sent on location to obtain videotapes, which later must be transported, processed, and edited. A script must be written. The order of stories must be decided, as well as the amount of time to be given to each of them. All of these tasks require advance decision-making. These advance decisions usually reflect current liberal issues: concern for the poor and blacks, environmental protection, and consumerism; opposition to defense spending and support for arms control; hostility toward foreign governments which are noncommunist but "authoritarian"; criticism of "big oil companies," tax loopholes, and the moral majority; opposition to nuclear energy; and so on. Ideally, a story should capture wide audience attention through shock or fear, provide good "visuals" (something dramatic to observe), and at the same time advance liberal values.

Television news can be categorized as either "spontaneous" or "preplanned." Spontaneous news includes fires, floods, accidents, shootings, and so on, which actually occurred the day of the news broadcast and was not planned by the media to occur on that day. In contrast, preplanned events may have occurred days or weeks before the broadcast, or may have been planned by the media and others for coverage on that day. The most common preplanned events are congressional hearings and investigations, meetings of government leaders, and press conferences. These are usually coordinated by government press agents and network producers. Ideally, they try to predict "slow" news days to schedule these media events. They are not always successful; if a hurricane, assassination, or violent eruption occurs (and if film of it is available), then a spontaneous event may push the preplanned event off the evening news.

Almost 70 percent of all television news stories are preplanned. One careful study of stories presented on ABC, NBC, and CBS weekday evening newscasts in 1978 reported the following breakdown of stories:[19]

	Percent of Time
Preplanned events	31.8
Commentary on preplanned events	38.1
Spontaneous events	19.8
Commentary on spontaneous events	10.3
	100.0

The requirement to preplan television news helps create the "media event"—an activity arranged primarily for media coverage. It is not only the press secretaries, public relations professionals, "spokespersons," and politicians who benefit from media events. It is also the network executives and producers who are searching for dramatic, sensational, or bizarre activities to videotape, and who appreciate notification well in advance of these activities so they can assign camera crews and broadcast time.

In addition to selecting topics for media coverage, there are other techniques of creating bias in the news:

[19]Robert Rutherford Smith, "Mythic Elements in Television News," *Journal of Communication,* 29 (Winter 1979), pp. 78–82.

Invoking anonymous "high Washington sources" who express the newscasters' own opinions, or using phrases such as "observers point out..." and "experts believe..." to express their opinions.

Suppressing information that might clash with a liberal interpretation of the news. Thus, Eldridge Cleaver's criminal conviction as a rapist was never mentioned, and he was presented as "a noted black nationalist."

Presenting glamorous, articulate spokespersons for the liberal side of an argument and "balancing" it with ugly, harsh, offensive spokespersons for the other side.

Winding up coverage of a controversy by a "summary" or "recapitulation" which directs humor, sarcasm, or satire at the other side.

"Mind-reading," in which newscasters glibly describe the motives and aspirations of large numbers of people—students, blacks, suburbanites, or whatever—and express the causes of society's discontents and other social and political ideologies.

SELECTIVE PERCEPTION: *ALL IN THE FAMILY*

Many have argued, however, that the viewer's psychological mechanism of "selective perception" defends him or her against some portion of television bias. Indeed, one of the reasons why political scientists pay little heed to the political impact of television newscasting is their belief in the theory of selective perception. This is the notion that viewers mentally screen out information, statements, or images with which they disagree, and see only what they want to see on the tube. The proponents of this theory argue that television rarely produces attitudinal or behavioral changes in viewers.[20] If this theory is true, newsmakers exercise little real power. But many of these studies have directed their inquiries to political *campaigns*, not to *issues* and *policies*. Many have ignored the *visual* impact of television. Only recently has a small number of political scientists come to grips with the real power of the mass media.[21]

But there is just enough evidence of selective perception, and enough evidence of network executive blunders, to keep alive the notion that television cannot completely control public opinion. Consider the example of the enormously popular CBS television show *All In The Family*. Producer Norman Lear and the leadership of CBS believed that the crude, bumbling, working-class, conservative, superpatriotic, racist Archie Bunker would be an effective weapon against prejudice. Bigotry would be

---

[20]See Herbert Simon and Frederick Stern, "The Effect of Television upon Voting Turnout in Iowa in the 1952 Election," *American Political Science Review*, 49 (1955), pp. 470–477; J. Blumer and T. McQuail, *Television in Politics* (Chicago: University of Chicago Press, 1969); Harold Mendelsohn and Irving Crespi, *Polls, Television and the New Politics* (Scranton: Chandler, 1970).

[21]For an excellent summary, see Doris A. Graber, *Mass Media and American Politics* (Washington: Congressional Quarterly Inc., 1980).

made to appear ridiculous; Archie would always end up suffering some defeat because of his bigotry; and the masses would be instructed in liberal reformist values. But evidence soon developed that many viewers applauded Archie's bigotry, believing he was "telling it like it is."[22] They missed the satire altogether. Sixty percent of the viewers liked or admired the bigoted Archie more than his liberal son-in-law, Mike. Vidmar and Rokeach's study indicated that highly prejudiced people enjoy and watch the show *more* than less-prejudiced people; and few people believed that Archie was being "made fun of." When these trends in public opinion became apparent, the show was sharply attacked by the *New York Times.*[23] But by that time, *All In The Family* had become the number one rated show on television. CBS optimistically predicted that eventually the humor of the program would help break down bigotry.[24] But it seems clear that the network vastly underestimated "selective perception."

"TELEVISION MALAISE"

The networks' concentration on scandal, abuse, and corruption in government has not always produced the desired liberal, reformist notions in the minds of the masses of viewers. Contrary to the expectations of network executives, their focus on governmental scandals—Watergate, illicit C.I.A. activities, F.B.I. abuses, congressional sex scandals, and power struggles between Congress and the executive branch—has produced feelings of general political distrust and cynicism toward government and "the system." These feelings have been labeled "television malaise"—a combination of social distrust, political cynicism, feelings of powerlessness, and disaffection from parties and politics which seems to stem from television's emphasis on the negative aspects of American life.[25]

Network executives do not *intend* to create "television malaise" among the masses. But scandal, sex, abuse of power, and corruption attract large audiences and increase "ratings." "Bad" news is placed up front in the telecast, usually with some dramatic visual aids. Negative television journalism "... is concerned with what is *wrong* with our governmental system, our leaders, our prisons, schools, roads, automobiles, race relations, traffic systems, pollution laws, every aspect of our society. In Europe,

[22]See Neil Vidmar and Milton Rokeach, "Archie Bunker's Bigotry: A Study in Selective Perception and Exposure," *Journal of Communication,* Winter 1974, pp. 36–47.

[23]I.Z. Hobson, "As I Listened to Archie say 'Hebe,'" *New York Times,* September 12, 1972.

[24]Norman Lear, "As I Read How Laura Saw Archie," *New York Times,* October 10, 1971.

[25]Michael J. Robinson, "Public Affairs Television and the Growth of Political Malaise," *American Political Science Review,* 70 (June 1976), pp. 409–432; and "Television and American Politics," *The Public Interest,* Summer 1977, pp. 3–39.

there is much less emphasis on exposing what is wrong, much more satisfaction with the status quo."[26] The effect of negative television coverage of the American political system is to turn off" the masses from participation in government. The long-run effects of this elite behavior may be self-defeating in terms of elite interest in maintaining a stable political system.

SUMMARY

The people who control the flow of information in America are among the most powerful in the nation. Television network broadcasting is the first form of truly *mass* communication; it carries a visual image with emotional content as well as information. Television news reaches virtually everyone, and for most Americans it is the major source of information about the world.

Control of the television media is highly concentrated. Three private corporations (CBS, NBC, and ABC) determine what the people will see and hear about the world; they feed 700 local TV stations that account for 90 percent of the news and entertainment broadcasts. Most of the nation's 1,748 daily newspapers receive their news from the AP and/or UPI wire services. The ten largest newspaper chains account for one third of the total newspaper circulation in the country.

Those at the top of the mass media include both inheritors and individuals who worked their way up the management ladder. Among the media elite are the heads of CBS, NBC, and ABC; AP and UPI; the *New York Times; Washington Post—Newsweek;* Time, Inc.; and the ten largest newspaper chains.

Television programming is uniformly liberal—within an establishment framework—which means that elite values of those in positions of power predominate. Bias is introduced primarily in the selection of topics to be treated as "news," but there are other ways in which liberal values are incorporated into newsmaking. While claiming to present merely a "mirror of society," newsmakers credit themselves with the success of the civil rights movement, ending the Vietnam War, exposing Watergate, and ousting two Presidents from office.

The major counterbalance to the power of the media is the "selective perception" of the mass viewing audience. Viewers often mentally screen out information or images they do not want to see. Network executives have blundered in creating certain undesired issues and attitudes by underestimating selective perception.

[26]Merritt Panitt, "America Out of Focus," *TV Guide,* January 15, 1972. p. 6.

5

The civic establishment

In a complex, industrial society, there are many specialized institutions and organizations that exercise power. In addition to economic organizations (corporations, banks, insurance companies, and utilities), governmental and military bureaucracies, television networks and news organizations, there are other less visible institutions which also provide bases of power in American society. An operational definition of a national elite must include individuals who occupy positions of power in influential law firms, major philanthropic foundations, recognized national civic and cultural organizations, and prestigious private universities. We shall refer to these institutions collectively as the civic establishment.

The identification of a "civic establishment" involves many subjective judgments. We shall try to defend these judgments, but we recognize that equally valid defenses of alternative judgments might be made in many cases.

THE "SUPERLAWYERS"

As modern societies grow in scale and complexity, the need for rules and regulations increases geometrically, and so does the power of people whose profession it is to understand those rules and regulations. As early as 1832, deTocqueville felt that the legal profession in this country would become the "new aristocracy" of the Republic. C. Wright Mills asserts that lawyers are indeed a key segment of the nation's aristocracy of power:

> The inner core of the power elite also includes men of the higher legal and financial type from the great law factories and investment firms who are professional go-betweens of economic, political, and military affairs, and who thus act to unify the power elite.[1]

The predominance of lawyers among political elites has already been noted. Within the corporate elite—presidents and directors of the nation's largest industries, banks, utilities, and insurance companies—over 15 percent are lawyers. But neither the politician-lawyer nor the businessman-lawyer really stands at the top of the legal profession. The "superlawyers" are the senior partners of the nation's largest and most highly esteemed New York and Washington law firms. these are the firms that represent clients such as General Motors, AT&T, DuPont, CBS, and American Airlines,[2] not only in the courts, but perhaps more importantly, before Congress and the federal regulatory agencies. Of course, the nation's largest corporate and financial institutions have their own legal departments; but attorneys in these departments, known as "house counsels," usually handle routine matters. When the stakes are high, the great corporations turn to the "superlawyers."

Sociologist Erwin O. Smigel argues persuasively that the largest New York and Washington law firms are emerging as the dominant force in the legal profession:

> As our society has grown increasingly complex, the legal tools for social control have indeed increased beyond the possible total comprehension of a single individual. And the lawyers, like the scientists, have increasingly, although on a much smaller scale, met the problem of specialization within large law firms.[3]

Identification of the "top" New York and Washington law firms is necessarily a subjective task. Professional ethics prevent firms from listing their clients, so we cannot be certain what firms actually represent the nation's largest corporations. The listing in Table 5–1 was compiled from a variety of sources and represents our best estimate of the nation's legal elite. The senior partners of these firms are our "superlawyers."

The names of the firms themselves, of course, do not always identify

---

[1]C. Wright Mills, *The Power Elite* (New York: Oxford, 1956), p. 289.

[2]Quoted as clients of Covington and Burling by Joseph C. Goulden, *The Superlawyers* (New York: Dell Publishing Co., 1971), p. 27.

[3]Erwin O. Smigel, *The Wall Street Lawyer* (New York: Free Press, 1964), p. 9.

Table 5-1   The Top Law Firms

Wall Street	Washington
Shearman & Sterling	Arnold & Porter
Cravath, Swaine & Moore	Covington & Burling
White & Case	Arrent, Fox, Kintner, Plotkin & Kahn
Dewey, Ballantine, Bushby, Palmer & Wood	Wilmer, Cutler & Pickering
Simpson, Thacher & Bartlett	Clifford, Warnke, Glass, McIlwain & Finney
Davis, Polk, & Wardwell	Fried, Frank, Harris, Shriver & Kampelman
Milbank, Tweed, Hadley & McCloy	Califano, Ross & Heineman
Cahill, Gordon & Reindel	
Sullivan & Cromwell	
Chadbourne, Parke, Whiteside & Wolff	
Breed, Abbott & Morgan	
Winthrop, Stimson, Putnam & Roberts	
Cadwalader, Wickersham & Taft	
Wilkie, Farr & Gallagher	
Donovan, Leisure, Newton & Irvine	
Lord, Day & Lord	
Dwight, Royall, Harris, Koegel & Caskey	
Mudge, Rose, Guthrie & Alexander	
Kelley, Drye & Warren	
Cleary, Gottlieb, Steen & Hamilton	

the senior partners. Firms often retain the names of deceased founders, and most large firms have so many senior partners (twenty or thirty is not uncommon) that it would be impossible to put all their names in the title of the firm. Then, too, some firms change names upon the resignation of partners, so it is sometimes difficult to maintain the identity of a firm over time.[4]

The great law firms are, of course, the "spokesmen" for big business. But it would be naive to believe that they oppose government regulation, consumer laws, antitrust laws, labor laws, or corporate tax legislation. On the contrary, the top law firms gain in power and influence as the interaction between business and government heightens. New laws mean new business for lawyers. Even the founder of one of Washington's most conservative and dignified firms, Judge J. Harry Covington of Covington and Burling, confided before his death: "I disagreed with the New Deal

[4]For example, Mudge, Stern, Baldwin & Todd placed the name of Richard M. Nixon at the head of the firm during his Wall Street years, and later added John Mitchell's name to the firm. The result was "Nixon, Mudge, Rose, Guthrie, Alexander & Mitchell." When Nixon became President and Mitchell became Attorney General, the firm went back to Mudge, Rose, Guthrie & Alexander. Despite the legal difficulties of its former partners, the firm remains one of the most powerful on Wall Street. Likewise, when one of Arnold, Fortas & Porter's clients, Lyndon Johnson, became President of the United States, and named his personal attorney Abraham Fortas to the Supreme Court (and then later tried unsuccessfully to make him chief justice), the Fortas name was removed from the firm. The firm is now Arnold & Porter, but it is still one of the most powerful in Washington.

strongly. But it was a great benefit to lawyers because so many businessmen all over the country began squealing about what was happening and had to have lawyers. So when you ask me about bureaucracy, I say, 'Oh, I'm for it. How would I eat otherwise?' "[5]

Prestigious law firms do not provide lists of clients, claiming that to do so would violate lawyer-client "confidentiality." Nonetheless, a partial listing of the clients of the Washington firm of Arnold & Porter confirms the big business orientation of the major firms:[6]

Allis-Chalmers Mfg. Co.
American Brands, Inc.
American Council of Learned Societies
American Farm Lines
American Home Products Corp.
American Safety Razor Co.
American Trading & Production Corp.
Bank of America
Braniff Airways, Inc.
Chesebrough-Pond's, Inc.
Chris-Craft Industries, Inc.
Clark Oil & Refining Corp.
The Coca-Cola Co.
Commissioner of Baseball
Common Cause
Cresca, Inc.
Crown Cork & Seal Co., Inc.
Democratic National Committee
Fairchild Camera & Instrument Corp.
Federated Department Stores, Inc.
Florida East Coast Railway Co.
Gulf & Western Industries, Inc.
Hoffmann-LaRoche, Inc.
R.A. Holman & Co., Inc.
HRH Construction Corp.
Insurance & Securities, Inc.
Koppers Co., Inc.
Kroger Co.
Lever Brother Co.
Ling-Temco-Vought Inc.
Martin Marietta Corp.
National Retail Merchants Assoc.

---

[5]Quoted in Goulden, *The Superlawyers*, p. 36.
[6]From Jonathan Cotton, "Washington Pressures," *National Journal*, January 8, 1972, p. 46.

Northwest Industries, Inc.
Philip Morris, Inc.
Playboy Magazine
Recording Industry Assoc. of America, Inc.
North American Rockwell
State Farm Mutual Automobile Insurance Co.
Xerox Corp.

The senior partners of the nation's top law firms generally feel an obligation to public service. According to superlawyer Arthur Dean, the experience of serving in such a firm provides "an exceptional opportunity to acquire a liberal education in modern government and society. Such partnerships are likely in the future, as they have in the past, to prepare and offer for public service men exceptionally qualified to serve." The arrogance of such an assertion has too much basis in fact to be dismissed as mere self-congratulation.

Earlier we identified several superlawyers among the "serious men" who have been called upon for governmental leadership:

John Foster Dulles, Secretary of State (Sullivan & Cromwell)
Dean Acheson, Secretary of State (Covington & Burling)
Clark Clifford, Secretary of Defense (Clifford, Warnke, Glass, McIlwain & Finney)
Cyrus Vance, Secretary of State (Simpson, Thacher & Bartlett)

In an even earlier era, the New York Wall Street law firms supplied presidential candidates:

John W. Davis, Democratic Party nominee for President of the United States, 1928 (Davis, Polk, Wardwell, Sunderland & Kiendl)[7]
Wendell Willkie, Republican Party nominee for President of the United States, 1940 (Willkie, Farr, Gallagher, Walton & Fitzgibbon)
Thomas E. Dewey, Republican Party nominee for President of the United States, 1944 and 1948 (Dewey, Ballantine, Bushby, Palmer & Wood)

Equally important are the top lawyers who are called upon to represent the United States itself in periods of crisis where matters are too serious to be left to State Department bureaucrats.

Paul Warnke. Arms control and disarmament adviser under President Carter. U.S. negotiator in the Strategic Arms Limitation Talks (SALT). Partner in

---

[7]Davis unsuccessfully argued the case for racial segregation on behalf of the Board of Education of Topeka, Kansas, in the famous case of *Brown* v. *Board of Education* (1954); opposing counsel for Brown, of course, was Supreme Court Justice Thurgood Marshall.

Clifford, Warnke, Glass, McIlwain & Finney. Former Assistant Secretary of Defense, 1967–69. A member of the Trilateral Commission and a director of the Council on Foreign Relations.

John J. McCloy. Special Adviser to the President on disarmament, 1961–63. Chairman of the Coordinating Committee on the Cuban Crisis, 1962. Member of the President's commission on the assassination of President Kennedy. U.S. High Commissioner for Germany, 1949–52. President of the World Bank, 1947–49. Partner in Milbank, Tweed, Hadley & McCloy. Member of the board of directors of Allied Chemical Corp., AT&T, Chase Manhattan Bank, Metropolitan Life Insurance Co., Westinghouse Electric, E.R. Squibb and Sons. Member of the board of trustees of the Ford Foundation, Council on Foreign Relations, and Amherst College.

Arthur H. Dean. Chairman of the U.S. Delegation on Nuclear Test Ban Treaty. Chief U.S. negotiator of the Korean Armistice Agreement. Partner, Sullivan and Cromwell. Member of the board of directors of American Metal Climax, American Bank Note Co., National Union Electric Corp., El Paso Natural Gas Co., Crown Zellerbach Corp., Lazard Fund, Inc. and Bank of New York. Member of the board of trustees of New York Hospital, Cornell Medical Center, Cornell Medical College, Cornell University, Carnegie Foundation, and Council on Foreign Relations.

Still other superlawyers are called upon from time to time to head major domestic programs.

R. Sargent Shriver, Jr. Former director of the Peace Corps, the Office of Economic Opportunity (President Johnson's "war on poverty"), and Democratic vice-presidential nominee in 1972. Canterbury School, Yale, Yale Law School. Senior partner in the Washington law firm of Fried, Frank, Harris, Shriver, and Kampelman. Married Eunice Kennedy, sister of John F., Robert F., and Edward M. Kennedy. He began work for Joseph P. Kennedy after World War II and eventually married his boss's daughter. He managed the Kennedy's Merchandise Mart in Chicago until President John F. Kennedy asked him to organize the Peace Corps. The Peace Corps was a popular success, so President Lyndon Johnson asked him to organize the "war on poverty" in 1964. But the poverty program was less successful, and Shriver was shipped off as ambassador to France in 1968. He was McGovern's second choice for Vice-President in 1972, after Senator Thomas Eagleton revealed a history of mental illness. Shriver was defeated by Jimmy Carter in the Democratic presidential primaries in 1976. He settled into his Washington law practice and remains an influential superlawyer today. He is a member of the Council on Foreign Relations.

The typical path to the top of the legal profession starts with a Harvard or Yale Law School degree, clerkship with a Supreme Court Justice, and then several years as an attorney with the Justice Department or a federal regulatory commission. Young government lawyers who are *successful* at defeating a top firm in a case are *more* likely to be offered lucrative junior partnerships than those who lose to big firms. Poorly paid but talented younger government lawyers are systematically recruited by the top firms.

CLARK CLIFFORD: WASHINGTON SUPERLAWYER

Flavor the style of the nation's top Washington lawyer, Clark Clifford:

> There is one point I wish to make clear. This firm has no influence of any kind in Washington. If you want to employ someone who has influence, you will have to go somewhere else.... What we do have is a record of working with the various departments and agencies of the government, and we have their respect and confidence, and that we consider to be a valuable asset.[8]

Clifford's "valuable assets" have brought him clients such as Standard Oil of California, American Broadcasting Company, Hughes Tool Co. (Howard Hughes), Time, Inc., General Electric, Penn Central Railroad. DuPont Corporation, Phillips Petroleum, W.R. Grace Shipping, El Paso Natural Gas, TWA, and so forth. A former personal client was John F. Kennedy. The Clifford firm is Clifford, Warnke, Glass, McIlwain & Finney.

Clifford was the son of an auditor for the Missouri-Pacific Railroad. He attended Washington University and St. Louis Law School, graduating in 1928. He promptly established a successful law practice in St. Louis, and included in his contacts Missouri Senators Harry S. Truman and Stuart Symington. Clifford enlisted in the Navy in World War II, but when Truman became President, he was called to the White House as counsel to the President. Clifford's title never changed, but he soon became a dominant figure on Truman's staff. He supervised foreign and domestic policy in the White House, as well as Truman's successful 1948 presidential campaign. In 1950, he left the White House, after five years of service, to open his own Washington firm. The decision to leave was fortunate, since the White House staff was shortly thereafter shaken by scandal.

Bureaucrats had become accustomed to answering Clifford's phone calls when they came from the White House, so they answered them when he called from his firm. His first big clients were Phillips Petroleum, Pennsylvania Railroad, Standard Oil of California, and Howard Hughes. Even during the Republican years under President Dwight Eisenhower, Clifford prospered: his close friend Senator Stuart Symington was chairman of the Senate Armed Forces Committee. McDonnell-Douglas Aircraft became a Clifford client. After DuPont had lost its complex ten-year antitrust case and was ordered to sell its ownership of General Motors, it called upon Clifford in desperation. (Covington & Burling had unsuccessfully represented DuPont.) If DuPont were forced to sell its stock in GM immediately, the price of GM stock would plummet, and income from the sale would be heavily taxed. Clifford obtained passage of a special congressional act allowing distribution of the GM stock to DuPont stock-

---

[8]Quoted in Goulden, *The Superlawyers*, p. 78.

holders as a capital gain—and a tax savings to DuPont of $.5 billion (which of course was a tax loss to the U.S. Treasury of an equal amount). Clifford's modest legal fee—$1 million.

When President Kennedy prepared to take over the reins of government from his predecessor, Dwight Eisenhower, he sent his personal attorney, Clark Clifford, to arrange the transition. He also sent Clifford to investigate the Bay of Pigs disaster and reorganize the C.I.A. and Defense intelligence operations. Later he sent Clifford to the headquarters of U.S. Steel to force a rollback of steel prices by threatening tax audits, contract cancellations, and F.B.I. investigations. But Clifford did not accept any formal government appointment under Kennedy; by then his annual earnings regularly exceeded $1 million per year.

When the Vietnam War controversy had shattered the Johnson Administration and Robert McNamara was forced to resign as Secretary of Defense, Johnson persuaded his friend Clark Clifford to assume leadership of the Defense Department. Clifford reluctantly accepted the position of Secretary of Defense, reversed the policy of escalation in Vietnam, and began America's slow and painful withdrawal. Thus, the policy of military disengagement from Southeast Asia had already been started under Clifford when the Nixon Administration came to Washington in 1969.

Clifford returned to his Washington law firm; he subsequently accepted the directorships of Phillips Petroleum and the Knight-Ridder newspapers. His partner, Paul Warnke, was arms control and disarmament adviser to President Carter, with special responsibilities for the SALT negotiations with the Soviet Union. When President Carter's personal friend and banker, Bert Lance, who Carter had named as Director of the Office of Management and Budget, was charged with banking irregularities, Lance turned to Clifford to get him out of trouble. Lance was forced to resign his office, but he avoided conviction under banking laws. Clifford himself remains at the top of the hierarchy of Washington "superlawyers."

THE FOUNDATIONS

The power of the nation's largest foundations derives from their support of significant *new* research projects in social problems, arts, and humanities. Actually, the foundations spend far less for research and development than does the federal bureaucracy. But the principal research components of the federal bureaucracy—the National Science Foundation, Energy Research and Development Administration, U.S. Public Health Service, the National Institute of Education—are generally conservative in their support of social research. These government agencies frequently avoid sensitive, controversial issues and avoid projects that would lead to major social innovations. Thus, it has been the role of the nation's largest foundations to support and direct innovations in the scientific, intellectual, and cultural life of the nation.

Most foundations consider themselves to be in the forefront of national policy-making. "The foundations' best role," said Dr. Douglas D. Bond of the W.T. Grant Foundation, "is to identify, support, and bring to fruition certain ideas that government may later implement....Government is beset by crises of a social and political nature that divert it and its money from the nurturing of new ideas and new discoveries. It is the foundation's task to remain steady in its aim and to sacrifice immediate goals for the more distant."[9]

The foundations channel corporate and personal wealth into the policy-making process, providing both financial support and direction for university research and the activities of various policy-planning groups. Foundations are tax-exempt: Contributions to foundations may be deducted from federal corporate and individual income taxes, *and* the foundations themselves are not subject to federal income taxation.

Foundations can be created by corporations or by individuals. These corporations or individuals can name themselves and their friends as directors or trustees of the foundations they create. Large blocks of corporate stock or large amounts of personal wealth can be donated as tax-exempt contributions to the foundations. The foundations can receive interest, dividends, profit shares, and capital gains from these assets without paying any taxes on them. The directors or trustees, of course, are not allowed to use foundation income or assets for their personal expenses, as they would their own taxable income. Otherwise, however, they have great latitude in directing the use of foundation monies—to underwrite research, investigate social problems, create or assist universities, establish "think tanks," endow museums, theaters, operas, symphonies, and so on.

According to *The Foundation Directory*, there are 3,138 foundations large enough to deserve recognition and listing in 1980; these are the foundations with at least $1 million in assets or $100,000 in yearly distributions. (There are tens of thousands of other smaller foundations and trusts, some established as tax dodges by affluent citizens and therefore not having any appreciable effect on public policy except to reduce tax collections.) In 1979 these foundations controlled $32.4 billion in assets.

But as in other sectors of society, these foundation assets are concentrated in a small number of large foundations. *The Foundation Directory* reports: "One of the outstanding facts concerning assets is the degree of their concentration in a small number of large organizations."[10] The 50 largest foundations control over 40 percent of all foundation assets in the nation (see Table 5–2).

[9]"Medicine's Philanthropic Support," *Medical World News*, December 8, 1972, p. 65.

[10]*The Foundation Directory*, 3rd ed. (New York: Russell Sage Foundation, 1967), p. 16.

Table 5–2   The 50 Leading Foundations (Ranked by Assets)

Rank	Foundation	Assets (millions)	Cumulative percent
1	Ford Foundation	2,300	7.0
2	Pew Memorial Trust	890	9.8
3	Robert Wood Johnson Foundation	877	12.5
4	Andrew W. Mellon Foundation	827	15.1
5	Lilly Endowment	812	17.6
6	Rockefeller Foundation	805	20.0
7	W.K. Kellogg Foundation	792	22.5
8	Kresge Foundation	608	24.4
9	Duke Endowment	363	25.5
10	Carnegie Corporation of New York	295	26.4
11	Richard King Mellon Foundation	274	27.2
12	Houston Endowment (Jesse H. Jones family)	263	28.1
13	Alfred P. Sloan Foundation	252	28.8
14	Bush Foundation	217	29.5
15	Moody Foundation	210	30.2
16	James Irvine Foundation	208	30.8
17	Frank E. Gannett Newspaper Foundation	201	31.4
18	Edna McConnel Clark Foundation	199	32.0
19	Henry J. Kaiser Family Foundation	186	32.6
20	Rockefeller Brothers Fund	160	33.1
21	Commonwealth Fund (Harkness family)	129	33.5
22	Robert A. Welch Foundation	123	33.9
23	John A. Hartford Foundation	118	34.2
24	Surdna Foundation (Andrus family)	116	34.6
25	Northwest Area Foundation	114	34.9
26	Charles Stewart Mott Foundation	107	35.3
27	Amon G. Carter Foundation	102	35.6
28	William Penn Foundation (Hass Family)	101	35.9
29	William R. Kenan, Jr. Charitable Trust	100	36.2
30	Sarah Scaife Foundation	97	36.5
31	Charles A. Dana Foundation	96	36.8
32	John Simon Guggenheim Memorial Foundation	85	37.1
33	F. Smith Reynolds Foundation	83	37.3
34	Callaway Foundation	82	37.6
35	George Gund Foundation	80	37.8
36	Henry Luce Foundation	78	38.1
37	Howard Heinz Endowment	77	38.3
38	Charles F. Kettering Foundation	74	38.5
39	Claude Worthington Benedum Foundation	74	38.8
40	Smith Richardson Foundation	73	39.0
41	El Pomar Foundation	72	39.2
42	Charles Hayden Foundation	71	39.4
43	Danforth Foundation	68	39.6
44	Mary Flagler Cary Charitable Trust	65	39.8
45	William T. Grant Foundation	61	40.0
46	Vincent Astor Foundation	54	40.2
47	John and Mary R. Markle Foundation	47	40.3
48	Research Corporation	44	40.5
49	Tinker Foundation	28	40.6
50	Elliot White Springs Foundation	18	40.6

Total number of foundations with $1 million in assets = 3,138
Total asset value of these foundations = $32.4 billion.

Historically, the largest and most powerful foundations have been those established by the nation's leading families—Ford, Rockefeller, Carnegie, Mellon, Kresge, Pew, Duke, Lilly, Danforth. Over the years, some foundations—for example, the Ford Foundation and the Carnegie Corporation—have become independent of their original family ties; independence occurs when the foundation's own investments prosper and new infusions of family money are not required. However, Rockefellers, Mellons, Lillys, Danforths, Kresges, and other wealthy individuals still sit on the boards of directors of their family foundations. A number of foundations limit their contributions to specific fields; the Johnson Foundation, for example, sponsors research in medicine, and the Lilly Foundation supports advances in education and religion. This specialization, however, tends to reduce a foundation's power to shape national goals and policy directions. In contrast, the Ford, Rockefeller, and Carnegie Foundations deliberately attempt to focus on key national policy areas. This latter group of foundations plays a more influential role in national policy-making, because they concentrate their attention on broad social issues such as poverty, health care, welfare reform, and foreign affairs.

The Rockefeller Foundation.   A glance at the members of the Rockefeller Foundation board of directors confirms its ties to other top institutions.

John D. Rockefeller IV. Son of John D. Rockefeller, III, who served many years as chairman of the Rockefeller Foundation, United Negro College Fund, Lincoln Center for the Performing Arts, and the Population Council. Young Rockefeller is governor of West Virginia.

Theodore Hesburgh. Chairman of the Rockefeller Foundation. President of Notre Dame and chairman of the U.S. Civil Rights Commission.

Robert V. Roosa. Partner, Brown Brothers, Harriman & Co. (investment firm) and a director of American Express, Owens-Corning Fiberglass, and Texaco.

Clifford M. Hardin. Former Secretary of Agriculture and chairman of Ralston Purina.

Vernon Jordan. Executive director of the National Urban League.

Lane Kirkland. Secretary-treasurer of the AFL-CIO.

Clifton W. Wharton, Jr. Chancellor of the State University of New York. Former President of Michigan State University and a director of Ford Motors, Burroughs Corp., and Equitable Life Assurance.

William Moyers. Former presidential press secretary under Lyndon B. Johnson.

Kenneth N. Dayton. Chairman of Dayton-Hudson Corp. and a director of General Mills and Northwest Bancorp.

James P. Grant. Executive director of UNICEF.

Richard W. Lyman. President of Washington University, St. Louis.

Henry B. Schacht. Chairman of the board of Cummins Engine and a director of CBS.

Eleanor B. Sheldon. A sociologist who is a director of the Rand Corporation, Equitable Life Assurance Society, Citicorp, and Mobil Oil.

Paul A. Volcker. Chairman of the board of the Federal Reserve System and former Chase Manhattan vice-president.

The Ford Foundation.   The president of the Ford Foundation is Franklin A. Thomas, a black New York attorney (Columbia Law School), who made his mark as president of the Bedford Stuyvesant Restoration Corporation (urban renewal). He is a director of Citicorp, CBS, Aluminum Company of America, Allied Stores, and Cummins Engine; he is also a trustee of Columbia University. Until his resignation in 1977, the driving force behind the foundation was Henry Ford II himself. Others include:

Walter A. Haas. President of Levi Strauss & Co. and a director of BankAmerica.

Robert S. McNamara. Former president of Ford Motor Co., Secretary of Defense, and president of the World Bank.

Andrew F. Brimmer. Former member of the Federal Reserve Board and a director of BankAmerica, American Security Bank, International Harvester, United Air Lines, and DuPont.

Donald S. Perkins. Chairman of the board of Jewel Companies, Inc. and a director of Time, Inc., AT&T, Inland Steel, Corning Glass, Cummins Engine, and Morgan Guarantee Bank; also a trustee of The Brookings Institution and Business Roundtable.

Harriet S. Rabb. Columbia Law School professor and civil rights attorney.

Alexander Heard. President of Vanderbilt University, and a director of Time, Inc.

Joseph Irwin Miller. Chairman of Irwin-Union Bank & Trust and a director of AT&T, Purity Stores, Equitable Life Insurance, and Chemical Bank of New York.

The Carnegie Foundation.   For many years, the president of the Carnegie Foundation was John W. Gardiner, who went on to become Secretary of Health, Education, and Welfare under President Lyndon B. Johnson. Gardiner now uses his top connections to solicit support for the nation's heaviest spending congressional lobby, Common Cause. The Carnegie Corporation board includes persons at the top such as:

Caryl P. Haskins. Former president of the Carnegie Corporation; a director of DuPont, RAND Corp., Yale University, Smithsonian Institute, and the Council on Foreign Relations.

Carl M. Mueller. Chairman of the board of Bankers Trust of New York, and a director of Cabot Corporation, MacMillan Inc., and M.I.T.

Harding F. Bancroft. Executive vice-president of the New York Times Company.

Louis W. Cabot. (of the original Boston Cabots who explored America). Chairman of the board of the Cabot Corporation.

THE CULTURAL ORGANIZATIONS

The identification of the nation's leading civic and cultural institutions requires qualitative judgments about the prestige and influence of a variety of organizations. Six cultural organizations were selected:

Metropolitan Museum of Art
Museum of Modern Art
Lincoln Center for the Performing Arts
Smithsonian Institution
National Gallery of Art
John F. Kennedy Center for the Performing Arts

It is difficult to measure the power of particular institutions in the world of art, music, and theater. Certainly there are a number of viable alternatives that might be added to or substituted for our choices.

The Metropolitan Museum of Art.   This organization in New York City is the largest art museum in the United States, with a collection of nearly one-half million *objets d'art*. Decisions of the Metropolitan Museum regarding exhibitions, collections, showings, and art objects have tremendous impact on what is or is not to be considered valued art in America. These decisions are the formal responsibility of the governing board. This board includes names such as:

C. Douglas Dillon. Chairman, former Secretary of the Treasury, Under Secretary of State, and a director of Chase Manhattan.

Mrs. Vincent Astor. Wealthy philanthropist and trustee of New York Public Library, New York Zoological Society, Pierpont Morgan Library, and Rockefeller University.

Daniel P. Davison. President of Morgan Guaranty Trust and a director of Burlington Northern, Portland Cement, and Scovill.

J. Richardson Dilworth. Chairman of the board of Rockefeller Center, New York, and a director of Macy & Co., Chase Manhattan, and Chrysler Corporation.

Roswell Gilpatrick. Partner in Cravath, Swaine & Moore and a director of CBS, Eastern Air Lines, Fairchild Camera, and Corning Glass.

Henry A. Kissinger. Former Secretary of State.

Mrs. Henry J. Heinz II. Spouse of the chairman of the H.J. Heinz Company.

R. Manning Brown, Jr. Chairman of the board of New York Life Insurance and a director of Avon, J.P. Morgan & Co., and Union Carbide.

Richard S. Perkins. Former chairman of the board of Citicorp, and a director of Allied Chemical, New York Life Insurance, Southern Pacific, ITT, and Hospital Corporation of America.

The Museum of Modern Art.   This museum in New York City is the leading institution in the nation devoted to collecting and exhibiting contemporary art. It houses not only paintings and sculpture, but also films, print, and photography. Its loan exhibitions circulate art works throughout the world. The determination of what is to be considered "art" in the world of modern art is extremely subjective. The directors of the Museum of Modern Art, then, have great authority in determining what is or is not to be viewed as art. Its directors include illustrious names such as:

William S. Paley. Chairman, chairman of the board of CBS.

Mrs. John D. Rockefeller III. Widow of the oldest of four sons of John D. Rockefeller, Jr.

David Rockefeller. Former chairman of the board of Chase Manhattan.

Frank T. Cary. Chairman of the board of IBM.

Thomas S. Carroll. President of Lever Brothers.

Peter G. Peterson. Chairman of the board of Lehman Brothers, Kuhn Loeb (investments), and a director of RCA, General Foods, Minnesota Mining and Manufactory, Black and Decker, and Cities Service.

The Lincoln Center for the Performing Arts.   The Lincoln Center in New York City is a major influence in the nation's serious theater, ballet, and music. The Lincoln Center houses the Metropolitan Opera, the New York Philharmonic, and the Juilliard School of Music. It also supports the Lincoln Repertory Company (theater), the New York State Theater (ballet), and the Library-Museum for Performing Arts.

The Metropolitan Opera, which opened in 1883, is the nation's most influential institution in the field of serious operatic music. Decisions about what operas to produce influence greatly what is, or is not, to be considered serious opera in America, and indeed, in the world. Such decisions are the formal responsibility of a board that includes luminaries such as the following:

William Rockefeller. Chairman of the Metropolitan Opera. A cousin of the Rockefeller brothers. Senior partner in Shearman and Sterling, a top Wall Street law firm.

Richard R. Shinn. Chairman of the board of Metropolitan Life.

Norborne Berkeley, Jr. President of Chemical Bank of New York.

Anthony A. Bliss. Senior partner in Milbank, Tweed, Hadley & McCloy.

John T. Conner. Former chairman of the board of Allied Chemical, and a director of General Motors, Chase Manhattan, ABC, and Warner Lambert.

The Smithsonian Institution.   The Smithsonian Institution in Washington supports a wide variety of scientific publications, collections, and exhibitions. It also exercises nominal control over the National Gallery of Art, the John F. Kennedy Center for Performing Arts, and the Museum of Natural History, although these component organizations have their own boards of directors. The Smithsonian itself is directed by a board consisting of the Vice-President of the United States, the Chief Justice of the Supreme Court, three U.S. senators, three U.S. representatives, and six "private citizens."

Its "private citizens" turn out to be people such as:

J. Paul Austin. Chairman of the board of the Coca Cola Company.

Carl P. Haskins. Former president of the Carnegie Foundation and a director of DuPont and the RAND Corporation.

William G. Bowen. President of Princeton University.

Carlisle H. Humelsine. Chairman of the board of Colonial Williamsburg Foundation.

William S. Anderson. Chairman of the board of National Cash Register (NCR).

Carla Hills. Former Secretary of Housing and Urban Development and a director of IBM, American Airlines, Signal Companies, and Standard Oil of California.

The National Gallery of Art.   The capital's leading art institution was begun in 1937 when Andrew W. Mellon made the original donation of his art collection together with $15 million to build the gallery itself. Since then it has accepted other collections from wealthy philanthropists, and it exercises considerable influence in the art world. Its permanent trustees are the Chief Justice of the Supreme Court and the Secretary of State and the Secretary of the Treasury. Its "citizen" trustees include:

Paul Mellon. A son of Andrew Mellon and a director of Mellon National Bank and Trust and the Mellon Foundation.

Franklin D. Murphy. Chairman of the board of the Times-Mirror Company and a director of BankAmerica, Ford Motors, and Hallmark cards.

The John F. Kennedy Center for the Performing Arts. The Kennedy Center in Washington, which was begun in 1964, also has considerable influence on the arts in America. It describes itself as a "national showcase for the performing arts" (music, opera, drama, dance). It is officially part of the Smithsonian Institution, but it is administered separately by a forty-five member board, most of whom are appointed by the President. The board is largely "political" in origin and includes:

Edward M. Kennedy. U.S. senator from Massachusetts.

Mrs. J.W. Marriott. Wife of the president of Marriott Motor Hotels, a heavy financial contributor to political candidates.

Charles H. Percy. U.S. senator from Illinois.

Mrs. Howard H. Baker, Jr. Spouse of the Republican leader of the U.S. Senate.

Abe Fortas. Former U.S. Supreme Court Justice.

J. William Fulbright. Former U.S. senator.

Mrs. Patricia Roberts Harris. Former Secretary of Health Education and Welfare and senior partner in a top Washington law firm.

Melvin R. Laird. Former Secretary of Defense.

Mrs. Jean Kennedy Smith. Sister of John F., Robert F., and Edward M. Kennedy.

Roger L. Stevens. Chairman of the board of the John F. Kennedy Center for the Performing Arts. Producer of *West Side Story, Cat on a Hot Tin Roof, Bus Stop, Tea and Sympathy, A Man for All Seasons.* Former chairman of the National Endowment for the Arts. A director of the Metropolitan Opera.

THE CIVIC ASSOCIATIONS

Our judgments about power and influence in the civic arena are necessarily qualitative, as they were for cultural organizations. We shall focus particular attention on the political power of the nation's leading policy-planning organizations—the Council on Foreign Relations, the Business Roundtable, the Committee for Economic Development, and The Brookings Institution—both in this chapter and later in Chapter 9. These organizations are central coordinating mechanisms in national policy-making. They bring together people in top positions from the corporate world, the universities, the law firms, and the government, to develop explicit policies and programs for submission to Congress, the President, and the nation.

The Council on Foreign Relations. The most influential policy-planning group in foreign affairs is the Council on Foreign Relations. The origins of the CFR go back to the Versailles Treaty in 1919 ending World War I. Some Americans, including Woodrow Wilson's key adviser, Edward M. House, believed that top leadership in the United States was not sufficiently informed about world affairs. The Council on Foreign Relations was founded in 1921 and supported by grants from the Rockefeller and Carnegie Foundations and later the Ford Foundation. Its early directors were internationally minded Wall Street corporation leaders such as Elihu Root (who was Secretary of State), John W. Davis (1924 Democratic presidential nominee) and Paul Cravath (founder of the famous law firm of Cravath, Swaine & Moore).

The CFR is designed to build consensus among elites on foreign policy questions. It initiates new policy directions by first commissioning scholars to undertake investigations of foreign policy questions. Its studies are usually made with the financial support of foundations. Upon their completion, the CFR holds briefings and discussions among its members and between its members and top government officials.

The history of the CFR accomplishments is dazzling: it developed the Kellogg Peace Pact in the 1920s, stiffened U.S. opposition to Japanese Pacific expansion in the 1930s, designed major portions of the United Nations' charter, and devised the "containment" policy to halt Soviet expansion in Europe after World War II. It also laid the groundwork for the NATO agreement and devised the Marshall Plan for European recovery. While originally supporting U.S. involvement in Vietnam, the CFR worked out the plan that became the U.S. negotiating position at the Paris Peace Talks, which led to U.S. withdrawal in 1973. The CFR planned the Carter Administration's "human rights" campaign, as well as restrictions on international arms sales. Even before the election of Ronald Reagan, the CFR was calling for reassessment of U.S.–Soviet relations in view of the large Soviet arms buildup.

CFR publishes the journal *Foreign Affairs*, considered throughout the world to be the unofficial mouthpiece of U.S. foreign policy. Few important initiatives in U.S. policy have not been first outlined in articles in this publication. It was in *Foreign Affairs* in 1947 that George F. Kennan, chief of the policy-planning staff of the State Department, writing under the pseudonym of "X," first announced U.S. intentions of "containing" Communist expansion in the world. When top elites began to suspect that the U.S. was over-reliant on nuclear weapons in the late 1950s and unable to fight theater-type wars, the CFR commissioned a young Harvard professor to look into the matter. The result was Henry Kissinger's *Nuclear Weapons and Foreign Policy*, urging greater flexibility of response to aggression.

The CFR by-laws limit membership to 700 individual resident members (New York and Washington) and 700 nonresident members. However, there are now over 2,000 members and a long waiting list of individuals seeking membership in this prestigious organization. The CFR's list of former members includes every person of influence in foreign affairs from Elihu Root, Henry Stimson, John Foster Dulles, Dean Acheson, Robert Lovett, George F. Kennan, Averell Harriman, and Dean Rusk, to Henry Kissinger, Cyrus Vance, Alexander Haig, and George Bush.

The CFR describes itself as "a unique forum for bringing together leaders from the academic, public, and private worlds." Evidence of CFR interaction with the corporate and financial world, as well as with universities, foundations, the mass media, and government, is found in extensive interlocking between the leadership of CFR and the leadership of these other elements of the policy-making process. In 1976, the CFR board of directors included:

David Rockefeller. Chairman of the board of directors of the Council on Foreign Relations. Former chairman of the board and chief executive officer of Chase Manhattan Bank.

Gabriel Hauge. Former chairman of the board of Manufacturers Hanover Trust Co., former editor of *Business Week.* A director of New York Life Insurance, America Metal Climax, Chrysler Corp., Royal Dutch Petroleum, SAS Inc.; a trustee of the Committee for Economic Development, Juilliard School of Music, and the Carnegie Endowment for International Peace.

William P. Bundy. Editor of the Council on Foreign Relations' official journal *Foreign Affairs.* Senior partner of Covington & Burling (Washington law firm). Former deputy director of the C.I.A.; Assistant Secretary of Defense, 1961–64; Assistant Secretary of State for the Far East, 1964–68. A trustee of the Committee on Economic Development and the American Assembly. (His brother McGeorge Bundy was dean of Harvard College, Special Assistant to President Johnson for national security affairs, and president of the Ford Foundation.)

Robert O. Anderson. Chairman of the board of Atlantic Richfield Co; a director of the American Petroleum Institute. He is trustee of the California Institute of Technology, University of Chicago, the University of Denver, and Cal Tech.

Nicholas DeB. Katzenbach. Former Attorney General of the United States, 1964–66; former University of Chicago law school professor. He is director and general counsel of the IBM Corporation.

Theodore M. Hesburgh. President of the University of Notre Dame. Former chairman of the U.S. Civil Rights Commission. A director of the American Council on Education, the Rockefeller Foundation, the Carnegie Corporation, the Woodrow Wilson National Fellowship Foundation, the United Negro College Fund, and the Freedom Foundation.

Robert V. Roosa. Senior partner of the New York investment firm of Brown Brothers, Harriman & Co. (which was founded by Averell Harriman). A director of American Express Co., Anaconda Copper, Owens-Corning Fiberglass, and Texaco. He was former Under Secretary of the Treasury.

Peter G. Peterson. Chairman of the New York investment firm of Lehman Bros. Former chairman of the board of Bell and Howell Co., and former assistant to the President for international economic affairs, 1971–72. A director of Minnesota Mining & Mfg., General Foods, and Federated Department Stores. He is a trustee of the Museum of Modern Art and the University of Chicago.

W. Michael Blumenthal. Chairman of the board of the Burroughs Corp. Former chairman of the board of Bendix Corporation. A naturalized U.S. citizen whose parents fled Nazi Germany in 1938; an earned Ph.D. in economics from Princeton; a director of Equitable Life Insurance and Pillsbury, and a trustee of Princeton University.

Lucian W. Pye. Professor of political science, M.I.T.

Henry A. Kissinger. International adviser for Chase Manhattan. Former Secretary of State; former National Security Adviser. An earned Ph.D. in government from Harvard University.

James F. Hoge. Editor-in-chief of the *Chicago Sun Times* and the *Chicago Daily News.*

Richard L. Gelb. Chairman of the board of Bristol Meyer. A director of Charter Corp., Banking Trust of N.Y., and the *New York Times.*

Graham T. Allison. Dean of the John F. Kennedy School of Government at Harvard University.

William D. Ruckelshaus. Vice-president of Weyerhaeuser Co.; former Director of the Environmental Protection Agency; a director of Cummins Engine.

Lane Kirkland. President of the AFL-CIO.

George P. Schultz. President of the Bechtel Corp. (world's largest construction company). Former Secretary of the Treasury, former Director of the Office of Management and Budget, former Secretary of Labor. A director of Morgan Guaranty Trust and Sears Roebuck & Co. An earned Ph.D. in economics from M.I.T.

Stephen Stamas. Vice-president of Exxon Corp.

Martha R. Wallace. Vice-president of Time, Inc. and the Henry Luce Foundation Inc. A director of American Can, American Express, Bristol Meyers, Chemical Bank, and the New York Stock Exchange.

Marina VonNeumann Whitman. Daughter of John VonNeumann, developer of first modern computers. Vice-president of General Motors; a director of Manufacturers Hanover Trust and Procter and Gamble; an earned Ph.D. in economics from Columbia University.

C. Peter McColough. Chairman of the board of Xerox Corporation and a director of Citicorp and Union Carbide.

Franklin Hall Williams. Former NAACP attorney. Former U.S. Ambassador to Ghana. A director of Chemical Bank, Consolidated Edison, and Borden Co.

Of the twenty-five current (1980) directors and eighteen "directors emeriti," the Council now, according to fashion, boasts of two women and one black. The women are Martha R. Wallace of Time, Inc. and Marina VonNeumann Whitman of General Motors. The black is Franklin Hall Williams.

Committee on Economic Development. The Committee on Economic Development (CED) is a central organization for developing consensus among business and financial leaders on domestic public policy, and communicating their views to government officials. The CED does not restrict itself to fiscal and monetary policy, nor to business regulation, but instead it works on a wide range of domestic issues. There are many interlocks between CFR and CED members. A brief listing of CED trustees indicates their extensive interlocking with business, financial, foundation, and governmental institutions. The trustees include:

William H. Franklin. Chairman of the board of trustees of the Committee on Economic Development. Chairman of the Board of Caterpillar Tractor Co. and a director of Exxon Corp.

Peter G. Peterson. Chairman of the New York investment firm of Lehman Bros. Former chairman of the board of Bell and Howell Co., and former assistant to the President for international economic affairs, 1971–72. A director of Minnesota Mining & Mfg., General Foods, and Federated Department Stores. He is a trustee of the Museum of Modern Art and the University of Chicago.

J.L. Scott. Chairman of the board of Great Atlantic and Pacific Tea Co. (A & P).

George P. Schultz. Former Secretary of Labor, 1969–70; Director of the Office of Management and Budget, 1970–72; and Secretary of Treasury, 1972–74. Currently president of Bechtel Corporation and a director of J.P. Morgan & Co. and the Morgan Guaranty Trust Co. Former dean of the Graduate School of Business, University of Chicago; an earned Ph.D. in economics from M.I.T.

Joseph L. Black. Chairman and chief executive officer of Inland Steel Company. A director of the Chicago Board of Trade, Commonwealth Edison Co., Chicago First National Bank. A trustee of the National Merit Scholarship Fund, Illinois Institute of Technology, American Iron and Steel Institute.

Jevis J. Babb. Former president and chairman of the board of Lever Brothers. A director of Sucrest, Universal Foods, Gruen Industries, Guardian Life Insurance, American Can, Bank of New York.

Chauncey J. Medberry III. Chairman of the board of BankAmerica and a director of Getty Oil Co.

John B. M. Place. Chairman of the board of Anaconda Copper Co., and a director of Celanese Corp, Chemical Bank of New York, Communications Satellite Corp., Lever Brothers, and the Union Pacific Railroad.

Business Roundtable.   The Business Roundtable provides direct representation of the chief executive officers of the nation's 200 largest corporations in the policy process. Unlike other policy-planning groups, which emphasize policy formation and consensus-building, the Roundtable engages in direct lobbying on behalf of specific bills it wants passed by the Congress and supported by the President. The Roundtable was formed in 1972 to successfully lobby Congress on labor laws in the construction industry. Later, the Roundtable was successful in defeating the establishment of a Consumer Protection Agency in both the Ford and Carter administrations. The Roundtable has been instrumental in making "deregulation" a key item in the Washington policy agenda in recent years. It has also supported social spending cuts, general tax cuts, and faster depreciation schedules for business tax purposes.

The Business Roundtable claims a membership of 200 chief executive officers in corporations from a variety of industries. The Roundtable has formed task forces on a wide variety of policy issues—antitrust, energy, environment, inflation, government regulation, health, social security, taxation, welfare, and so on. These task forces submit their policy recommendations to a powerful forty-five member policy committee. The strength of the organization is derived from the willingness of its member chiefs to appear *in person* in Washington. Congresspersons are impressed with the personal appearance of luminaries such as:

Clifton C. Garvin. Chairman of the Business Roundtable. Chairman of the board of Exxon.
Walter B. Wriston. Chairman of the board of Citicorp.
Charles L. Bain. Chairman of the board of AT&T.
Frank T. Cary. Chairman of the board of IBM.
Alden W. Clausen. Chairman of the board of BankAmerica.
Justin Dart. Chairman of the board of Dart Industries.
Thomas A. Murphy. Chairman of the board of General Motors.
Irving S. Shapiro. Chairman of the board of DuPont.
Rawleigh Warner. Chairman of the board of Mobil Oil.
Ralph Lazarus. Chairman of the board of Federated Department Stores.
Theodore Brophy. Chairman of the board of GTE.
Phillip M. Hawley. Chairman of the board of Carter Hawley Hale Stores.

John F. Bookout. Chairman of the board of Shell Oil.

Reginald H. Jones. Chairman of the board of General Electric.

David M. Roderick. Chairman of the board of United States Steel.

Richard R. Shinn. Chairman of the board of Metropolitan Life.

Robert A. Beck. Chairman of the board of Prudential.

The Brookings Institution. Over the years, the foremost policy-planning group in domestic affairs has been The Brookings Institution. Since the 1960s, it has overshadowed the CED, the American Enterprise Institution, the American Assembly, the Twentieth Century Fund, the Urban Institute, and all other policy-planning groups. Brookings has been extremely influential in planning the War on Poverty, welfare reform, national health care, defense programs, and taxation. The Brookings Institution is generally regarded as moderate-to-liberal in its policy orientation. The American Enterprise Institute (AEI) was reorganized in the 1970s to try to offset Brookings' influence by providing moderate-to-conservative advice on public policy. While the AEI has enjoyed a resurgence in Washington in the Reagan Administration, its long-term influence is no match for the well-established Brookings Institution.

The Brookings Institution directors today are as impressive a group of top elites as assembled anywhere:

Robert V. Roosa. Chairman of board of trustees of The Brookings Institution. Senior partner, Brown Brothers, Harriman & Co. (New York investment firm). He is a director of American Express Co., Anaconda Copper, Owens-Corning Fiberglass Co., and Texaco. He is a former Under Secretary of the Treasury and a director of the Council on Foreign Relations. Roosa has an earned Ph.D. in economics from the University of Michigan and was a Rhodes scholar. A trustee of the Rockefeller Foundation.

Louis W. Cabot. Chairman of the board of the Cabot Corporation. A director of Owens-Corning Fiberglass Co., and New England Telephone, and chairman of the Federal Reserve Bank of Boston. A trustee of the Carnegie Corporation, M.I.T., and Northeastern University, and a member of the Council on Foreign Relations.

Robert S. McNamara. Former President of the World Bank. Former Secretary of Defense, 1961–67. Former president of Ford Motor Company.

Frank T. Cary. Chairman of the board of IBM.

John D. DeButts. Former Chairman of the board of AT&T. A director of Citicorp, U.S. Steel, Kraft, General Motors, and trustee of the Duke Endowment.

Carla A. Hills. Senior partner of Latham Watkins & Hills.

Lane Kirkland. President of the AFL-CIO.

James D. Robinson. Chairman of the board of American Express.

Arjay Miller. Former president of Ford Motor Company; dean of the Graduate School of Business at Stanford University.

Herbert P. Patterson. Former president of Chase Manhattan Bank. A director of American Machine & Foundry and the Urban Coalition.

Edward W. Carter. President of Broadway Hale Stores. A director of AT&T. Southern California Edison, Del Monte Corporation, Western BanCorporation, and Pacific Mutual Life Insurance Company.

Two women are listed among the twenty-one trustees and one honorary trustee of The Brookings Institution: Carla Hills, a Washington attorney who was formerly Secretary of Housing and Urban Development, and is currently a director at IBM, American Airlines, Signal Companies, and Standard Oil of California; and Phyllis A. Wallace, a professor of management at M.I.T.

If the names are growing repetitious by now, it is for good reason. Those who occupy top posts in the leading corporate, governmental, and mass media institutions are frequently the same individuals who direct the leading foundations, civic associations, and cultural organizations. In the next few pages, we shall see many of their names again, when we examine the trustees of the nation's leading universities. The purpose of "naming names," even when they become repetitive, is to suggest frequent interlocking of top elites in different institutional sectors. In Chapter 6, we will examine interlocking in greater detail.

THE UNIVERSITIES

The growth of public higher education since World War II—the creation of vast state university, state college, and community college systems in every state in the nation—has diminished the influence of the prestigious private universities. There are now over 2,500 separate institutions of higher education in America, enrolling over eleven million students—about half of all high school graduates. Only about a quarter of these students are enrolled in *private* colleges and universities. Moreover, some leading public universities—for example, the University of California at Berkeley, the University of Wisconsin, and the University of Michigan—are consistently ranked with the well-known private universities in terms of the quality of higher education offered. Thus, the leading private universities in the nation no longer exercise the dominant influence over higher education that they did before World War II.

Nonetheless, among private colleges and universities it is possible to identify those few top institutions which control most of the resources available to private higher education. The twenty-five universities listed in Table 5–3 control two thirds of all private endowment funds in higher education; this was the formal basis for their selection. (Only three *public* universities rank with the top twenty-five private universities in endowments. These are the University of Texas, which like Harvard has over $1 billion in endowment funds, the University of Delaware, and the University of Virginia.) Moreover, they are consistently ranked among the "best" educational institutions in the nation. Finally, as we will see, a disproportionate number of the nation's top leaders attended one or another of these institutions.

Table 5–3   Private Universities with Largest Endowments

	Assets (millions)
1. Harvard University	$1,457
2. Yale University	577
3. Columbia University	504
4. Princeton University	473
5. Stanford University	450
6. Massachusetts Institute of Technology	374
7. University of Rochester	323
8. University of Chicago	311
9. Cornell University	288
10. New York University	272
11. Rice University	270
12. Northwestern University	256
13. Washington University	220
14. Rockefeller University	201
15. Dartmouth College	173
16. University of Pennsylvania	168
17. Johns Hopkins University	164
18. California Institute of Technology	164
19. University of Notre Dame	137
20. University of Southern California	130
21. Wellesley College	126
22. Duke University	122
23. Case Western Reserve University	118
24. Carnegie-Mellon University	113
25. Wesleyan University	106

Source: *Chronicle of Higher Education,* March 24, 1980.

The presidents and trustees of these institutions, then, can exercise significant influence over higher education and thus over the quality of life in America. A brief look at the careers of some of these people who head our institutions of higher education tells us a great deal about the educational elite. Note how their careers involve two or more similar positions, and note their close ties with other fields—notably business, culture, and government. We will list some names of trustees for the nation's top three private universities—Harvard, Yale, and the University of Chicago.

Harvard University

Thorton F. Bradshaw. Chairman of the board of RCA.

Albert V. Casey. Chairman of the board of American Airlines.

William T. Coleman. Former Secretary of Transportation and director of IBM, Chase Manhattan, Pepsico, Pan American, and Philadelphia Electric.

John C. Culver. U.S. Senator (D. Iowa).

Augustus Peabody Loring. Trustee of the Peabody Museum.

Colman M. Mockler, Jr. Chairman of the board of Gillette Company and director of First National Boston Corp., John Hancock Mutual Life, and Raytheon.

Frank Stanton. Former president of CBS and a director of Atlantic Richfield, Pan American, American Electric Power, New York Life Insurance.

Stephen Stamas. Vice-president of Exxon (Harvard Ph.D., 1957, and Rhodes scholar).

Lewis Thomas. M.D., president of Memorial Sloan-Kettering Cancer Center.

Yale University

J. Richardson Dilworth. Chairman of the board of Rockefeller Center and a director of Macy's, Chase Manhattan, and Chrysler Corp.

Vernon R. Loucks, Jr. Chairman of the board of Baxter, Travenol Labs, Inc. and a director of Continental Illinois Bank, Dun & Bradstreet, and Marshall Field.

John B. Madden. Senior partner, Brown Brothers, Hamman and Company.

Bayless Manning. Senior partner, Paul, Weiss, Rifkind, Wharton and Garrison, and a director of Aetna Life and Scovill.

William S. Beinecke. Chairman of the board of Sperry and Hutchinson (S & H green stamps).

Cyrus R. Vance. Former Secretary of State. Senior partner, Simpson, Thacher and Bartlett.

University of Chicago

David Rockefeller. Former chairman of the board of Chase Manhattan.

Robert O. Anderson. Former chairman of the board of Atlantic Richfield Co.

Katherine Graham. Publisher of *Washington Post-Newsweek*.

Robert S. Ingersoll. Former chairman of board of Borg-Warner Corp.

David M. Kennedy. Former Secretary of the Treasury; former chairman of the board of Continental Illinois National Bank & Trust.

Charles H. Percy. U.S. senator from Illinois.

Ellmore C. Patterson. Former president of Chase Manhattan.

Max Palevsky. Former chairman of the board of Xerox Corp.

Philip D. Block Jr. Former chairman of the board of Continental Illinois Bank.

Peter G. Peterson. Chairman of the board of Lehman Brothers, Kuhn Loeb and Company investments.

Jay A. Pritzker. Chairman of the board of Hyatt Corp.

We have already acknowledged the growing importance in higher education of the nation's leading *state* universities. Is there any reason to believe that their rise to prominence since World War II has distributed power in education more widely and opened positions of authority to persons whose elite credentials are not necessarily as impressive as the ones we have seen again and again in our lists of top leaders? Our answer is a very qualified "yes": State boards of regents for state universities are on the whole composed of individuals who would probably *not* be among the top institutional elites according to our definition in Chapter 1. Many of these regents hold directorships in smaller corporations, smaller banks, and smaller utility companies; they frequently have held state rather than national political office; their legal, civic, cultural, and foundation affiliations are with institutions of state rather than with prestigious and powerful national institutions.[11]

University presidents, particularly the presidents of the nation's top institutions, are frequently called upon to serve as trustees or directors of other institutions and to serve in high government posts. Most university presidents today have come up through the ranks of academic administration, suggesting that universities themselves may offer channels for upward mobility into the nation's elite. We must keep in mind, however, that presidents are hired and fired by the trustees, not the students or faculty.

THE INTELLECTUAL ELITE

The intellectual "community" is not sufficiently organized or institutionalized to provide its leadership with formal control over any significant portion of society's resources. Indeed, "intellectuals" do not

---

[11]David N. Smith, *Who Rules the Universities?* (New York: Monthly Review Press, 1974), pp. 30–33.

even have much control over universities, the institutions that house the largest group of the nation's intellectuals. Some intellectuals, of course, have "influence" because directors of large institutions read their books and listen to their lectures and are persuaded by them. But intellectuals per se have no direct control over the institutional structure of society, *unless they are recruited into top institutional positions.* Our formal definition of elites as individuals in positions of control over institutional resources, then, means that we can count as intellectual elites only those intellectuals who have been recruited to high institutional positions—particularly in government, the foundations, and the civic and cultural organizations.

Historian Richard Hofstadter has categorized intellectuals in a fashion that reflects our own notion about treating those in power differently from those not in power. Hofstadter expressed the hope that "the intellectual community will not become hopelessly polarized into two parts, one part the technicians concerned with power and accepting the terms of power put to them, and the other of willfully alienated intellectuals more concerned with maintaining their own sense of purity than with making their ideas effective."[12]

Actually, it is difficult to define precisely who is an intellectual. Seymour Martin Lipset defines intellectuals as

> all of those who create, distribute, and apply culture, that is, the symbolic world of man, including art, science, and religion. Within this group there are two main levels; the hard core of creators of culture—scholars, artists, philosophers, authors, some editors and some journalists; and the distributors—performers in the various arts, most teachers, and most reporters.[13]

Such a broad definition includes millions of individuals with a wide range of institutional affiliations.

Perhaps the most systematic attempt to identify an intellectual *elite* is found in the work of Charles Kadushin and his associates at Columbia University.[14] According to Kadushin, "An elite intellectual may be defined roughly as one who is an expert in dealing with general ideas on questions of values and esthetics and who communicates his judgments on these matters to a fairly general audience." (Note that Kadushin excludes many specialists, particularly in the physical and biological sciences, who deal with specific scientific questions and communicate to a very specialized

[12]Richard Hofstadter, *Anti-Intellectualism in American Life* (New York: Knopf, 1963), p. 429.

[13]Seymour Martin Lipset, *Political Man* (New York: Doubleday, 1960), p. 310.

[14]Charles Kadushin, Julie Hover, and Monique Richy, "How and Where to Find an Intellectual Elite in the United States," *Public Opinion Quarterly,* 35 (Spring 1971), 1–18; see also Charles Kadushin, "Who Are the Elite Intellectuals?" *The Public Interest* (Summer 1972), pp. 109–125.

audience; this may be the greatest weakness in his definition.) To operationalize this definition, Kadushin employed a reputational approach to select 20 leading intellectual journals of general interest, excluding specialized or technical ones. A sample of professors, writers, and editors selected the following publications:

New York Review of Books	*Daedalus*
New Republic	*Ramparts*
Commentary	*Yale Review*
New York Times Book Review	*Dissent*
New Yorker	*American Scholar*
Saturday Review	*Hudson Review*
Partisan Review	*Village Voice*
Harpers	*The Progressive*
The Nation	*Foreign Affairs*
Atlantic	*The Public Interest*

It turns out that nearly 8000 persons had contributed articles to these intellectual journals in a four-year period. A second sample was then asked to identify those intellectuals "who influenced them on cultural or social-political issues, or who they believed had high prestige in the intellectual community." The result was the listing in Table 5-4. Unfortunately, this work was done in the early 1970s, and no comparable studies are available for the 1980s. Nonetheless, we can make some observations about the nation's intellectual elite.

A few intellectuals have occupied high places in government— Galbraith, Moynihan, Schlesinger, Gardner—but most have remained on the sidelines, perhaps exercising "influence" from time to time, but not "power" in terms of institutional authority. About half of America's intellectuals are Jewish (less than three percent of the nation's total population is Jewish). Their median income (about $70,000 in current dollars) is considerably less than other elites identified in this book. There are very few women among the nation's top intellectuals, and only one black—Bayard Rustin.

The American intellectual elite is far more liberal than any other segment of the nation's elite. Richard Hofstadter writes: "If there is anything that could be called an intellectual establishment in America, this establishment has been, though not profoundly radical (which would be unbecoming in an establishment), on the left side of center."[15] Kadushin confirms this judgment; most of his intellectuals are left-liberal and generally critical of the government and the economic system. Only about one quarter are "neoconservatives." About 20 percent could be classified as

[15]Hofstadter, *Anti-Intellectualism.*

Table 5-4 The Most Prestigious American Intellectuals in the 1970s

Ranks 1 to 10 (2 tied for 10th place)

Daniel Bell
Noam Chomsky
John Kenneth Galbraith
Irving Howe
Dwight MacDonald
Mary McCarthy

Norman Mailer
Robert Silvers
Susan Sontag
Lionel Trilling
Edmund Wilson

Ranks 11 to 20

Hannah Arendt
Saul Bellow
Paul Goodman
Richard Hofstadter
Irving Kristol

Herbert Marcuse
Daniel Patrick Moynihan
Norman Podhoretz
David Riesman
Arthur Schlesinger, Jr.

Ranks 21 to 25 (numerous ties)

W.H. Auden
Norman O. Brown
Theodore Draper
Jason Epstein
Leslie Fiedler
Edgar Friedenberg
John Gardner
Eugene Genovese
Richard Goodwin
Michael Harrington

Pauline Kael
Alfred Kazin
Murray Kempton
George Lichtheim
Walter Lippmann
Marshall McLuhan
Hans Morgenthau
I. F. Stone
C. Vann Woodward

Ranks 26 and 27 (numerous ties)

Edward Banfield
Isaiah Berlin
Barbara Epstein
R. Buckminster Fuller
Nathan Glazer
Elizabeth Hardwick
Robert Heilbroner
Sidney Hook
Ada Louise Huxtable
George F. Kennan
Christopher Lasch
Seymour Martin Lipset
Robert Lowell
Robert K. Merton
Barrington Moore

Willie Morris
Lewis Mumford
Reinhold Niebuhr
Robert Nisbet
Phillip Rahv
James Reston
Harold Rosenberg
Philip Roth
Richard Rovere
Bayard Rustin
Franz Schurman
John Simon
George Steiner
Diana Trilling
James Q. Wilson

Source: Charles Kadushin, "Who Are the Elite Intellectuals?" *The Public Interest,* Number 29 (Fall 1972), p. 123. Copyright © 1972 by National Affairs, Inc.

"radical"—that is, convinced that the overthrow of capitalism is essential to improvement in the quality of life in America. Kadushin found that the few elite intellectuals who rose from working-class backgrounds are somewhat more conservative than the majority of intellectuals who came from middle-class, upper-middle-class, and upper-class families. But he adds, "The elite intellectuals have so long been involved in the culture of intellectuals that their past backgrounds have become almost irrelevant."[16]

SUMMARY

Using the term *civic establishment,* we refer collectively to the nation's top law firms, its major foundations, its national cultural institutions, influential civic organizations, and prestigious private universities. At the top of the legal profession, the senior partners of the nation's largest and best known New York and Washington law firms exercise great power as legal representatives of the nation's largest corporations. These "superlawyers" generally reflect the same liberalism and concern for public welfare that prevail among other segments of the nation's elites. Superlawyers are frequently called upon for governmental leadership, particularly when high-level, delicate negotiations are required. Many superlawyers have been educated at Ivy League law schools and serve apprenticeships in governmental agencies before entering law firms.

The power of the nation's large foundations rests in their ability to channel corporate and personal wealth into the policy-making process. They do this by providing financial support and direction over university research and the activities of policy-oriented, civic associations. There is great concentration of foundation assets: Twelve of the nation's 6,803 foundations control 40 percent of all foundation assets. There is also a great deal of overlapping among the directorates of the leading foundations and corporate and financial institutions, the mass media, universities, policy-planning groups, and government.

A small number of cultural organizations exercise great power over the nation's art, music, theater, and ballet. A brief glance at the directors of these institutions confirms that they are the same group of people identified earlier as influential in business, finance, government, and the mass media.

The civic associations, particularly the leading policy-planning groups—The Council on Foreign Relations, the Business Roundtable, the Committee on Economic Development, and The Brookings Institution—play key roles in national policy-making. They bring together leaders at the top of various institutional sectors of society to formulate recommenda-

---

[16]*Ibid.,* p. 120.

tions on major policy innovations. More will be said about the important role of policy-planning groups in Chapter 9. But we have noted here that the directors of these groups are top leaders in industry, finance, government, the mass media, law, and the universities.

There may not be as much concentration of power in higher education as in other sectors of American life. The development of state universities since World War II has diminished the influence of the private, Ivy League-type universities. However, among *private* universities, only twenty-five institutions control over two thirds of all private endowment funds. A glance at some of the trustees of three of these institutions—Harvard, Yale, and Chicago—suggests heavy overlapping of those in power in corporations, government, the mass media, the foundations, and civic organizations. The intellectual "community" does not exercise any formal control over any significant portion of the nation's resources. Only when an intellectual is recruited to high position, as in the case of Henry Kissinger or Zbigniew Brzezinski, can he or she be said to have power.

PART THREE

The structure
of
institutional elites

6

Interlocking
and specialization
at the top

CONVERGENCE OR SPECIALIZATION AT THE TOP?

Is there a convergence of power at the top of an institutional structure in America, with a single group of individuals, recruited primarily from industry and finance, who occupy top positions in corporations, education, government, foundations, civic and cultural affairs, and the military? Or are there separate institutional structures, with elites in each sector of society having little or no overlap in authority and many separate channels of recruitment? In short, is the structure of power in America a pyramid or a polyarchy?

Social scientists have differed over this important question, and at least two varieties of leadership models can be identified in the literature on power.[1] A *hierarchical model* implies that a relatively small group of

[1]This literature is voluminous, and any characterization of positions results in some oversimplification. For good summary statements of positions, see the works of Mills, Hunter, Berle, Kolko, and Dahl, cited elsewhere in chapter notes. See also Arnold M. Rose, *The Power Structure* (New York: Oxford University Press, 1967); Suzanne Keller, *Beyond the Ruling Class* (New York: Random House, 1963); G. William Domhoff, *Who Rules America?* (Englewood Cliffs, N.J.: Prentice-Hall, Inc., 1967); Nelson Polsby, *Community Power and Political Theory* (New Haven: Yale University Press, 1963); and David Ricci, *Community Power and Democratic Theory* (New York: Random House, 1971).

individuals exercises authority in a wide variety of institutions—forming what has been called a "power elite." In contrast, a *polyarchical model* implies that different groups of individuals exercise power in various sectors of society and acquire power in separate ways.

The hierarchical model derives from the familiar "elitist" literature on power. Sociologist C. Wright Mills argues that "the leading men in each of the three domains of power—the warlords, the corporation chieftains, and the political directorate—tend to come together to form the power elite of America."[2] According to Mills, leadership in America constitutes "an intricate set of overlapping cliques." And Hunter, in his study *Top Leadership, U.S.A.*, concludes: "Out of several hundred persons named from all sources, between one hundred and two hundred were consistently chosen as top leaders and considered by all informants to be of national policy-making stature."[3] The notion of interlocking directorates has widespread currency in the power elite literature. Kolko writes that "interlocking directorates, whereby a director of one corporation also sits on the board of one or more other corporations, are a key device for concentrating corporate power...."[4] The hierarchical model also implies that top leaders in all sectors of society—including government, education, civic and cultural affairs, and politics—are recruited primarily from business and finance.

In contrast, "pluralist" writers have implied a polyarchical leadership structure, with different sets of leaders in different sectors of society and little or no overlap, except perhaps by elected officials responsible to the general public. According to this view, leadership is exercised in large measure by "specialists" who limit their participation to a narrow range of societal decisions. These specialists are believed to be recruited through separate channels—they are not drawn exclusively from business and finance. Generally, pluralists have praised the dispersion of authority in American society. Dahl writes: "The theory and practice of American pluralism tends to assume, as I see it, that the existence of multiple centers of power, none of which is wholly sovereign, will help (may indeed be necessary) to tame power, to secure the consent of all, and to settle conflicts peacefully."[5] But despite the theoretical (and ideological) importance of the question of convergence versus specialization in the leadership structure,

---

[2]C. Wright Mills, *The Power Elite* (New York: Oxford University Press, 1956), p. 9.

[3]Floyd Hunter, *Top Leadership, U.S.A.* (Chapel Hill: University of North Carolina Press, 1959), p. 176.

[4]Gabriel Kolko, *Wealth and Power in America* (New York: Praeger, 1962), p. 57.

[5]Robert A. Dahl, *Pluralist Democracy in the United States* (Chicago: Rand McNally, 1967), p. 24.

there has been very little *systematic* research on the concentration of authority or the extent of interlocking among top institutional elites.

"INTERLOCKERS" AND "SPECIALISTS"

Earlier we identified 7,314 top institutional positions in 12 different sectors of society which we defined as the nation's elite (see Chapter 1). Individuals in these positions control half of the nation's industrial and financial assets, nearly half of all the assets of private foundations, and over two thirds of the assets of private universities; they control the television networks, the news services, and leading newspapers; they control the most prestigious civic and cultural organizations; and they direct the activities of the executive, legislative, and judicial branches of the national government.

These 7,314 top positions were occupied by 5,778 individuals. In other words, there were fewer top individuals than top positions—indicating multiple holding of top positions by some individuals. Table 6-1 presents specific data on this phenomenon which we shall call *interlocking*.

Approximately 15 percent of those we identified as the nation's elite held more than one top position at a time. These are our "interlockers." Most of them held only two top positions, but some held six, seven, eight, or more! Eighty-five percent of the people at the top are "specialists"—individuals who hold only one top position. Many of these specialists hold other corporate directorships, governmental posts, or civic, cultural, or university positions, but not *top* positions as we have defined them. Thus, our "specialists" may assume a wide variety of lesser positions: director-ships in corporations below the top hundred; positions on governmental

Table 6-1   Interlocking and Specialization in Top Institutional Positions

	Number of top institutional positions	Percent of total positions	Number of indi-viduals in top positions	Percent of total individuals
Total	7,314	100.0	5,778	100.0
Specialized	4,981	68.1	4,911	85.0
Interlocked	2,333	31.9	867	15.0
Number of Interlocks:				
Two	1,046	14.3	520	9.0
Three	614	8.4	202	3.5
Four	278	3.8	69	1.2
Five	197	2.7	40	0.7
Six	110	1.5	17	0.3
Seven or more	88	1.2	11	0.2

boards and commissions; trusteeships of less well-known colleges and foundations; and directorships of less influential civic and cultural organizations. We will also observe that over a lifetime many of our specialists tend to hold a number of top positions, serially, rather than concurrently.

About 32 percent of all top *positions* are interlocked with other top positions. The reason that 32 percent of the top positions are interlocked, but only 15 percent of the top individuals hold more than one position, is that some individuals are "multiple interlockers"—they hold three or more positions.

The multiple interlockers turned out to be individuals of considerable stature, as the listing in Table 6–2 indicates. This list was compiled from extensive data collected and analyzed in 1980–81. These individuals comprised our top group of "multiple interlockers"—individuals occupying *six or more* top positions concurrently. By any criteria whatsoever, these individuals must be judged important figures in America. The fact that our investigation of positional overlap revealed such impressive names lends some face validity to the assertion that interlocking is a source of authority and power in society. However, despite the impressive concentration of interlocking authority in this top group, it should be remembered that most of the remaining 85 percent of top position-holders were "specialists."

Table 6–2   Multiple Interlockers in Top Institutional Positions, 1980

A. Robert Abboud. President, Occidental Petroleum. Former chairman of the board of First National Bank of Chicago; a director of Hart Schaffner & Marx, Inland Steel, Standard Oil of Indiana. A director of the Committee for Economic Development, a trustee of the University of Chicago, and member of the Council on Foreign Relations.

J. Paul Austin. Chairman of the board of Coca Cola Co. A director of Federated Department Stores, Morgan Guaranty Trust, General Electric, Trust Company of Georgia, Dow Jones & Co.

Thorton Bradshaw. Chairman of the board of RCA. Former president of Atlantic Richfield. A director of Security Pacific Corp., NBC, Los Angeles Philharmonic, Aspen Institute, American Petroleum Institute, and a trustee of Howard University.

Andrew F. Brimmer. President of Brimmer & Co. A director of BankAmerica, American Security Bank, International Harvester, United Airlines, DuPont Corp., the Trilateral Commission, Committee for Economic Development, the Ford Foundation, Urban League, the Council on Foreign Relations.

Ralph Manning Brown, Jr. Chairman of the board of New York Life Insurance Co. A director of Union Carbide, Morgan Guaranty Trust Co., A & P, and Avon Products. Is also a trustee of the Sloan Foundation, Princeton University, a director of the Metropolitan Museum of Art.

Edward W. Carter. Chairman of the board of Carter Hawley Hale Stores (including Nieman Marcus, Bergdorf, etc.). A director of AT&T, Del Monte, Lockheed Corp., Pacific Mutual Life Insurance, Southern California Edison, Western Bancorp. A trustee of Brookings Institution, Committee for Economic Development, Rockefeller University, Howard University.

Table 6–2 Multiple Interlockers in Top Institutional Positions, 1980 (Cont.)

Frank T. Cary. Chairman of the board of IBM. A director of J.P. Morgan & Co. and the American Broadcasting Company. A director of the Brookings Institution, Business Roundtable, and Committee for Economic Development.

Catherine B. Cleary. Former chairman of the board of First Wisconsin Corp. A Director of Northwestern Mutual Life Insurance, General Motors, Kohle Corp., Kraft.

William T. Coleman. Former Secretary of Transportation. Washington Attorney. A director of IBM, Chase Manhattan, Pepsi Co., American Can, Pan American World Airways, Philadelphia Electric. A trustee of The Brookings Institution and Harvard University, and a member of the Trilateral Commission and the Council on Foreign Relations.

John D. Debutts. Former chairman of the board of AT&T. A director of Citicorp, U.S. Steel, Kraft, General Motors, Hospital Corporation of America. A trustee of The Brookings Institution, Business Roundtable, Duke Endowment, and Duke University.

Clifton C. Garvin. Chairman of the board of Exxon. A director of Citicorp, Pepsi Co., Sperry Rand. Chairman of the Business Roundtable. A trustee of Committee for Economic Development, Sloan Kettering Institute for Career Research, Vanderbilt University.

J. Richardson Dilworth. Chairman of the board of the Rockefeller Center. A director of R.H. Macy & Co., Chase Manhattan, Chrysler. A trustee of colonial Williamsburg and Yale University.

Harry Jack Gray. Chairman of the board of United Technologies. A director of Exxon, Citicorp, Aetna Life & Casualty, Carrier Corp., Otis Elevator, Pratt & Whitney.

Fred L. Hartley. Chairman of the board of Union Oil Co. A director of Rockwell International, Union Bank, Daytona International Speedway. A trustee of Cal Tech., Pepperdine University, Council on Foreign Relations, and the Committee for Economic Development.

Gabriel Hauge. Former chairman of the board of Manufacturers Hanover Trust. A director of New York Life Insurance, Amax, N.Y. Telephone, Chrysler, Royal Dutch Petroleum. A trustee of the Committee for Economic Development and Juilliard School of Music.

Robert S. Hatfield. Chairman of the board of Continental Can. A director of Citicorp, Johnson & Johnson, New York Stock Exchange, Kennecott Copper, General Motors, Eastman Kodak. A director of the Business Roundtable and a trustee of the Committee for Economic Development and Cornell University.

Carla A. Hills. Former Secretary of Housing and Urban Development. Washington Attorney. A director of IBM, American Airlines, Signal Companies, Standard Oil of California. A trustee of The Brookings Institution and the University of Southern California.

George P. Jenkins. Chairman of the board of Metropolitan Life. A director of Citicorp, ABC, St. Regis Paper, Bethlehem Steel, W.R. Grace & Co., and a trustee of the University of Southern California.

Howard W. Johnson. Former president of M.I.T. A director of Federated Department Stores, John Hancock Mutual Life Insurance, DuPont Corp., Morgan Guaranty Trust, Champion International. A trustee of the Committee for Economic Development and Radcliffe College.

J. Paul Lyet. Chairman of the board of Sperry Rand Corp. A director of Armstrong Cork, Continental Can, Manufacturers Hanover Trust, Hershey Trust, Eastman Kodak, and a trustee of the University of Pennsylvania.

173

Table 6–2   Multiple Interlockers in Top Institutional Positions, 1980 (Cont.)

Lee L. Morgan. Chairman of the board of Caterpillar Tractor. A director of 3 M, Commercian National Bank, Mobil Oil.

Elmore C. Patterson. Former chairman of the board of Morgan Guaranty Trust. A director of General Motors, Bethlehem Steel, Acheson Topeka and Santa Fe Railroad, J.P. Morgan & Co., Standard Brands, and Comsat. A trustee of the Alfred P. Sloan Foundation, Memorial Sloan-Kettering Cancer Center, University of Chicago, and M.I.T.

Donald S. Perkins. Chairman of the board of Jewel Companies. A director of Time Inc., AT&T, Inland Steel, Corning Glass, Cummins Engine. A trustee of the Ford Foundation, the Business Roundtable, and The Brookings Institution.

Richard S. Perkins. Former chairman of the board of Citicorp. A director of Allied Chemical, New York Life, Southern Pacific, ITT, Hospital Corporation of America. A trustee of Chapin School, Miss Porter's School, and Metropolitan Museum of Art.

Peter G. Peterson. Chairman of the board of Lehman Brothers, Kuhn Loeb Inc. Former Secretary of Commerce. A director of RCA, Black & Decker, Cities Service, 3 M Co. General Foods, Federated Department Stores. A trustee of the Museum of Modern Art, Council on Foreign Relations, and the University of Chicago.

Edmund T. Pratt. Chairman of the board of IBM. A director of Chase Manhattan, International Paper Co., General Motors. A trustee of the Committee for Economic Development, Duke University.

David Rockefeller. Chairman of the board of Chase Manhattan Bank. Chairman of the Council on Foreign Relations. A trustee of the Rockefeller Foundation, the Museum of Modern Art, Rockefeller Center, Downtown Lower Manhattan Association, University of Chicago, and Howard University.

Robert V. Roosa. Senior partner, Brown Brothers, Harriman & Co. A director of American Express, Owens-Corning Fiberglass, Texaco. Chairman of The Brookings Institution. A trustee of the Rockefeller Foundation, Memorial Sloan-Kettering Cancer Center, and the National Bureau of Economic Research.

Irving Saul Shapiro. Chairman of the board of E.I. Dupont de Nemours & Co. A director of Citicorp, Bank of Delaware, IBM, Continental American Insurance. A director of the Business Roundtable and a trustee of the Conference Board, the University of Delaware, and the Ford Foundation.

Richard R. Shinn. Chairman of the board of Metropolitan Life Insurance. A director of Allied Chemical, Sperry Rand, Norton Simon. A director of the Business Roundtable and the Committee for Economic Development. A trustee of the Metropolitan Opera and University of Pennsylvania.

Rawleigh Warner. Chairman of the board of Mobil Oil. A director of Caterpillar Tractor, AT&T, Chemical Bank of New York, American Express, Wheelabrator. A trustee of Princeton University.

THE INNER GROUP: AN ELITE WITHIN THE ELITE

Let us label these multiple interlockers as the *inner group* of the nation's institutional leadership.[6] These individuals are only a small percentage of the total number of leaders who we identified, but they are in a unique position to communicate and coordinate the activities of a variety of institutions. The members of the inner group have significant "connections" with corporations, banks, media, cultural organizations, universities, foundations, and civic associations. The inner group is really a metaphor, and the boundary between it and other top leaders is not sharp. The individuals listed in Table 6–2 have *six* or more *top* institutional positions; they certainly can be thought of as the central core of the inner group. But we might also picture concentric rings surrounding the inner group—these persons with five, four, three, or two interlocking positions.

The existence of a "core elite," or an "elite within the elite," has been suggested by several social scientists.[7] However, there is no clear-cut definition of these terms. Our notion of an *inner group* involves not only multiple directorships of large corporate and financial institutions, but also the governance of large, influential foundations, universities, cultural organizations, and civic associations.

Members of the inner group are differentiated from other leaders in that their multiple position-holding encourages them to take a broader view of business problems. "They move from the industrial point of interest and outlook to the interest and outlook of the class of all big corporate property as a whole."[8] Indeed, members of the inner group cannot take narrow positions based upon the interests of a single firm, but instead they must consider the well-being of a wide range of American institutions.

Members of the inner group know each other socially. They come together not only in multiple corporate boardrooms, but also at cultural and civic events, charitable endeavors, foundation meetings, and university trustee and alumni get-togethers. They are also members of the same exclusive social clubs—the Links, Century, Knickerbocker, Burning Tree, Metropolitan, Pacific Union.

Most importantly, the inner group plays a major role in linking the

---

[6]Maurice Zeitlin, "Corporate Ownership and Control," *American Journal of Sociology*, 79 (September 1974), pp. 1073–1119; Michael Patrick Allen, "Continuity and Change Within the Core Corporate Elite," *Sociological Quarterly*, 19 (Autumn 1978), pp. 510–521.

[7]W. Lloyd Warner and James D. Abegglen, *Big Business Leaders in America* (New York: Harper, 1955) pp. 000; Michael Patrick Allen, "Continuity and Change Within the Core Corporate Elite," *Sociological Quarterly*, 19 (Autumn 1978), pp. 510–521.

[8]C. Wright Mills, *The Power Elite*, p. 121.

corporate world with government, foundations, universities, cultural organizations, and civic associations. Members of the inner group are highly valued and generally preferred as members, advisers, and trustees of government and non-profit organizations. "The multiple corporate connections place inner group members in an exceptionally good position to help mobilize the resources of many firms on behalf of policies they favor—and institutions whose governance they assist—making inner group members preferable to other businessmen when appointments to positions of governance are decided."[9] Indeed, it turns out that multiple corporate directors have a participation rate in government and non-profit organizations which is more than twice the participation rate of single directors ("specialists").[10]

IS POWER BECOMING MORE CONCENTRATED OVER TIME?

There is conflicting evidence over whether or not power is becoming more concentrated or more dispersed over time. Certainly over the long run— since 1900—the growth of the modern corporation and government bureaucracy has ensured that large institutions dominate both private and public life. But over the short run—since 1970—it is difficult to determine whether the largest institutions are increasing their share of the nation's assets and whether fewer individuals are exercising control over these assets.

If we consider *industrial* assets only, our own figures show that the top 100 corporations held 52.3 percent of all industrial assets in 1970 and 55.0 percent in 1980. This modest increase over ten years suggests increasing concentration of assets among industrial corporations. However, the *federal government's* share of the gross national product has remained fairly constant at about 22 percent between 1970 and 1980. Finally, it must be noted that the top 50 *banks* held 65.6 percent of all banking assets in 1970 but only 61.4 percent in 1980, a modest decline.

Interlocking of directorates appears to have declined modestly over the last ten years. In 1970, we estimated that about 20 percent of all top leaders were "interlockers." In 1980, our estimate is only 15 percent. While the two samples are not exactly comparable (1980 is larger), we believe that this modest decline in interlocking is "real," and not merely a product of

[9]Michael Useem, "The Social Organization of the American Business Elite," *American Sociological Review*, 49 (August 1979), p. 557.

[10]*Ibid.*

methodology.[11] Over time, increasing proportions of top leaders are "specialists."

PREVIOUS INSTITUTIONAL EXPERIENCE
OF INDIVIDUALS AT THE TOP

How many positions of authority in all types of institutions have top leaders *ever held* in a lifetime? We carefully reviewed the biographies of our top position-holders to see how many authoritative positions—president, director, trustee, and so on—were ever held by these men. The record of leadership of an average top official turned out to be truly impressive. The average corporate leader held 10.5 positions in a lifetime; the average foundation trustee, 10.2; the average civic group leader, 11.4; the average governmental leader, 8.0 (see Table 6–3). Of course, these positions are not all in *top-ranked* institutions. But it is clear that top leaders occupy a number of institutional positions in their lifetime.

This impressive record of position-holding is found among leaders in all sectors of society. (The only exception is military leaders, whose experience is generally limited to the military itself.) Table 6–3 shows the average number of authoritative positions ever held by top leaders in each sector of society. Leaders in government have held somewhat fewer top positions in their lifetime than leaders in the corporate world, but nonetheless their record of leadership experience is impressive. However, governmental leaders tended to gain their experience in *governmental* or *public interest* positions—over 70 percent of governmental leaders had held previous governmental posts and had held posts in the public interest sector. Only about one quarter of top governmental elites had previously held any top positions in the corporate world.

The tradition of public service is very much alive among top institutional leaders in every sector. Both corporate and governmental elites reported one or more public appointments during their lifetime. Nearly 40 percent of corporate elites held at least one government post at some time during their careers.

As we might expect, corporate directorships are common among top leaders in industry, communications, utilities, and banking. It is common for these individuals to have held four or more directorships in a lifetime.

---

[11]However, for evidence that interlocking among all corporations remained fairly constant from 1935 to 1970, see Michael Patrick Allen, "The Structure of Interorganizational Elite Corporation: Interlocking Corporate Directorates," *American Sociological Review,* 39 (June 1974), pp. 393–406.

Table 6–3 Institutional Experience of Top Leaders

	Corporate					Public Interest					Government		All
	Industry	Banking	Utilities	Insur.	Invest.	Media	Law	Found.	Education	Civic	Government	Mil.	
Average Number of Positions Ever Held:													
Total	10.5	6.6	10.9	9.1	4.6	7.1	7.9	10.2	7.9	11.4	8.0	1.0	9.3
Corporate	5.9	4.1	6.0	5.1	3.1	2.1	2.0	5.2	3.2	6.0	1.0	.0	5.2
Public Interest	3.8	2.0	3.9	3.1	1.2	3.8	4.2	4.0	3.8	4.2	3.8	0.8	3.1
Governmental	.8	.5	1.0	.9	.3	1.2	1.7	1.0	.9	1.2	3.2	0.2	1.0
Percent Having Ever Held Positions in:													
Corporate	99.8	88.8	99.6	86.5	72.4	48.1	46.8	96.2	76.2	98.6	25.2	.0	80.2
Public Interest	76.9	59.0	72.5	69.1	59.6	76.5	80.2	88.0	70.8	82.2	72.2	38.6	78.4
Governmental	39.2	24.8	40.6	38.0	19.2	40.2	56.5	45.1	42.5	58.6	76.6	14.5	42.3

In contrast, top government officials have *not* held many corporate directorships. Their experience in institutional positions is derived mainly from public service and government.

AT&T AND ITS FRIENDS:
CONVERGENCE AT THE TOP

Our aggregate data indicate that a majority of the people at the top are specialists, that corporate and governmental elites are not closely locked, and that there appear to be multiple, differentiated structures of power in America. Earlier we suggested that many corporate, governmental, and public-interest leaders were self-made managerial elites rather than "inheritors" who started at the top. All of these findings tend to undermine confidence in the hierarchical model, at least as it is represented in the traditional power elite literature.

Nonetheless, there are important concentrations of combined corporate, governmental, and social power in America. The best evidence of concentration is found in interlocking directorates of major corporations. Figure 6–1 is our own diagram of the interlocking of AT&T directors with industrial corporations, banks, and insurance companies in 1980. We are fortunate that AT&T publically lists what it calls its "principal corporate affiliations."[12] Most corporations do *not* publish such information.

It might be possible to greatly expand Figure 6–1 and observe all of the corporate interlocks of corporations that interlock with AT&T. We might observe "indirect" interlocking of AT&T with any corporation that has an interlocking board member with any of the corporations in Figure 6–1. An "indirect" interlock does not mean that a director serves on two boards (this is a direct interlock); it means instead that a director of one corporation and a director of another both belong to the board of a third corporation. For example, AT&T and IBM are competitors in satellite communications. The AT&T and IBM boards are *not* interlocked. However, an AT&T director and an IBM director may meet on the board of an oil company. Is this evidence of collusion? Probably not. It requires "a touch of paranoia" to believe that "indirect" interlocks can create a concentration of power that would threaten the corporate structure.

The pattern of interlocking directorates with AT&T is illustrative of relationships and interests in the boardrooms of major corporations. AT&T, like many other giant corporations, has direct contacts with a wide variety of industrial corporations—oil, autos, steel, retail stores, foods, clothing, publishing, and so on—as well as banks and insurance companies.

---

[12]*Moody's Public Utility Manual.*

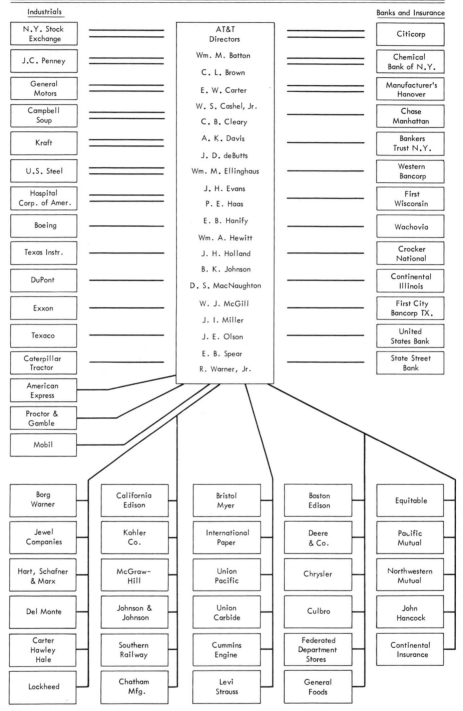

Figure 6–1   AT&T and its Friends.

Each line represents an interlocking directorship with AT&T in 1980. A double line represents two interlocks with AT&T. Board members for 1980 are listed.

These boardroom contacts provide AT&T with information about their business and financial environment and permit the corporation to coordinate its activities with the activities of other large institutions.

In 1982, AT&T settled a long-standing anti-trust suit with the U.S. Justice Department by agreeing to divest itself of ownership of twenty-two telephone companies.[13] These companies provide the basic telephone service to the nation's homes, factories, schools, and offices. They represent $87 billion in assets—two-thirds of AT&T's total assets. In the future AT&T will concentrate on long distance service, communication equipment made by its subsidiary, Western Electric; research and development in Bell Laboratories; and new high-technology enterprise in electronics and computers.

DAVID ROCKEFELLER:
THE VIEW FROM CHASE MANHATTAN

Certainly no better illustration of convergence of power can be found than the Rockefeller network of industrial, financial, political, civic, and cultural institutions, headed by David Rockefeller of the Chase Manhattan Bank.

The Rockefeller family fortune was founded by John D. Rockefeller, originator of the Standard Oil Company. With his partners, H.M. Flagler and S.V. Harkness, Rockefeller created the company that controlled 90 percent of the nation's oil production by the 1880s. A series of antitrust cases, culminating in the Supreme Court in *U.S.* v. *Standard Oil* (1911), resulted in the forced dissolution of the company into several separate corporations: Exxon, formerly Standard Oil of New Jersey (the nation's number-one-ranked industrial corporation), Standard Oil of California (ranked number 7), Standard Oil of Indiana (ranked number 9), Standard Oil of Ohio (ranked number 18), Atlantic Richfield (ranked number 13), Mobil Oil (ranked number 3), and the Marathon Oil Company (ranked number 50).[14] The best available evidence suggests that the Rockefeller family continues to hold large blocks of stock in each of these companies.[15] But the key to Rockefeller power today is no longer the oil industry, however impressive the holdings in this industry may be. The center of Rockefeller power is banking and finance.

---

[13]Pacific Tel., Southwest Bell, N.Y. Tel., Southern Bell, South Central Bell, Mountain States, Illinois Bell, New England Tel., Bell of Penn., Northwestern Bell, Michigan Bell, New Jersey Bell, Pac. NW Bell, Ohio Bell, Ches & Pot. Va., Ches, & Pot. Md., Indiana Bell, Wisconsin Bell, Ches & Pot. W. Va., C&P Wash. D.C., Diamond State Tel., Bell of Nevada.

[14]See Table 2–1 for rankings.

[15]House of Representatives, Banking and Currency Committee, Tax-Exempt Foundations (Washington, DC: Government Printing Office, 1968).

The core financial institution of the Rockefeller family is Chase Manhattan Bank, which David Rockefeller supervised for nearly thirty years. However, the family is also interested in Citicorp, which was headed for many years by James Stillman Rockefeller, a cousin of David's.

The Rockefeller financial influence in corporate decision-making is felt in several ways: by giving or withholding loans to corporations, by placing representatives on corporate boards of directors, and by owning or controlling blocks of common stock of corporations. Chase Manhattan directors (there are 25 of them) are interlocked with over 100 major industrial corporations, banks, utilities, and insurance companies. These include giants such as Exxon, AT&T, ITT, Metropolitan Life, Equitable Life, and United States Steel. In addition, Chase Manhattan owns or holds in trust over 5 percent of the corporate stock of many other large companies, including Eastern Airlines, Pan American World Airways, Boeing, TWA, Mobil Oil, Sperry Rand, ABC, and CBS. The rules of the Securities and Exchange Commission presume that 5 percent of a corporation's stock can give the holder dominant influence in the corporation.

Corporations are dependent upon bank loans for capital expansion. Often the banks dictate specific aspects of corporate policy as a condition of granting a loan (in the same fashion that federal agencies often dictate policies of state and local governments as a condition of receiving federal grants-in-aid). Frequently, banks will also require corporations that borrow money to appoint bank officers or directors to the boards of the corporation. This allows the bank to continuously oversee the activities of the debtor corporation. Finally, the trust departments of major banks hold large blocks of common stock of industrial corporations on behalf of individuals, pension funds, and investment companies. Generally, the banks vote the shares held in trust in corporate elections.

The Rockefeller interest in foreign affairs is particularly strong. The oil companies, which have long been the industrial core of Rockefeller holdings, require constant attention to foreign sources of supply. In addition, Chase Manhattan is deeply involved in overseas banking and investment activities. The Rockefellers have supplied many of the top foreign affairs personnel for the nation, including Secretaries of State John Foster Dulles, Dean Rusk, and Henry Kissinger. Dulles, Secretary of State under President Eisenhower, was a senior partner in the Wall Street law firm of Sullivan & Cromwell, whose principal client for many years was Standard Oil Company (Exxon). Dulles was also chairman of the trustees of the Rockefeller Foundation. Dean Rusk, Secretary of State under Presidents Kennedy and Johnson, served seven years as president of the Rockefeller Foundation. John J. McCloy, a Chase Manhattan director, served as U.S. High Commissioner for Germany during the post-war occupation; in 1962, he was chairman of the Coordinating Committee on the Cuban Missile Crisis. Henry Kissinger was director of the Rockefeller Brothers Special Studies Project, and personal adviser on foreign policy to Nelson Rockefeller before becoming special assistant for national security affairs and later Secretary of State under President Richard Nixon. Cyrus Vance, Secretary of State under President Carter, was a Wall Street lawyer and a director of the Rockefeller Foundation, as well as Pan American World Airlines, Aetna Life Insurance, and IBM. Zbigniew Brzezinski, President Carter's National Security Adviser, was director of the Trilateral Commission—David Rockefeller's influential group of top leaders from industrialized nations of the world. Secretary of State Alexander Haig was Deputy National Security Adviser under Henry Kissinger. David Rockefeller himself serves as chairman of the influential Council on Foreign Relations, which is responsible for many of the nation's most important foreign policy initiatives (see the section "The Policy-Planning Establishment" in Chapter 9).

The single most powerful private citizen in America today is David Rockefeller,—"the only man for whom the presidency of the United States would be a step down." David Rockefeller is the youngest of five sons of John D. Rockefeller, Jr., himself the only son of the founder of the Rockefeller empire, John D. Rockefeller. Despite the seniority of his brothers,[16] it was recognized that David was the serious and scholarly one. It was to David that the family wisely entrusted more of its wealth; this is the really convincing evidence of his recognized leadership.

David was raised with his brothers at the Rockefeller's 3,500-acre Pocantico Hills estate, east of Tarrytown, New York. He attended nearby Lincoln School. His early interest in art continues today. As a child, he traveled about to Rockefeller holdings—the Seal Harbor, Maine retreat, the Virgin Islands estate, the Venezuela ranch, the Grand Teton Mountains ranch—and collected beetles as a hobby. It soon became clear to David's father and grandfather that Nelson, Lawrence, and Winthrop were more interested in politics and pleasure than hard work, and that John D. III was content to pursue cultural interests. The elder Rockefellers wanted a businessman to care for the family fortune, and they were successful in motivating David in this direction.

David's undergraduate career at Harvard was undistinguished. But later he spent a year at the Harvard Graduate School of Business and a year at the London School of Economics. He married Margaret "Peggy" McGrath, whose father was a senior partner in the esteemed Wall Street

---

[16]John D. III (deceased), former chairman of the Rockefeller Foundation and the Lincoln Center for the Performing Arts; Nelson A. (deceased), former vice-president of the United States and four-term governor of New York; Lawrence S., family dilettante in "venture capitalism" and "conservationist"; and Winthrop (deceased), former governor of Arkansas and cattle rancher.

law firm of Cadwalader, Wickersham & Taft. He enrolled at the Rockefeller-funded University of Chicago and *earned* a Ph.D. in economics in 1940. He returned to New York for a short stint in public service as an unpaid assistant to Mayor Fiorello La Guardia. In 1942 he enlisted in the Army as a private, went through Officers Training School, and served in North Africa and Europe as an intelligence officer. He speaks French, Spanish, and German.

After the war he began his banking career in his uncle Winthrop W. Aldrich's bank, the Chase Manhattan. His first post was assistant manager of the foreign department; three years later he became vice-president and director of the bank's business in Latin America. When his uncle became ambassador to England in 1952, David became successively executive vice-president, vice-chairman of the board, and finally, president and chairman of the board.

Of course, David Rockefeller is active in civic and cultural affairs. He is, or has been, chairman of the Museum of Modern Art, president of the Board of Overseas Study of Harvard University, a trustee of the Carnegie Endowment for International Peace, a trustee of the University of Chicago, a trustee of the John F. Kennedy Library, and so forth.

Above all, David Rockefeller is an internationalist. His active intervention in American foreign policy has produced remarkable results. He was personally involved in Nixon's arrangement of detente with the USSR, the Strategic Arms Limitations Talks (SALT), and the "normalization" of U.S. relations with the mainland Peoples Republic of China. He is chairman of the board of the Council on Foreign Relations, and he formed the Trilateral Commission in 1972. Through the CFR, Rockefeller has been instrumental in most of the nation's important foreign policy initiatives of recent years: from the Paris Peace Agreement ending the Vietnam War, through "detente" with the Soviet Union and the international "human rights" campaign, to new concerns over U.S.–Soviet relations in the 1980s. David Rockefeller was personally involved in the decision to permit the Shah of Iran to come to the U.S. for medical treatment, the decision not to hand over the dying Shah to ransom the U.S. hostages, and the financial agreement that finally secured the release of the hostages.

Under David Rockefeller's direction, Chase Manhattan developed a reputation in the business world for "social responsibility" which included the active recruitment and promotion of blacks, women, and other minorities; granting a large number of loans to minority-owned business enterprises; and active involvement in a variety of social projects. Indeed, this may be one reason why Chase Manhattan has fallen behind Bank-America and Citicorp as the nation's leading banks. Another reason for Chase's performance may be that David Rockefeller is so deeply involved in national and international affairs that he did not devote full attention to banking matters.

Rockefeller himself believes that his own power, and the power of business and financial institutions, is limited by public opinion:

> I don't believe a bank such as ours, for example, could long fly in the face of welfare consideration—welfare in the broader sense—without having major problems with Congress and with all kinds of groups in our society who would resent us and would do their best to take steps to force us to act differently.[17]

But Rockefeller's liberal concern for "doing good" is constrained by his institutional responsibilities in a capitalist system, and he recognizes this fact:

> I don't think one has to go to extremes. We don't feel that we can do everything for the community that we'd like to, nor do we feel it's wise to go all out 100 percent for the highest profits disregarding the best interests of the community. We have to find some kind of middle ground. We're very much bottom-line conscious,[18] but we also feel we have responsibilities to the community.[19]

David Rockefeller exercises great power, with *modesty,* of course, as one would expect of a man who has no reason to try to impress anyone. Indeed, he consistently understates his own power:

> I feel uncomfortable when you ask how I exert power. We accomplish things through cooperative action, which is quite different than exerting power in some mysterious and presumably evil way. I have no power in the sense that I can call anybody in the government and tell them what to do. Because of my position, I'm more apt to get through on the telephone than somebody else, but what happens to what I suggest depends on whether they feel this makes sense in terms of what they are already doing.[20]

David Rockefeller's own views on power tend to reinforce the importance of achieving consensus among separate groups of leaders. In commenting on the redevelopment of downtown New York City— Rockefeller Plaza and the World Trade Center—Rockefeller characteristically sees himself as a *catalyst* rather than as a *chieftain:*

> If you are interested in the analysis of power [says Rockefeller], I would think this is somewhat relevant: I'm not sure it is the power of an individual or even an institution, but more the power of cooperation and ideas....

[17]The Dilemma of Corporate Responsibility and Maximum Profits: An Interview with David Rockefeller," *Business and Society Review,* Spring 1974, p. 10.

[18]A businessman's phrase meaning concern with whether the last line on a quarterly or annual financial account shows a profit or loss. [Footnote added.]

[19]"The Dilemma of Corporate Responsibility," p. 11.

[20]"Beyond Wealth, What?" *Forbes,* May 15, 1972, pp. 250–252.

...We got the community and government working together in the development of a plan that was of common interest to all parties involved. This isn't so much power; it is organization, coordination, cooperation. The reason we could do this is this group exists. The city couldn't have pulled this thing off by itself. Certainly neither could we. But working together, we could.

I didn't do this thing myself; this is a joint undertaking where I have been to some extent the catalyst in the sense of bringing others together, and I certainly served as chairman of the committee, but the strength of it is the unity and sense of cooperation.[21]

Of course, what Rockefeller is really saying is that when David Rockefeller is calling, people answer their phone; when he asks them to serve on a committee, they are flattered to be asked; when he suggests that they do something, they do it.

In 1981, David Rockefeller retired as chairman of the board of Chase Manhattan and turned over control to his hand-picked successor, Willard Butcher. It is likely that David Rockefeller will retain dominant influence in the bank; the Rockefeller family continues to hold a controlling block of stock in Chase Manhattan. Moreover, David Rockefeller vows to retain his interest in international affairs. He named himself as the new chairman of Chase's international advisory board, replacing his old friend Henry Kissinger. And Rockefeller continues to defend his international activism:

"Looking back, it seems clear to me that one of the strengths I have contributed to the bank is its international expansion, without which we would not be in the strong position we are today. Every time I saw some prominent figure around the world, I'd get my picture in the paper. But the hours I spent working for the future of the bank were not very well publicized.[22]

EVIDENCE OF POLYARCHY:
INTERLOCKING CORPORATE GROUPS

The Rockefeller story is suggestive of concentration of industrial, financial, governmental, and social power. Yet there is also considerable evidence of "polyarchy"—multiple, differentiated groupings of corporate power. This evidence can be gleaned from close observation of the network of interlocking directorates in corporate America. Recent advances in the application of statistical methods allow us to observe some interesting

---

[21]*Ibid.*, pp. 251–252.
[22]Quote from Jack Egan, "The Money Men," *New York*, December 1, 1980, p. 36.

groupings of corporate interlocks.[23] These groupings suggest the existence of a series of corporate groupings—industries, banks, utilities, and insurance companies—centered around distinct *geographic* areas.

Ten major interlocking groupings are identified in Table 6–4. These groupings, systematically described by sociologist Michael Patrick Allen,[24] indicate the most heavily interlocked groupings, the location of each corporation, the total number of interlocks each corporation maintains with other corporations, and the number of interlocks it maintains with corporations within its own grouping.

Table 6–4   Ten Principal Interlock Groups

GN	Corporation	IC	Location	PCS	TI	GI
1	Chemical New York	B	New York	5.3	47	12
	New York Life	L	New York	5.0	32	8
	Consolidated Edison	U	New York	5.0	22	11
	Southern Pacific	T	San Fran	2.8	24	4
	Equitable Life Assurance	L	New York	2.7	41	6
	Borden	I	New York	2.5	12	5
2	Continental Illinois	B	Chicago	5.2	29	15
	International Harvester	I	Chicago	4.8	22	11
	Commonwealth Edison	U	Chicago	4.0	12	10
	First Chicago Corp.	B	Chicago	3.5	25	11
	Sears Roebuck	R	Chicago	2.8	18	5
	Standard Oil (Indiana)	I	Chicago	2.6	11	6
	Inland Steel	I	Chicago	2.6	10	6
	Illinois Central, Inc.	I	Chicago	2.6	18	5
	Borg-Warner	I	Chicago	2.1	10	5
3	Mellon National Bank	B	Pittsburgh	5.6	30	14
	Gulf Oil	I	Pittsburgh	5.4	11	10
	Aluminum Co. of America	I	Pittsburgh	4.3	10	6
	Pittsburgh Plate Glass, Inc.	I	Pittsburgh	3.4	7	6
	Westinghouse Electric	I	Pittsburgh	2.5	19	4
4	Morgan Guaranty Bank	B	New York	5.1	38	11
	General Electric	I	New York	3.2	26	7
	General Motors	I	Detroit	2.8	27	5
	Continental Oil	I	New York	2.5	20	4
	Scott Paper	I	Philadelphia	2.5	12	4
	U.S. Steel	I	New York	2.0	27	3
	Procter & Gamble	I	Cincinnati	2.0	18	4

[23]A variation of factor analysis applied to sociometric data permits the extraction of a matrix of relationships based on interlocking among corporations. The matrix systematically identifies relatively independent and cohesive cliques. See Duncan MacRae, Jr., "Direct Factor Analysis of Sociometric Data," *Sociometry*, 23 (1960), pp. 360–371; also Philip M. Lankforth, "Comparative Analysis of Clique Identification Methods," *Sociometry*, 37 (1974), pp. 287–305.

[24]Michael Patrick Allen, "Economic Interest Groups and the Corporate Elite Structure," *Social Science Quarterly*, 58 (March 1978), pp. 597–615.

Table 6–4   Ten Principal Interlock Groups (Cont.)

GN	Corporation	IC	Location	PCS	TI	GI
5	Citicorp	B	New York	4.6	51	11
	Monsanto	I	St. Louis	2.6	13	6
	National Cash Register	I	Cleveland	2.6	17	5
	Westinghouse Electric	I	Pittsburgh	2.4	19	3
	Kimberly-Clark	I	Milwaukee	2.2	7	5
	Pan-American World Airways	T	New York	2.1	22	4
	AT&T	U	New York	2.0	33	2
6	Republic Steel	I	Cleveland	5.2	21	13
	Avco	I	Greenwich	4.1	13	10
	Metropolitan Life	L	New York	2.8	39	7
	Standard Oil (Ohio)	I	Cleveland	2.7	9	4
	Chemical New York	B	New York	2.6	47	7
	International Business Machines	I	Armonk	2.2	25	7
	Illinois Central, Inc.	I	Chicago	2.1	18	6
	Olin	I	Stamford	2.0	9	6
7	Chase Manhattan	B	New York	4.8	37	9
	General Foods	I	New York	2.8	20	5
	Metropolitan Life	L	New York	2.6	39	5
	International Paper	I	New York	2.1	15	5
	AT&T	U	New York	2.0	33	4
8	Western Bancorporation	B	Los Angeles	4.1	19	6
	Southern California Edison	U	Los Angeles	3.4	11	9
	Union Oil of California	I	Los Angeles	3.2	18	6
	BankAmerica	B	San Francisco	2.8	17	5
	North American Rockwell	I	Los Angeles	2.7	13	6
	Security Pacific National Bank	B	Los Angeles	2.5	13	5
	Getty Oil	I	Los Angeles	2.0	14	5
9	Pennsylvania Mutual	L	Philadelphia	5.1	21	12
	First Pennsylvania	B	Philadelphia	4.1	11	7
	Girard	B	Philadelphia	3.2	8	6
	Philadelphia Electric	U	Philadelphia	3.2	10	8
	Philadelphia National Bank	B	Philadelphia	2.6	7	5
	Atlantic Richfield	I	New York	2.4	15	4
10	National Bank of Detroit	B	Detroit	4.7	21	10
	Burroughs	I	Detroit	2.8	8	6
	Detroit Edison	U	Detroit	2.8	10	4
	National Steel	I	Detroit	2.5	10	4
	Bendix	I	Detroit	2.2	7	4
	S.S. Kresge	R	Detroit	2.2	7	4

Legend   GN = Group Number   U = Utility
           IC = Industry Code   T = Transportation
           PCS = Principal Component Score   R = Retailing
           TI = Total Interlocks   B = Banking
           GI = Group Interlocks   L = Life Insurance
           I   = Industrial

Source: Michael Patrick Allen, "Economic Interest Groups and the Corporate Elite Structure," *Social Science Quarterly*, 58 (March 1978), pp. 608–609.

There is an obvious tendency for corporations to maintain interlocks with other corporations in the same geographic area, even though many New York based corporations occur across the board. Five interlocking groups involve corporations based primarily in Chicago, Pittsburgh, Los Angeles, Philadelphia, and Detroit. Four others are based primarily in New York. This finding, generally supportive of the polyarchical model of corporate power, suggests that geography rather than financial or family interests plays a major role in creating concentrations of corporate power.

However, another way of identifying the interlocking corporate groups in Table 6–4 would be by the major banks which provide the largest number of interlocking directors within each group. The banks which appear to lead corporate groupings include Citicorp, Chase Manhattan, Mellon, Morgan Guaranty, Chemical New York, Continental Illinois, Western Bancorp, and the National Bank of Detroit.

Thus, the systematic analysis of corporate interlocking suggests (1) multiple concentrations of financial and industrial power, (2) based in part upon geographic proximity, and (3) dominated by large commercial banks.

SUMMARY

The question of hierarchy versus polyarchy in America's elite structure is a familiar one in the literature on power. The "elitist" literature describes a convergence of power at the top, with a single group of leaders recruited primarily from industry and finance, exercising power in many different sectors of society. The "pluralist" literature describes many separate structures of power in different sectors of society with little or no overlap in authority and many separate channels of recruitment.

Our findings do not all fit neatly into either the elitist or the pluralist leadership model. The fact that roughly 7,000 persons in 6,000 positions exercise formal authority over institutions that control over half of the nation's resources is itself an indication of a great concentration of power. But despite institutional concentration of authority, there is considerable specialization among these 7,000 leaders. Eighty-five percent of them hold only one "top" position. Only 15 percent are "interlockers"—holders of two or more top positions. However, because of "multiple interlockers," about 30 percent of all top positions were found interlocked with another top position. Moreover, the top multiple interlockers (those people with six or more top positions) turned out to be impressive figures in America, lending support to the notion of an "inner group" of national leaders.

There is very little overlap among people at the top of the corporate, governmental, and military sectors of society. To the extent that high government officials are interlocked at all, it is with civic and cultural and educational institutions. It is *within* the corporate sector that interlocking is most prevalent. If there is a "coming together" of corporate, governmental, and military elites as C. Wright Mills contends, it does not appear to be by means of interlocking directorates.

The notion of hierarchy is strengthened, however, if we examine the record of leadership experience of top institutional elites *over a lifetime.* Most top leaders have held more than one top position in their career. Governmental leaders, however, have generally gained their leadership experience in governmental positions or in the law; only one quarter of top governmental leaders have ever held high positions in the corporate world.

These aggregate figures suggest specialization rather than convergence at the top of the nation's institutional structure. However, we agree that there are special cases of concentrated corporate, governmental, and social power. AT&T, for example, is linked through its board of directors to a wide variety of manufacturing companies, as well as to banks and insurance companies. Moreover, the Rockefeller family, through its dominance of Chase Manhattan bank and its family holdings in many large corporations, utilities, and insurance companies, together with its activities in cultural organizations, universities, foundations, and civic associations, represents a very important concentration of power. Nonetheless, there is also evidence of polyarchy in identifiable groupings of corporations with extensive interlocking directorates. These groupings each appear to be geographically defined yet dominated by large banks.

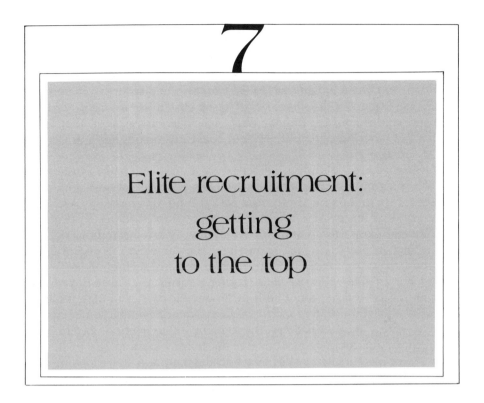

7

Elite recruitment: getting to the top

A RULING CLASS OR AN OPEN LEADERSHIP SYSTEM?

Are there opportunities to rise to the top of the institutional structure of America for individuals from all classes, races, religions, and ethnic groups, through multiple career paths in different sectors of society? Or are opportunities for entry into top circles limited to white, Anglo-Saxon Protestant, upper- and upper-middle-class individuals whose careers are based primarily in industry and finance?

Social scientists have studied data on the social backgrounds of corporate and governmental leaders for many years. But there is still disagreement on the interpretation of the data. A "ruling class" school of thought stresses the fact that elites in America are drawn disproportionately from among wealthy, educated, "well-employed," socially prominent, "WASP" groups in society. These "ruling class" social scientists are impressed with the fact that leadership in industry, finance, government, education, the law, the mass media, and other institutional sectors is recruited primarily from society's upper social classes. Many of the elite have been educated at a few esteemed private prep schools and gone to Ivy League colleges and universities. They have joined the same private clubs, and their families have intermarried. Moreover, a disproportionate share of the top leadership in all sectors of society has made its career mark in industry and finance. "Ruling class" social scientists infer that these similarities contribute to cohesion and consensus among the institutional leaders in America.

By contrast, "pluralists" describe an open leadership system that enables a significant number of individuals from the middle and lower classes to rise to the top. High social background, or wealth, or WASPishness *itself* does not provide access to top leadership positions. Instead, top institutional posts go to individuals who possess outstanding skills of leadership, information, and knowledge, and the ability to organize and communicate. Admittedly, opportunities to acquire such qualities for top leadership are unequally distributed among classes. But lower-class origin, the "pluralists" believe, is not an insurmountable barrier to high position.

Classical elitist writers such as Mosca acknowledge that some "circulation of elites" is essential for the stability of a political system. The opportunity for the brightest among the lower classes to rise to the top siphons off potentially revolutionary leadership, and the elite system is actually strengthened when talented and ambitious individuals enter top positions. The fact that only a minority of top leaders are drawn from the lower classes is not really important. It is the availability of a modicum of opportunity that encourages talented people to believe they can rise to the top and strengthens support for the system throughout all social classes.

Defenders of the pluralist theory also argue that social background, educational experience, and social group membership are poor predictors of decision-making behavior. Members of the social elite often hold very different views about policy questions, differences that can be attributed to a variety of factors, all of which are more influential than social background. Among these are the nature of the top position occupied; the individual's perception of his or her own role; the institutional constraints placed upon the individual; systems of public accountability; interest-group pressures; public opinion; and so forth. Thus, pluralists argue that the class homogeneity among top leaders that is reported in many social background studies is meaningless, since the class background-decision-making behavior linkage is weak.

In contrast, the evidence of social class influence on behavior is truly impressive.[1] Social scientists have shown that social background affects

---

[1] The following evidence was compiled from the numerous sources cited by psychologist Richard L. Zweigenhart, "Who Represents America?" *The Insurgent Socialist,* 5 (No. 3), p. 119.

whether or not you shoplift[2] or use LSD.[3] It has an important influence on whom you date and marry,[4] how happy your marriage is likely to be,[5] how you vote,[6] how many children you have,[7] and how you go about raising them.[8] It largely determines your values,[9] how happy you are,[10] and how long you're likely to live.[11] It can even influence how large you think the circumference of a quarter is![12] In our opinion, it would be most unlikely that social class membership could affect all these varied attitudes and behaviors and *not* affect decision-making behavior.

The recruitment of some non-upper-class individuals to elite positions may be essential to society, because these individuals bring new and different perspectives to societal problems. Sociologist Suzanne Keller speaks of "two irreconcilable tendencies in social life—the need for order and the need for change":

> If the social leadership becomes so conservative as to be immune to new ideas and social developments, the pressure for unfulfilled needs mounts until that leadership declines, resigns, or is violently displaced. If it is so receptive to the new as to neglect established traditions, social continuity is endangered.[13]

[2]George Won and George Yamamoto, "Social Structure and Deviant Behavior: A Study of Shoplifting," *Sociology and Social Research*, 53, No. 1 (1968), pp. 44–45.

[3]Reginald G. Smart and Dianne Fejer, "Illicit LSD Users: Their Social Backgrounds, Drug Use and Psychopathology," *Journal of Health and Social Behavior*, 10, No. 4 (1969), pp. 297–308.

[4]A. B. Hollingshead, *Elmtown's Youth: The Impact of Social Classes on Adolescents* (New York: John Wiley & Sons, Inc., 1949).

[5]William J. Goode, "Marital Satisfaction and Instability: A Cross-Cultural Class Analysis of Divorce Rates," *International Social Science Journal*, 14, No. 3 (1962), pp. 507–526.

[6]P. F. Lazarsfeld, B. Berelson, and H. Caudit, *The People's Choice*, (New York: Columbia University Press, 1948). Also G. J. Selznick and Stephen Steinberg, "Social Class, Ideology, and Voting Preferences: An Analysis of the 1964 Presidential Election," in *Structural Social Inequality: A Reader in Comparative Social Stratification*, ed. Celia S. Heller (New York: Macmillan, 1969).

[7]Dennis H. Wrong, "Trends in Class Fertility in Western Nations," *The Canadian Journal of Economics and Political Science*, 24, No. 2 (May 1958), pp. 216–229.

[8]R. R. Scars, E. MacCoby, and H. Levin, *Patterns of Child Rearing* (New York: Harper & Row, 1957).

[9]Herbert H. Hyman, "The Value Systems of Different Classes: A Social Psychological Contribution to the Analysis of Stratification," in *Readings on Social Stratification*, ed. Melvin M. Tumin (Englewood Cliffs, N.J.: Prentice-Hall, Inc., 1970), pp. 186–203.

[10]Alex Inkeles, "Class and Happiness," in Tumin, *Readings on Social Stratification*, pp. 180–186.

[11]I.M. Moriyama and L. Guralnick, "Occupational and Social Class Differences in Mortality," in Tumin, *Readings on Social Stratification*, pp. 170–178.

[12]J. S. Bruner and L. Postman, "Symbolic Value as an Organizing Factor in Perception," *Journal of Social Psychology*, 27, (1948), pp. 203–208.

[13]Suzanne Keller, *Beyond the Ruling Class: Strategic Elites in Modern Society* (New York: Random House, 1968), p. 172.

Thus, we would expect to find some recruitment of non-upper-class individuals to elite positions even in an essentially hierarchical society. The question remains, *how much* opportunity exists in America for middle- and lower-class individuals to climb to the top?

GETTING AHEAD IN THE SYSTEM

The American ideal is not a classless society, but rather a society in which individuals are free to get ahead on the basis of merit, talent, hard work, and good luck. Upward mobility is valued very highly in American culture. The nation is portrayed in its own literature as a "land of opportunity" where individuals can better themselves if they work at it.

Table 7–1   Social Mobility: Occupational Mobility of Sons in Relation to Fathers by Educational Level

	Upward	*Stable*	*Downward*
Total	54%	11%	35%
College	69	17	14
High School	49	6	45
Some High School	52	12	36
Grade School	48	11	41

Source: Derived from Chicago Labor Mobility Sample figures reported by Otis Dudley and Robert W. Hodge, "Education and Occupational Mobility," *American Journal of Sociology*, 79 (May 1963), 629–644.

And, indeed, there is a great deal of upward social mobility in America. Research on social mobility reveals that every major occupational category contains a majority of individuals whose fathers followed other occupations. The results of a typical study of social mobility are shown in Table 7–1. These figures suggest that very few sons have occupations with the same prestige as their fathers. Table 7–1 shows that on average 54 percent of sons have jobs with higher prestige than their fathers, while only 35 percent have jobs with lower prestige. There is more upward mobility than downward mobility in the American system, a phenomenon that can be attributed to an economic growth that has permitted upward mobility for successive generations of Americans.

Does this evidence of general social mobility tell us much about opportunities for getting to the *top*? Not really. There are several important reservations concerning this generally rosy picture of opportunity and mobility in America.

Most social mobility occurs within a very narrow range of occupations. Few individuals start life on the bottom rung of the social ladder and climb all the way to the top in their lifetime. Most upward mobility occurs step by

step—from unskilled labor to skilled labor, from clerk to manager, from small businessperson to professional, and so forth.

In summary, although there is a great deal of social mobility in America, we can expect a majority of the individuals at the top to be recruited from the upper social classes. Even those who have experienced considerable upward mobility are likely to have risen from middle- or upper-middle-class families rather than working-class families.

SOCIAL CHARACTERISTICS
OF INSTITUTIONAL LEADERS

What do we know about the people who occupy top institutional positions in American society? There are a number of excellent studies of the social backgrounds of political decision makers,[14] federal government executives,[15] military officers,[16] and corporate executives.[17] These studies consistently show that top institutional leaders are *atypical* of the American public. They are recruited from the well-educated, prestigiously employed, older, affluent, urban, white, Anglo-Saxon, upper- and upper-middle-class male populations of the nation. We expected our top institutional elites to conform to the pattern, and we were not at all disappointed (see Table 7–2).

Age. The average age of all the corporate leaders identified in our study is sixty. Leaders in foundations, law, education, and civic and cultural organizations are slightly older—average age sixty-two. Top positions in the governmental sector are filled by slightly younger people—average age fifty-six. This means that America's elites in the 1980s were born in the 1920s and grew up during the Great Depression. World War II was an important event in their early careers; over half of our elites report military service.

Sex. The feminine sector of the population is seriously underrepresented at the top of America's institutional structure. Male dominance in top positions is nearly complete in the corporate world. But even in government, women hold less than 10 percent of the key posts. Two women served in the Carter cabinet, and only one woman has Cabinet rank in the Reagan Administration—U.N. Ambassador Jeane Kirkpatrick. Sandra Day O'Conner is the only woman to serve on the U.S. Supreme

---

[14]Donald R. Matthews, *The Social Background of Political Decision-makers* (New York: Doubleday & Co., 1954).

[15]David T. Stanley, Dean E. Mann, and Jameson W. Doig, *Men Who Govern* (Washington: The Brookings Institution, 1967).

[16]Morris Janowitz, *The Professional Soldier* (New York: Free Press, 1960).

[17]Lloyd Warner and James C. Abegglen, *Big Business Leaders in America* (New York: Harper & Row, 1955).

Table 7-2 Social Characteristics of Top Leaders

	Corporate					Public Interest					Government		All
	Industry	Banking	Utilities	Insur.	Investment	Media	Law	Foundation	Education	Civic	Government	Mil.	All
Average Age	61	61	61	62	58	61	64	62	62	60	56	56	60
Female %	2.4	2.3	4.3	1.1	.9	6.8	1.8	14.7	10.6	9.0	7.7	0	4.3
Education													
Non-College %	3.0	5.8	7.6	5.0	.9	18.4	0	5.1	4.3	3.6	8.8	4.7	5.7
College %	42.7	43.0	40.6	42.7	51.3	39.2	–	24.9	32.8	37.0	10.7	30.2	37.4
Law %	22.6	22.2	25.1	22.6	8.8	20.9	100.0	26.9	28.1	24.8	41.0	9.3	25.8
Advanced %	29.8	29.0	26.7	29.8	39.0	21.6	5.3	43.1	34.7	34.7	33.5	55.8	31.1
Schools													
Public %	25.3	28.5	28.3	25.3	21.2	28.5	8.4	13.7	15.5	21.4	37.9	23.3	24.9
Private %	18.2	20.7	18.8	18.2	17.7	13.9	8.4	19.8	10.2	17.9	17.2	7.0	16.9
Prestigious* %	54.9	49.5	51.0	54.9	61.1	51.9	83.2	66.5	73.7	59.7	41.9	20.9†	56.1

*Harvard, Yale, Chicago, Stanford, Columbia, M.I.T., Cornell, Northwestern, Princeton, Johns Hopkins, Pennsylvania, and Dartmouth.

†U.S. Military Academy (West Point) and U.S. Naval Academy (Annapolis) account for an additional 48.8 percent.

Court in the 200-year history of that institution. No women served as chairpersons of any of the standing committees of the House or Senate in 1980. Only in cultural affairs, education, and foundations are women found in significant numbers among the top position-holders.

Ethnicity. WASP's are preeminent in America's institutional structure. Our own data does not include ethnic identification, but the work of sociologists Richard Alba and Gwen Moore confirm the disproportionate representation of WASP's in high positions in business and government. Their studies revealed that WASP's (who made up only 22.9 percent of all persons born before 1932) made up 57.3 percent of top business leaders and 53.4 percent of Congress. ("Other Protestants" increase these figures to 79.4 for business and 72.4 for Congress.) However, ethnics have made some inroads: 37 percent of union leaders are Irish Catholics, and 25.8 percent of mass media leaders are Jews. A WASP background, they conclude, is an "incremental advantage" in achieving elite status.[18]

Education. Nearly all our top leaders are college-educated, and more than half hold advanced degrees. Some 25.8 percent hold law degrees, and 31.1 percent hold advanced academic or professional degrees. (These are earned degrees only; there are a host of honorary degrees that were not counted.) Governmental leaders are somewhat more likely to hold advanced degrees than corporate leaders. What is even more impressive is the fact that 54 percent of the corporate leaders and 42 percent of the governmental leaders are graduates of 12 heavily endowed, prestigious, "name" private universities—Harvard, Yale, Chicago, Stanford, Columbia, M.I.T., Cornell, Northwestern, Princeton, Johns Hopkins, Pennsylvania, and Dartmouth. Elites in America are notably Ivy League.

Urban. Most of our top leaders were urban dwellers. Governmental leaders (notably congresspersons) are somewhat more likely to be drawn from rural areas than are leaders in business, finance, and law, but fewer than one third of the key government posts in our study were found to be filled by individuals from rural areas.

Preppy. Elites are notably "preppy." At least 10 percent of the corporate leaders and 6 percent of the governmental leaders attended one of only 33 prestigious private prep schools before entering college.[19]

---

[18]Richard D. Alba and Gwen Moore, "Ethnicity in the American Elite," *American Sociological Review* Vol. 47 (June, 1982).

[19]Andover, Buckley, Cate, Catlin, Choate, Cranbrook, Country Day, Deerfield, Episcopal, Exeter, Gilman, Groton, Hill, Hotchkiss, Kingswood, Kent, Lakeside, Lawrenceville, Lincoln, Loomis, Middlesex, Milton, St. Andrew's, St. Christopher's, St. George's, St. Mark's, St. Paul's, Shattuck, Taft, Thatcher, Webb, Westminster, Woodberry Forest. Listing courtesy of G. William Domhoff.

(Actually, the proportion of "preppies" among top leaders may be double these figures—up to 20 percent for corporate leaders and 10 percent for government leaders. The reason for suggesting these higher figures is that less than half of known preppies reported their prep school affiliation to *Who's Who in America*.[20] Thus, their prep school backgrounds would be overlooked in our biographical search.) It is astonishing to realize that these proportions of top leaders went to only thirty-three prep schools, since these schools educate an infinitesimal proportion of the nation's population. As *The Official Preppy Handbook* explains: "There are preparatory schools and then there are Prep Schools, those institutions that bless you with a certain luster along with your diploma."[21]

Among the Eastern establishment, the phrase "old school ties" refers to prep schools, not to colleges or universities. It is considered more prestigious to have attended Groton, Hotchkiss, Phillips Exeter, Loomis, Phillips at Andover, or Choate, than to have attended Harvard, Yale, Princeton, or Columbia. Most of the prestigious prep schools are in the northeast, although Woodberry Forest is in Virginia, Cate is in California, and St. Marks is in Texas.

These social background characteristics suggest a slight tendency for corporate elites to be more "upper-class" in origin than government elites. Among governmental leaders there are slightly fewer Ivy Leaguers. Moreover, there is a slight tendency for governmental leaders to have had more advanced professional education.

BLACKS AT THE TOP

There are very few blacks in positions of power in America. We are able to identify only 20 blacks in 7,314 positions of authority in top-ranked institutions. It is possible, of course, that some may have escaped identification in our biographical search.

Blacks are noticeably absent from top positions in the corporate world. The *Wall Street Journal* reported in 1980 that only 3 of 1,700 senior executives surveyed were black.[22] Corporations say that the main reason that blacks are not found in top management positions is that they did not enter the corporate ranks until the late 1960s, and it takes anyone, white or black, over twenty years to rise to the top. However, many blacks feel that discrimination continues to play a major role in obstructing black progress up the corporate ladder. White corporate executives feel more comfortable

---

[20]Unpublished reports by Michael Useem and G. William Domhoff, November 1980.

[21]Lisa Birnbach (ed). *The Official Preppy Handbook*, (New York: Workman Publishing Co., 1980), p. 50.

[22]*Wall Street Journal*, July 9, 1980, p. 1.

in dealing with other whites, and they do not aggressively recruit blacks into management. The Equal Employment Opportunity Commission, and other federal agencies assigned to investigate job discrimination, focus their attention on entry-level cases rather than on very subtle discrimination in the ranks of top corporate management. Instead of assigning promising black executives to key operating posts, many corporations tend to move them to positions overseeing personnel or affirmative action programs. This removes blacks from the "fast track" in corporate promotions.

On the positive side, however, it is important to note that the black proportion of the white-collar work force in America has grown from 4 to 8 percent since the 1960s. This is still less than the 12 percent of blacks in the nation's population. But Andrew F. Brimmer, one of the nation's few black corporate directors, is optimistic that black executives will climb the "pyramid of experience." "There are an awful lot of black assistant vice-presidents and black assistant treasurers.[23] Illustrative of blacks who have recently won positions at the top of the corporate structure are:

William T. Coleman. Former Secretary of Transportation under President Gerald Ford. Senior partner, O'Melveny and Myers, Washington. Attended the University of Pennsylvania and Harvard Law School. Chairman of the board of the NAACP Legal Defense and Education Fund. A director of IBM, Chase Manhattan, Pepsi Company, American Can, Pan American World Airways; Philadelphia Electric. A director of the Brookings Institution, a member of the Council on Foreign Relations and the Trilateral Commission, and a trustee of Harvard University.

Andrew F. Brimmer. Independent financial consultant. A director of Bank-America, International Harvester, United Airlines, and DuPont. A graduate of the University of Washington with a Ph.D. (economics) from Harvard. He taught at the Wharton School of the University of Pennsylvania and moved on to be Assistant Secretary of Commerce and later a member of the Federal Reserve Board. He now heads Brimmer and Company, an independent financial and managerial consulting firm. He is a member of the Council on Foreign Relations and the Trilateral Commission, and he is a trustee of Atlanta University, Tuskegee Institute, the Urban League, and the Ford Foundation.

Vernon Jordan. Executive director of the National Urban League. A graduate of DePauw University and Howard University Law School. He began his career in civil rights affairs as the Georgia field secretary of the NAACP in the early 1960s, and later became director of the Vote Education Project of the Southern Regional Council, leading black voter registration drives in the south. He served briefly as executive director of the United Negro College Fund before becoming head of the National Urban League in 1972. In recent years he has accepted directorships of Bankers Trust of New York, Celanese Corporation, J. C. Penney Co., and the Xerox Corporation. He is also a director of the Rockefeller Foundation.

[23]*Ibid.*

Vivian W. Henderson. President of Clark College, Atlanta. A graduate of predominantly black North Carolina Central University who earned a Ph.D. in economics at the University of Iowa. He became chairman of the department of economics at Fisk University and later (1965) president of predominantly black Clark College. He served on the Southern Regional Council in the 1960s. In recent years he has been appointed a director of Citizen and Southern Bank and the Bendix Corporation, and a trustee of the Ford Foundation.

Franklin A. Thomas. President of the Ford Foundation. Former president of the Bedford Stuyvesant Restoration Corporation in New York. He received his B.A. and law degree from Columbia University, and served as Deputy Police Commissioner under New York's mayor John Lindsay. He is a director of Citicorp, Columbia Broadcasting System, New York Telephone, Cummins Engine, and New York Life Insurance. He is also a director of the Carnegie Corporation, Lincoln Center for the Performing Arts, and the Urban Institute.

Clifton R. Wharton, Jr. Chancellor of the State University of New York. Educated at the private prestigious Boston Latin School and later Harvard and Johns Hopkins; he received his Ph.D. (economics) from the University of Chicago. Former president of Michigan State University. A director of Ford Motor Co., Burroughs Corp., Equitable Life. A director and later chairman of the board of the Rockefeller Foundation. A director of the Carnegie Corporation and a member of the Council on Foreign Relations.

No blacks have ever been *presidents* of a major industrial corporation, bank, utility, insurance company, investment firm, communication network, prestigious university, or top civic cultural organization. Black leadership has been confined to a small number of board members.

One black served in the Ford cabinet (Secretary of Transportation William Coleman), and one black served in the Carter cabinet:

Patricia Roberts Harris. Former Secretary of Housing and Urban Development. The daughter of a railroad dining car waiter and a graduate of Howard University (B.A., 1945). Received a law degree from George Washington University in 1960. She began her career as a YWCA director in Chicago and later as executive director of Delta Sigma Theta, a national black sorority. She was a delegate to the Democratic National Convention in 1964, and seconded the nomination of Lyndon Johnson; President Johnson appointed her ambassador to Luxembourg (1965–67). She returned to a brief, troubled tenure as dean of Howard University Law School and resigned during student protests. She became a law partner of Sargent Shriver (Kennedy brother-in-law) and a prominent Washington attorney. She was appointed a director of IBM, Chase Manhattan, and Scott Paper Co. She is a member of the Council on Foreign Relations and the NAACP Legal Defense Fund.

President Carter's 1977 appointment of Andrew Young as ambassador to the United Nations was widely heralded as a major breakthrough for blacks in high office. Young was an early member of Martin Luther King,

Jr.'s Southern Christian Leadership Conference; Young was beaten and jailed in Birmingham in 1963 with King. Young helped to bring King's father and widow into Carter's camp during the presidential campaign. But the U.N. ambassadorship is a traditional dumping ground for political figures who are too important to be ignored but who carry little influence with the President (for example, Adlai Stevenson, Daniel Patrick Moynihan, William Scranton). The surprise is that the handsome, articulate Young accepted this largely ceremonial position. Young later resigned in a disagreement with the Carter White House over his public statements, which frequently conflicted with Carter's announced policies. Young was later elected mayor of Atlanta.

President Reagan's Cabinet includes one black, Samuel R. Pierce, Secretary of Housing and Urban Development. Pierce was a senior partner in the New York law firm of Fowler, Jaffin, Pierce & Kneel and a governor of the American Stock Exchange. Pierce received his law degree from Cornell in 1949 and began his long career as an assistant district attorney in New York. He was named an assistant U.S. attorney under President Eisenhower and later assistant to the Under Secretary of Labor. He was a Ford Foundation Fellow at Yale for a year, and a New York City judge. Under Nixon, he was General Counsel for the U.S. Department of the Treasury (from 1970 to 1973). He has served as trustee for NAACP fundraising and for the RAND Corporation, Cornell University, Mt. Holyoke College, and the Hampton Institute. He was a director of General Electric, Prudential Insurance, First National Boston Corp., International Paper, and U.S. Industries.

WOMEN AT THE TOP

Less than 5 percent of the nation's top institutional leaders—presidents, directors, and trustees of the nation's largest industrial corporations, banks, utilities, insurance companies, television networks and newspaper chains, foundations, universities, civic and cultural organizations; full partners in the nation's leading law firms and investment houses; and top elected and appointed federal government officials—are women. Out of the 7,314 top institutional positions in 12 separate sectors of society, only 318 (or 4.3 percent) were occupied by women in 1980. As low as this proportion of female leadership may be, it represents more than double the proportion of women (1.9 percent) found in top institutional positions in 1970.

Most corporate boardrooms continue to resemble all-male clubs. In 1980, only 32 of the 100 largest *industrial corporations* had even one female member; the other 68 industrials remained exclusively male directed. The nation's two largest industrial corporations, Exxon and General Motors, had women on their boards of directors: Martha Peterson was an Exxon director, and General Motors had two female directors, Anne L. Armstrong and Catherine B. Cleary. RCA also had two women directors, Jane C. Pfeiffer and Cecily C. Selby, at the beginning of 1980 (although Ms. Pfeiffer was ousted in this year). General Foods and Norton Simon also had two female board members. However, overall, only 36 women occupied top industry positions in 1980 out of 1,499 positions identified in the 100 largest industrial corporations (see Table 2–1). This means that women occupied only 2.4 percent of the top industrial leadership posts. (No woman served as a president or chief executive officer of any of the 100 largest industrial corporations.) Nonetheless, these figures are an improvement over the 3 women who served as directors of the 100 largest industrial corporations in 1970, an infinitesimal 0.2 percent of the industrial leadership of America.

Women have also improved their leadership position in *banking*. In 1980, twenty one of the nation's fifty largest banks had at least one female director, including BankAmerica and Citicorp, the nation's two largest financial institutions. Yet women held only 2.3 percent of the total number of big bank directorships. Four major banks had two women among their directors. One major bank, First Wisconsin Corporation, had a female president—Catherine B. Cleary. Again, these figures represent an improvement over the *two* women (0.2 percent) who served on the boards of directors of major banks in 1970.

The nation's largest *utilities, transportation, and communication* corporations appear to have moved a little faster and further in recruiting women to top institutional positions than have industry, banking, or insurance. AT&T, the nation's largest corporation of any kind, appointed banker Catherine B. Cleary to its board of directors in the early 1970s. A total of 29 (or 4.3 percent) of the directors of this sector were women; there were *no* women identified as directors in this sector in 1970.

Only eight of the fifty largest *insurance* companies had a woman on their boards of directors. Only 9 women (or 1.1 percent) could be identified among the insurance company presidents and directors. However, the three largest companies—Prudential, Metropolitan, and Equitable—had women among their directors.

Large numbers of women are currently entering the *legal profession;* law schools currently report that over 25 percent of their students are female. However, few women have yet managed to penetrate the inner circles of the nation's largest and most prestigious New York and Washington law firms. These firms generally have forty or fifty or more full partners, but in 1980 only 1.8 percent were women. Seventeen of the twenty-five top firms had at least one woman partner. Washington's two top firms, Arnold and Porter, and Covington and Burling, led the way with three female partners each. It is important to note that there has been only a very modest increase in women as partners in top firms between 1970 and 1980. Indeed, the corporate sector has admitted more women to their boardrooms than the top law firms have admitted to full partnerships.

Women are still difficult to find on Wall Street. The nation's largest *investment* and *security* dealers do not include women as officers or directors, nor do they appear to be moving in that direction. In 1980, there were only five women (0.9 pecent) among the full partners in the nation's top investment firms.

Women have been more successful in the *mass media* than in law, investments, industry, utilities, banking, or insurance. In 1980, women held 6.8 percent of the officer and director posts in the 17 leading media corporations. For nearly twenty years, Katherine Graham, owner of the *Washington Post* and *Newsweek* magazine empire has served as chairman of the board of the Washington Post Company. Three women serve on the board of directors of the New York Times Co.; all of the them are "outside" directors. Each of the three television broadcasting networks have one woman on their board.

The nation's leading private *universities* have recently begun to appoint more women to their governing boards of trustees. In 1980, over 10 percent of the governing trustees of the nation's leading private universities were women, an increase over the 2 percent found in 1970. Six of Harvard's thirty-one trustees are women. All of the leading universities had at least one woman trustee.

Women are frequently encountered on the governing boards of trustees of leading *foundations.* Among the nation's fifty largest foundations, thirty had at least one woman trustee in 1980. The Ford and Rockefeller Foundations each had three women trustees, and the Carnegie Corporation had six women trustees on their sixteen member board. Some women, of course, have long served as foundation trustees because of their family associations: Mary Ethel Pew, Pew Memorial Trust; Doris Duke, Duke Endowment; Harriet Bush Melin, Bush Foundation; Mary Moody Northern, Moody Foundation; Josephine Hartford Bryce, Hartford Foundation; Mary Ann Mott Meynet, Mott Foundation; Ida Calloway, Calloway Foundation; Drue M. Heinz, Heinz Endowment.

Women are frequently encountered as trustees of *cultural organizations.* The influential *civic associations* may have one or two women trustees; for example, the Council on Foreign Relations and The Brookings Institution each had two women trustees in 1980. But the nation's leading cultural institutions appoint significant numbers of women to their governing boards. The John F. Kennedy Center for the Performing Arts has ten women on its twenty-five member board of trustees. Unlike most of the women in the corporate world who list themselves by their own name, many women in cultural organizations list themselves by their husbands' names (for example, Mrs. Howard H. Baker, Jr.; Mrs. Edward Finch Cox;

Mrs. Jean Kennedy Smith; Mrs. Bob Hope; Mrs. J. Clifford Folger). Likewise, among the trustees of the Metropolitan Museum of Art are listed Mrs. Charles W. Englehard, Mrs. Vincent Astor, Mrs. Henry J. Heinz II, Mrs. Charles Wrightsman, and so on, suggesting that these women are representing their husbands as much as themselves. Overall, however, about 9 percent of the trustees of the leading cultural and civic associations are women.

Finally, we can turn to the *federal government* itself to observe the under-representation of women in institutional leadership. Two women served in the Carter Cabinet: Patricia Roberts Harris, Secretary of Health and Human Services, and Shirley M. Hufstedler, Secretary of Education. No woman serves in the Reagan Cabinet, although U.N. Ambassador Jeane Kirkpatrick has Cabinet rank. Two women serve in the U.S. Senate: Nancy Landon Kassebaum (R. Kansas) and Paula Hawkins (R. Florida). *No woman served as chairperson or ranking minority member of any House or Senate standing committee in 1980.* Only 7.7 percent of the top positions in the federal government were filled by women.

The few women at the top deserve closer observation. This list of top women leaders includes:

Katherine Graham. Chairman of the board of the Washington Post Company. (See "Katherine Graham: The Most Powerful Woman in America" in Chapter 4.)

Patricia Roberts Harris. Former Secretary of Health and Human Services. (See "Blacks at the Top" in Chapter 7.)

Catherine B. Cleary. President and director of First Wisconsin Corporation. Earned a bachelor's degree from the University of Chicago and a law degree from the University of Wisconsin. She served as Assistant Treasurer of the United States in the Eisenhower Administration. She is a director of General Motors, AT&T, Kraft, and Northwestern Mutual Life Insurance.

Carla Anderson Hills. Partner in Latham, Watkins, and Hills (Washington law firm). Former Secretary of Housing and Urban Development. Earned a bachelor's degree from Stanford and a law degree from Yale. A director of IBM Corporation, American Airlines, Signal Companies, and Standard Oil of California. A member of the Council on Foreign Relations and the Trilateral Commission, and a trustee of The Brookings Institution.

Martha E. Peterson. Former president of Barnard College, and president of Beloit College. Has B.A., M.A., and Ph.D. degrees from the University of Kansas. A director of Exxon, Metropolitan Life Insurance, First Wisconsin Corporation, United Banks of Illinois, and R. H. Macy & Co. A trustee of the University of Notre Dame and Chatham College, and a member of the Committee on Economic Development.

Eleanor H. Sheldon. A director of Citicorp, Mobil Oil, Equitable Life Assurance, and the RAND Corporation. Earned a Ph.D. degree in sociology from the University of Chicago. A member of the Council on Foreign Relations, and a trustee of the Rockefeller Foundation.

Marina VonNeumann Whitman. Chief economist for General Motors Corporation and a director of Manufacturers Hanover Trust, Westinghouse Electric, and Procter and Gamble. Earned a bachelor's degree from Radcliffe and a Ph.D. from Columbia. A director of the Council on Foreign Relations, and a member of the Trilateral Commission.

Anne L. Armstrong. A director of General Motors, Braniff International, First City Bank Corporation of Texas, General Foods, Halliburton Company, and Boise Cascade. Has a bachelor's degree from Vassar College. Former co-chairperson of the Republican National Committee and former ambassador to Great Britain. A member of the Council on Foreign Relations. A trustee of the Smithsonian Institution and Southern Methodist University.

Jane Cahill Pfeiffer. Former chairman of the board of the National Broadcasting Company. A director of International Paper Company., J.C. Penney Company, Chesebrough-Ponds Inc., and the Bache investments group. A member of the Council on Foreign Relations. Earned a bachelor's degree from the University of Maryland. Former vice-president of I.B.M. A trustee of the University of Notre Dame, Catholic University, and the Rockefeller Foundation.

Jewel Stradford Lafontant. Partner in Lafontant, Wilkins, and Butler (Chicago law firm). Former Solicitor General of the United States. Has a bachelor's degree from Oberlin college and a law degree from the University of Chicago. A director of Trans World Airlines, Continental Bank, Bendix Corporation, Equitable Life Assurance.

SOCIAL CHARACTERISTICS OF WOMEN LEADERS

The educational level of top women leaders is very high; nearly half possess earned master's or doctorate degrees, and an additional quarter possess law degrees. (Honorary degrees were not counted.) Thus, a total of 71.0 percent of the women leaders earned advanced degrees; the comparable figure for male leaders is 55.8 percent. This strongly suggests that women need more education than men to compete effectively for top posts. (Only one woman in our entire group failed to indicate that she held a bachelor's degree. Marian Sulzberger Heiskell, the daughter of the owner of the *New York Times,* and a director of the New York Times Co., Consolidated Edison, Ford Motors, and Merck and Co., does not list an earned degree in her biography.)

Women are entering the business world in increasing numbers. In 1971, women numbered only 3.5 percent of all M.B.A. students; in 1981, women numbered 25.9 percent of all M.B.A. students.[24] But most women are still at the junior ranks of corporate management. Many feel pressures to outperform men in some jobs simply to stay even. And there is a fear among many women executives that they will be accused of using their

[24]*Newsweek,* September 14, 1981, p. 66.

Table 7–3 Social Characteristics of Women in Top Institutional Positions

	Total	Corp.	Gov't.	Law News	Civic, Cultural, Educ.
Average Age	54	55	49	55	54
Career					
Corporate %	15.9	19.0	17.6	–0–	4.3
Government %	19.6	8.5	58.8	9.1	17.4
Law %	13.1	11.9	5.9	18.2	21.7
News %	15.0	14.2	5.9	54.5	13.0
Education %	29.9	40.5	11.8	18.2	34.8
Other %	6.5	4.8	–0–	–0–	8.7
Education					
Advanced Degree %	46.7	47.6	47.0	18.2	52.2
Law Degree %	24.3	23.8	23.5	18.2	34.8
Bachelor's Degree %	28.0	28.6	29.4	54.5	13.0
No Degree %	0.8	–0–	–0–	9.1	–0–
Schools					
Women's Prestigious %	34.0	26.2	17.6	60.0	47.8
Prestigious %	26.4	28.6	17.6	20.0	39.1
Private %	9.4	7.1	29.4	–0–	4.3
Public %	30.2	38.1	35.3	30.0	8.7
Married %	76.2	69.2	70.6	100.0	87.0
Children, % with	61.0	57.7	52.9	90.9	61.0

sexuality to get ahead. Women are still excluded from membership in many of the nation's most prestigious private clubs. One top woman executive explains: "It's like integration of the races. People talk about it, but it happens very slowly."[25]

More than half of the nation's women leaders attended *prestigious* private colleges. About one quarter of them attended one of the "Seven Sisters": Vassar, Radcliffe, Smith, Wellesley, Barnard, Bryn Mawr, or Mt. Holyoke. Another one quarter attended one of the traditional prestigious private universities: Harvard, Yale, Chicago, Stanford, Columbia, Cornell, Northwestern, Princeton, Johns Hopkins, Pennsylvania. Thus, over half of our women leaders attended one of a handful of prestigious private colleges and universities. (Approximately the same proportion of men attended prestigious universities.)

The average age of top women leaders was fifty four in 1980. This is younger than the average age of men in comparable positions, which is

[25]*Ibid.*, p. 64.

sixty one. We suspect that this difference is largely a product of the recency of appointment of many of the women leaders to their positions. Newer members of an elite can be expected to be younger than established members.

An examination of the career backgrounds of women leaders reveals a number of separate recruitment paths. Table 7–4 includes the principal lifetime occupational activity of women at the top of each sector of society.

In the corporate world—industrials, banks, utilities, insurance companies, and investment firms—a surprising percentage of women are recruited to boards of directors from *universities*. Only 19 percent of female corporate directors were recruited from the corporate world itself; over 40 percent were recruited from universities. (This is *not* the pattern of recruitment of male corporate directors, most of whom [89 percent] are recruited from corporations, and few of whom [0.6 percent] come from universities.) This leads to the suspicion that many corporations deliberately reached out to universities in the 1970s to find talented women to join their boards. The corporations, in brief, raided the universities.

In contrast, women leaders in government tend to be recruited through government itself (58.8 percent). Only 17.6 percent of female governmental leaders are recruited from the corporate world. Likewise, top female lawyers are recruited through law firms, and top female leaders in the mass media are recruited from news organizations. The career backgrounds of civic, cultural, foundation, and educational leaders are balanced between various sectors of society. The largest single source of female leadership in these institutions is the academic world, supplying approximately one third of the trustees of the largest and most influential institutions.

We were able to identify only three black women out of our total of 318 top female leaders. One, of course, was Patricia Roberts Harris, former Secretary of Health and Human Services; another was former Congressperson Barbara C. Jordan, who sits (with Ladybird Johnson) on the board of Texas Commerce Bancshares; and the third was Margaret Bush Wilson, a civil rights lawyer who sits on the board of Monsanto, the Committee on Economic Development, the American Red Cross, and Washington University.

Finally, it is interesting to observe that three quarters of the nation's top women leaders are married and over 60 percent of them are mothers. Most of the women at the top today have combined marriage and family with careers that have taken them to the nation's highest institutional positions. Of course, these are extraordinary women. They compose less than 5 percent of the nation's top leadership. Most were born in the 1920s and reached adulthood in a period of history when marriage and family were seemingly more central to American culture.

SANDRA DAY O'CONNOR:
A WOMAN FOR THE HIGH COURT

For nearly 200 years the U.S. Supreme Court was America's most exclusive male club. After 101 male justices, Sandra Day O'Connor was named to the Supreme Court by President Reagan in 1981. At the time of her appointment, O'Connor was a fifty-one-year-old state appellate court judge in Arizona. Justice O'Connor had no previous experience as a federal court judge, but she had the active support of Arizona's senior U.S. Senator and Republican warhorse, Barry Goldwater. More importantly, she was a "she." Reagan was anxious to deflect attacks on his opposition to the Equal Rights Amendment and his failure to appoint many women in his own administration. As one Reagan aide put it: "This is worth 25 assistant secretaries, maybe more!" Feminist groups were forced to support the appointment, even though O'Connor's record in Arizona was moderately conservative.

Sandra Day grew up on her family's large Arizona ranch, graduated from Stanford with honors, and then went on to Stanford Law School. She finished near the top of her class, along with Supreme Court Justice William Rehnquist (who was first in the class) and Forrest Shumway, chairman of the Signal Companies. (When asked to name the *most* successful member of this 1952 Stanford class, Shumway replied, "I probably make the most money."[26]) She married John Jay O'Connor, a Phoenix attorney, and raised three sons. She entered Arizona politics about the time her youngest son entered school. She was appointed to the Arizona state senate in 1969 and was later elected twice to that body. She rose to majority leader in 1973. She left the Arizona legislature in 1975 to become a Phoenix trial judge. In 1979, she was appointed by a Democratic governor to the Arizona court of appeals. Work on this state intermediate court, however, does not involve major constitutional questions.

O'Connor has had some business experience: she was formerly a director of the First National Bank of Arizona and Blue Cross Blue Shield of Arizona. But until her appointment to the U.S. Supreme Court, O'Connor was an obscure state court judge. Her service as a Republican leader in the Arizona state senate qualified her as a moderately conservative party loyalist. However, it appears as if her professional and political friendships had more to do with bringing her to President Reagan's attention than her record as a jurist. She had known Justice William Rehnquist since her law school days. She had known Chief Justice Warren Burger for a long time. And Barry Goldwater had been her mentor in Arizona Republican politics. When Reagan's political advisers told him during the presidential campaign that he was not doing well among women voters, the candidate responded by pledging to appoint a woman to the

[26]*Newsweek*, July 20, 1981, p. 18.

Supreme Court. Reagan's fulfillment of his campaign pledge was a politically popular decision.

O'Connor replaced a moderately conservative Justice Potter Stewart, so it is not expected that she will bring many changes in the law to the high court. Nonetheless, her appointment has er ormous symbolic importance for women leaders.

MULTIPLE PATHS TO THE TOP

How do people at the top get there? Certainly, we cannot provide a complete picture of the recruitment process. But we can learn whether the top leadership in government is recruited from the corporate world, or whether there are separate and distinct channels of recruitment.

Biographical information on individuals occupying positions of authority in top institutions in each sector of society reveals that there are multiple recruitment paths to top institutional positions. Table 7–4 shows the principal lifetime occupational activity of individuals at the top of each sector of society. (This categorizing of people according to their lifework depends largely on their own designation of principal occupation in *Who's Who.*)

As we might expect, the corporate sector supplies most of the occupants of top positions in the corporate sector (over 80 percent). The corporate sector also supplies a majority of the top leadership in civic and cultural organizations (74.2 percent), a majority of the trustees of private and renowned educational institutions (66.5 percent); and about half of the trustees of the major foundations (47.7 percent). However, the corporate world provides less than 10 percent of governmental elites.

Top leaders in government are recruited primarily from the legal profession (61.5 percent); some have based their careers in government itself (15.7 percent) or in education (10.1 percent). This finding is important. Government and law apparently provide independent channels of recruitment to high public office. Thus, high position in the corporate world is not a prerequisite to high public office.

The mass media provide another separate path to elite membership. A majority of presidents and directors of television networks, wire services, and the influential press have been associated throughout their lives with the mass media. Of course, the nation's top lawyers have spent most of their lives in the legal profession.

Educators supply only a small fraction of the top leadership of the nation. Of the top governmental leaders, only 10.1 percent were educators, and educators compose about 8 percent of the trustees of civic and cultural associations and about 12 percent of the trustees of foundations. Indeed, educators do not even supply a majority of the membership of university boards of trustees; only 12 percent of our educational elites were drawn

Table 7-4 Recruitment to Top Institutional Positions

Sector From Which Top Elites Recruited*	Corporate					Public Interest					Government		All
	Industry	Banking	Utilities	Insur.	Invest.	Media	Law	Found.	Education	Civic	Government	Mil.	
Corporate %													
Industry	67.5	52.6	28.1	32.7	4.4	24.4	0	27.9	42.9	56.7	4.0	2.3	43.4
Banking	6.7	22.3	12.5	8.4	12.4	3.1	0	10.2	10.0	7.1	1.3	0	9.9
Utilities	3.8	7.6	36.2	6.7	0	1.2	0	3.0	6.1	4.8	0	0	7.3
Insurance	1.7	2.2	4.1	32.3	0	1.2	1.1	3.0	2.6	2.7	0	0	5.2
Invest.	2.6	2.1	3.0	1.6	77.0	3.1	0	3.6	4.9	2.9	.4	0	4.6
Total	82.3	86.8	83.9	81.7	93.8	33.0	1.1	47.7	66.5	74.2	5.7	2.3	70.4
Public Interest %													
Media	.7	0.9	1.9	.9	.9	55.6	0	6.6	5.5	3.6	3.1	2.3	4.2
Law	7.7	6.3	6.3	5.3	1.8	5.6	96.8	9.6	11.6	5.5	61.5	7.0	9.4
Found.	.6	0.3	.5	.9	0	0	0	6.6	1.8	1.1	.4	0	1.0
Educ.	7.7	4.0	6.5	9.5	1.8	4.4	2.1	23.4	12.0	8.2	10.1	7.0	8.2
Civic	.1	0.1	0	.2	0	0	0	2.0	.4	2.1	.4	0	0.5
Total	16.8	11.6	15.2	16.8	4.5	65.6	98.9	48.2	31.3	20.5	25.5	16.3	23.4
Governmental %													
Gov't.	.6	1.2	.3	.4	1.8	1.2	0	4.1	2.2	5.3	15.7	9.3	5.1
Mil.	.1	0	.5	.9	0	0	0	0	0	0	3.1	72.1	1.1
Total	.7	1.2	.8	1.3	1.8	1.2	0	4.1	2.2	5.3	18.8	81.4	6.2

*Columns may not total 100.0 because of rounding.

from the ranks of educators. Corporations only occasionally call upon educators to join corporate boards; less than 10 percent of corporate directors are educators.

LIFE AT THE TOP: COMPENSATION, TRAVEL, WORK

"All societies offer rewards to men assuming leadership positions," writes Suzanne Keller.

> Some rewards are tangible material benefits such as money, land, cattle, or slaves, while others are intangible such as social honor and influence.…
>
> Rewards play a two-fold role in the recruitment of elites: they motivate individuals to assume the responsibilities of elite positions; and they maintain the values of hierarchical social position.[27]

Institutional leaders receive compensation in many forms. Corporate executives usually receive a bonus based on company performance, in addition to their salary. Then there are stock options, low-interest loans, and deferred compensation paid out over future years to reduce the current tax bite. There are indirect forms of compensation too, the so-called perquisites of "perks," which may include personal aides and assistants, plush offices and equipment, paid club membership, expense accounts, and the use of company cars and planes.

In early 1980, top corporate executive salaries—exclusive of investments, interest on stock holdings, capital gains, or "perks"—clustered around $550,000 per year. Some top corporation executives were paid over $1 million per year. (Traditionally, bankers have been paid less than their counterparts in industry; presidents of major banks make only about $300,000.) These salaries must finance an expensive life-style. Most of this income is taxable and it is doubtful that many up-the-organization managers can accumulate great wealth from their salaries and bonuses.

Of course, "inheritors" generally receive much more compensation than the paltry $550,000 paid to a corporate president. Their income is mainly from dividends, interest, and capital gains on investments, including the companies in which they own controlling blocks of stock. Dividends and interest (except for interest on state and municipal bonds) are taxable as income, but capital gains are not taxed unless the asset (stock, real estate, and so on) is sold and the profit is realized in cash. Even then, capital gains are taxed at a lower rate than income. No one really acquires great wealth in America from *salary* income, even six-figure salary income. Instead, great fortunes are made through *capital gains*—investments in corporations, real estate, oil and gas and other minerals, which grow in value over

[27]Keller, *Beyond the Ruling Class*, pp. 183–184.

the years. Prior to the tax reductions passed by Congress at President Reagan's request in 1981, the top income tax bracket was 70 percent on unearned income. Now the top tax bracket is 50 percent on both earned (salaries) and unearned (interest, dividends, and so forth) income.

The salaries of governmental leaders are considerably lower than those of corporate executives, although the "perks"—aides, offices, cars, planes, expense accounts, secretaries, and so on—are roughly equivalent. The President of the United States receives a salary of $200,000, plus $50,000 for expenses, plus $112,000 for travel and official entertainment. Expenses of the White House staff, including salaries, expenses, and travel of special assistants, aides, and secretaries, run $10 million or more per year. The Vice-President receives $79,125 salary plus $19,000 for expenses. All Cabinet members receive $69,630 in salary. The Chief Justice of the Supreme Court receives $84,675; other justices receive $81,288. Congressmen—both Senators and Representatives—receive an annual salary of $60,622, but they are given another $200,000 or more to hire staff assistants and run their offices.(In 1975, Congress surreptitiously inserted an annual cost-of-living increase in their own salaries.) Committee chairmen have spent over $2 million per year running their committees.

A survey of the nation's top corporate executives by *Fortune* magazine, which included responses from half of the presidents of the nation's 500 largest corporations, reports many interesting tidbits about life at the top of the corporate world:

Over 60 percent of these corporate executives own or rent second "get-away" homes.

A surprisingly large number (48 percent) collect original works of art.

The most popular leisure activity is golfing (56 percent), followed by boating, hunting, tennis, and running. Few attend theatres, go to movies, or watch TV (other than the news).

A majority do not smoke, and contrary to popular impressions, most top executives live longer than the average American.[28]

Most people at the top are well traveled: four out of five travel outside the United States each year. Europe is the leading destination, but 20 percent travel to South America each year and 40 percent to Asia.

However, it is important to note that most top leaders in corporations and government work long and hard. The norm is sixty to seventy hours per week, traveling six to ten days per month, and spending many weekends devoted to business.[29] Most top elites put their jobs before their

[28]Robert S. Diamond, "Self-Portrait of the Chief Executive," *Fortune* (May 1970), pp. 181, 320–323.

[29]Based on a *Wall Street Journal—*Gallup Poll survey of chief executives of 1,300 large U.S. companies. *Wall Street Journal,* August 19, 1980, p. 31.

Table 7–5 Typical Corporate Compensation Packages

	Top Management	Middle Management	Lower Management
Base Salary	$300,000	$100,000	$40,000
Initial Bonus (To make up for costs in relocating and changing jobs)	1 year's salary	25–50% of one year's salary	$10,000 or relocation expenses only
Annual Bonus Expected Maximum	50% base 100% of base	40% of base 80% of base	25% of base 50% of base
Capital	25,000 stock options	7,500 stock options	2,000 stock options
Retirement	65% of final average 5-year gross pay (salary plus bonus)	40–50% of average 5-year gross pay	40–50% of average 5-year gross pay
Life Insurance	3 times base salary	1½ times base salary	1½ times base salary
Major Medical	company plan plus supp. benefits	company plan	company plan
Special Perks	car; luncheon club; country club; personal tax; financial planning service; bodyguard; office furnished as living-room with no desk; private lavatory.	luncheon club or country club; car; large offices with windows; carpeting and large desk.	no clubs or cars; small office or cubicle.

Sources: *Wall Street Journal*, November 17, 1980 p. 50; *Time*, June 2, 1980, p. 60.

families or themselves. On their way to the top, most have relocated six or more times. Most top leaders express the belief that their families' lives have suffered because of their careers. Because they have worked so hard all their lives, retirement is often difficult.

SOCIAL CLUBS: ELITES AT PLAY

Institutional leaders are "joiners." The overwhelming majority of those who hold top positions in America belong to one or more social clubs. More importantly, over one third of the people at the top belong to just a few very prestigious private clubs. Corporate directors, network moguls, Cabinet members, foundation presidents, and superlawyers rub shoulders at places such as the Links and the Knickerbocker in New York, and the Metropolitan and the Burning Tree in Washington. They relax together on a summer outing under California redwoods at the Bohemian Grove. These private clubs provide an opportunity for informal interaction among elites in different segments of society. The importance of these clubs in developing elite consensus and cohesion is the subject of a great deal of speculation. E. Digby Baltzell writes: "At the upper class level in America ... the club [a private voluntary association] lies at the very core of the social organization of the access to power and authority."[30] Ferdinand Lundberg says: "The private clubs are the most 'in' thing about the ... elite. These clubs constitute the societal control centers of the elite."[31]

Perhaps the most persuasive case for the importance of such private social clubs is set forth by sociologist G. William Domhoff:

> The Bohemian Grove [a luxury retreat on 2700 acres of giant redwoods maintained by the Bohemian Club of San Francisco], as well as other watering holes and social clubs, are relevant to the problem of class cohesiveness in two ways. First, the very fact that rich men from all over the country gather in such close circumstances as the Bohemian Grove is evidence of the existence of a socially cohesive upper class. It demonstrates that many of these men do know each other, that they have face-to-face communications, and that they are a social network. In this sense we are looking at [clubs] as a *result* of social processes that lead to class cohesion. But such institutions also can be viewed as facilitators of social ties. Once formed, these groups became another avenue by which the cohesiveness of the upper class is maintained.[32]

Ronald Reagan is a Bohemian, as are Vice-President George Bush, Defense Secretary Caspar Weinberger, and Attorney General William French Smith. The Bohemian Grove, seventy-five miles north of San Francisco, resembles a plush summer camp for overgrown and influential Boy Scouts. Here top government officials can relax comfortably with Leonard Firestone (tires), Ray Kroc (McDonald's), Alden Clausen (Bank-America), Justin Dart (Dart & Kraft), Reginald Jones (General Electric), Walter Wriston (Citicorp), Willard C. Butcher (Chase Manhattan), William A. Hewitt (Deere & Co.), George P. Shultz (Bechtel Corp.), former President Gerald R. Ford, and others of similar status. They may invite guests such as Henry Kissinger, Howard Baker, or Richard Nixon. The Grove itself is divided into a number of camps: the "Owls," "Mandalay," the

---

[30]E. Digby Baltzell, *The Protestant Establishment* (New York: Random House, 1964), p. 354.

[31]Ferdinand Lundberg, *The Rich and the Super-Rich* (New York: Bantam Books, 1968), p. 339.

[32]G. William Domhoff, *The Bohemian Grove and Other Retreats* (New York: Harper & Row, 1974), p. 88.

Table 7-6   Club Memberships of Top Leaders

	Corporate					Public Interest					Government		All
	Industry	Banking	Utilities	Insurance	Invest.	Media	Law	Found.	Education	Civic	Government	Mil.	
Club Membership %													
None	34.9	30.3	34.6	37.9	16.8	36.1	30.5	30.6	35.8	33.8	76.3	85.9	36.2
One to Four	33.3	37.1	39.8	40.2	51.3	39.3	48.4	43.3	29.0	32.8	20.7	11.8	35.4
Five or more	31.8	32.6	25.6	21.9	31.9	24.6	21.1	26.1	35.2	33.4	3.0	2.3	28.4
Exclusive Clubs* %													
None	64	57.4	65.4	70.9	57.5	65.8	65.3	65.8	56.3	63.0	95.7	95.1	64.7
One or More	36	42.6	34.6	29.1	42.5	34.2	34.7	34.2	43.7	37.0	5.3	4.9	35.3

*Links (N.Y.), Century (N.Y.), Knickerbocker (N.Y.), Piping Rock (N.Y.), River (N.Y.), Metropolitan (D.C.), Pacific Union-Bohemian (S.F.), Brook (N.Y.), Burlington (S.F.), California (L.A.), Casino (Chi.), Chagrin Valley (Clev.), Chicago (Chi.), Denver (Den.), Detroit (Det.), Eagle Lake (Hous.), Everglades (Fla.), Hartford (Conn.), Hope (R.I.), Idlewild (Dallas), Maryland (Md.), Milwaukee (Mil.), Minneapolis (Minn.), New Haven Town (Conn.), Philadelphia (Phil.), Rittenhouse (Phil.), Racquet (St. L.), Rainier (Seattle), Richmond (Va.), Cuyamuca (San Diego), Charleston (S.C.), Rolling Rock (Pitts.), Saturn (Buf.), St. Louis (St. L.), Somerset (Bos.), Union (Clev.), Woodhill (Minn.). Listing courtesy of G. William Domhoff.

"Hillbillies," "Cave Men," and so on (Ronald Reagan is an "Owl"). During an encampment, Bohemians try to forget their cares, listen to distinguished speakers, engage in games and skits, drink, and enjoy "good fellowship." Bohemians accept no women as members, or as guests, or even as employees.

It is our judgment, however, that club membership is a result of top position holding in the institutional structure of society rather than an important independent source of power. An individual is selected for club membership *after* he has acquired an important position in society; he seldom acquires position and power because of club memberships. Personal interaction, consensus building, and friendship networks all develop in the club milieu, but the clubs merely help facilitate processes that occur anyway. Nonetheless, the club memberships of persons at the top are worthy of attention.

Corporate leaders are more likely to be members of private social clubs than are governmental leaders. Table 7–6 shows that over two thirds of our corporate elites held private club memberships; nearly a third of them held five or more memberships. In contrast, only 23.7 percent of top governmental leaders held such memberships, and even fewer military chiefs were club members. Doubtless this differential reflects the greater importance of social interaction in the corporate world (and perhaps the fact that businesspersons can shift the exorbitant costs of such memberships to their corporations while government officials cannot). The fact that a majority of top governmental and military elites are *not* club members undercuts the importance attributed to club membership by many "power elite" writers. If a majority of top governmental elites do *not* sip cocktails at the Metropolitan Club, it is difficult to argue that the real decision-making in Washington takes place in that club's lounge.

Nonetheless, the fact that nearly half of the top elites in the corporate, legal, educational, foundation, and mass media sectors of society belong to one of *forty* selected clubs is impressive testimony to the prestige of these clubs.

SUMMARY

The "elitist" literature on power stresses the disproportionate numbers of top leaders drawn from the upper and upper-middle strata of society. But even classical elite theorists acknowledge the necessity of some opportunities for upward mobility in society, if only to maintain order and strengthen support for the political system. The "pluralist" literature on power describes a more open leadership system where individuals from all social backgrounds can rise to the top if they have the necessary skills, information, and talents. However, pluralists acknowledge that opportunities to acquire such qualities are unequally distributed among classes in society. Pluralists also argue that social class is a poor predictor of decision-making behavior. We have not resolved this debate, but perhaps we have added some more factual information about the social composition of top institutional leaders.

On the whole, those at the top are well-educated, older, affluent, urban, WASP, and male. Although a few blacks have recently been appointed to top corporate boards, in 1980 there were hardly more than 20 blacks among the 7,000 top position-holders in our study.

Blacks are noticeably absent from corporate boardrooms, and there are few blacks in government, although they represent 12 percent of the U.S. population. Likewise, there are very few women at the top of the nation's institutional structure. Overall, less than 5 percent of top leaders are women. Only recently have women been invited into the boardrooms of large corporations. Even in government, despite recent gains and a Supreme Court seat, women still occupy only about 8 percent of the key posts. Women are more likely to be found as trustees of universities, foundations, and cultural organizations, but even in these sectors women leaders are far outnumbered by men. Top women leaders are upper and upper-middle class in origin, like their male counterparts. However, women leaders tend to have more education and they are younger. Women leaders are more likely to have been recruited from education, the mass media, or law, than from the (mostly male) ranks of corporate management.

There is a slight tendency for corporate elites to be more urban and "upper-class" than governmental elites. There are more Ivy Leaguers in corporate boardrooms than in government, and there appear to be more private prep school types in corporate management than in government. Governmental leaders tend to have more advanced degrees, not only in law, but also in academic and professional fields.

There are multiple recruitment paths to the top of the nation's institutional structure. The corporate world, however, supplies a majority of the top leaders in the corporate sector itself, as well as in civic and cultural organizations, foundations, and universities. However, top governmental leaders are recruited primarily from the law, and to a lesser extent from government itself and education. The mass media, the law, and education all provide separate recruitment channels. In short, the corporate world, while an important recruitment channel, is not the exclusive road to the top.

8

Conflict and consensus among institutional leaders

CONFLICT OR CONSENSUS AMONG ELITES?

How much agreement exists among people at the top about the fundamental values and future directions of American society? Do America's top leaders agree on the *ends* of policies and programs and disagree merely on the *means* of achieving those ends? Or are there significant differences among American elites over the goals and purposes of our society?

Social scientists frequently give conflicting answers to these questions—not because of differences in the results of their research, but because of differences in the interpretation of these results. Although it is sometimes difficult to survey elite attitudes and opinions (individuals at the top do not have much time to spend with pollsters), nonetheless, social scientists have produced a number of good studies of the values of corporate executives, governmental officials, political party leaders, university intellectuals, and even newspersons.

Pluralists contend that these studies reveal significant conflicts between Democrats and Republicans, liberals and conservatives, corporate directors and labor leaders, intellectuals and bankers, and other leadership groups, over a wide range of policy issues. They cite studies showing significant differences between various segments of the nation's elite over tax policy, welfare programs, government regulation of business and labor, energy and environmental questions, alternative approaches to national health care, and the appropriate measures to deal with inflation and recession. The nation's leadership also appears divided over some foreign and defense policy issues: whether or not to build up new manned bombers or new missile systems, the appropriate posture of the U.S. in strategic arms limitation talks with the Soviets, whether or not the nation needs a draft or can rely on the All Volunteer Forces.

By contrast, elitists contend that despite these differences over *specific* policy questions, all segments of American leadership share a broader consensus about the *fundamental* values of private property, limited government, separation of church and state, individual liberty, and due process of law. Moreover, since the Roosevelt era, American elites have generally supported liberal social welfare programs, including social security, fair labor standards, unemployment compensation, a graduated income tax, a federally aided welfare system, government regulation of public utilities, and countercyclical fiscal and monetary policies. Today, elite consensus also includes a commitment to equality of opportunity for women and blacks and a desire to end direct, lawful discrimination. Finally, elite consensus includes a desire to exercise influence in world affairs, to oppose the spread of communism, to maintain a strong national defense, and to protect pro-Western governments from internal subversion and external aggression.

Both elitist and pluralist interpretations can be supported by available data. Most surveys conducted *within* the United States deliberately emphasize differences among elites by choosing public issues that are known to be sources of conflict. But there is indeed a fairly broad concensus among leaders on fundamental values and future directions of American society.

However, we do *not* contend that disagreement never occurs among top leaders. On the contrary, the multiple bases of power in American sources of conflict. But there is indeed a fairly broad consensus among ensure that different segments of America's elite will view public issues from slightly different vantage points. The notion of consensus on societal goals and conflict over specific means of their achievement is clearly expressed by sociologist Suzanne Keller:

> What is required for effective social life is moral accord among the strategic elites: they must have some loyalties and goals in common. As societies become more differentiated, a considerable degree of cohesion and consensus is needed at the top. . . . The point need not be labored that doubt and conflicts are necessary: societies advance both as a result of achievements and as a result of disagreements and struggles over the ways to attain them. This is where power struggles play a major and indispensable role. Loyalty to common goals does not preclude conflict over how they are to be realized.[1]

[1]Suzanne Keller, *Beyond the Ruling Class: Strategic Elites in Modern Society* (New York: Random House, 1963), p. 146.

Thus, we contend that disagreement occurs *within* a framework of consensus on fundamental values, that the range of disagreement among elites is relatively narrow, and that disagreement is generally confined to means rather than ends.

THE LIBERAL ESTABLISHMENT

The traditional philosophy of America's elite has been liberal and public-regarding. By this we mean that institutional leaders have shown a willingness to take the welfare of others into account as an aspect of their own sense of well-being: they have been willing to use governmental power to correct perceived wrongs done to others. This is a familiar philosophy— elite responsibility for the welfare of the poor and downtrodden, particularly minority populations. The liberal establishment believes that it can change people's lives through the exercise of governmental power: end discrimination, abolish poverty, eliminate slums, ensure employment, uplift the poor, eliminate sickness, educate the masses, and instill dominant culture values in all citizens. The prevailing liberal impulse is to *do good*, to perform public services, and to assist the poorest in society.

Historically, upper-class values in America have been liberal, public-regarding, and service-oriented. Society's elites are confident that with sufficient effort they can improve people's lives. They feel a strong obligation to improve not only themselves, but everyone else, whether they want to be improved or not.

Leadership for liberal reform has always come from America's upper social classes. This leadership is more likely to come from established "old families" rather than "new rich," self-made people. Before the Civil War, abolitionist leaders were "descended from old and socially dominant Northeastern families" and were clearly distinguished from the emerging "robber barons"—the new leaders of the Industrial Revolution. Later, when the children and grandchildren of the robber barons inherited positions of power, they turned away from the Darwinist philosophy of their parents and toward the social welfarism of the New Deal. Liberalism was championed not by the working class, but by men such as Franklin D. Roosevelt (Groton and Harvard), Adlai Stevenson (Choate School and Princeton), Averell Harriman (Groton and Yale), and John F. Kennedy (Choate School and Harvard).

The "elite consensus" defies simplistic Marxian interpretations of American politics; wealth, education, sophistication, and upper-class cultural values do *not* foster attitudes of exploitation, but rather of public service and do-goodism. Of course, such attitudes would be labeled by Marxists as merely more subtle and far more treacherous forms of class dominance, yet the fact remains that there is little evidence of overt conflict between the less privileged and America's liberal elites. Liberal elites are frequently paternalistic toward segments of the masses they define as "underprivileged," "culturally deprived," "disadvantaged," and so on, but they are seldom hostile toward them.

Today's upper-class liberalism was shaped in the era of Franklin Delano Roosevelt. Roosevelt came to power as a descendant of two of America's oldest families, the Roosevelts and the Delanos, original Dutch patrician families of New York whose landed wealth predates the English capture of New Amsterdam. The Roosevelts and other patrician families whose wealth was gained well before the Industrial Revolution never fully accepted the Social Darwinism "public be damned," rugged individualism of the industrial capitalists. They were not schooled in the scrambling competition of the upwardly mobile nouveau riche, but instead in the altruism and idealism of comfortable and secure wealth and assured social status. In describing FDR, historian Richard Hofstadter summarizes upper-class liberalism:

> At the beginning of his career he took to the patrician reform thought of the progressive era and accepted a social outlook that can best be summed up in the phrase "noblesse oblige." He had a penchant for public service, personal philanthropy, and harmless manifestos against dishonesty in government; he displayed a broad easy-going tolerance, a genuine liking for all sorts of people; he loved to exercise his charm in political and social situations.[2]

This liberal consensus, of course, is not strictly or necessarily altruistic. *The values of welfare and reform are functional for the preservation of the American political and economic system.* A radical criticism of the liberal establishment is that its paternalism toward the poor and minorities is in reality self-serving; it is designed to end poverty and discrimination while preserving the free enterprise system and the existing class structure.

THE NEOCONSERVATIVES

While American politics continues in the liberal tradition, that tradition is broad enough to encompass critics of "excessive" government interference in society. The war in Vietnam, the Great Society, urban rioting, campus unrest, Watergate, and inflation have all combined over the past twenty years to raise doubts about the size and scope of governmental power. A mood of disillusionment has penetrated elite circles and dampened enthusiasm for government intervention in society. Elite interest in liberal reforms has been tempered by the failures and costs of well-meaning yet

[2]Richard Hofstadter, *The American Political Tradition* (New York: Knopf, 1948), pp. 323–324.

ineffective (and sometimes harmful) public programs. Elites have learned that society's problems cannot be solved simply by passing a law, creating a new bureaucracy, and spending a few billion dollars. War, poverty, ill-health, discrimination, joblessness, inflation, crime, ignorance, pollution, and unhappiness have afflicted society for a long time. Elites no longer assume that these problems can be erased from society by finding and implementing the "right" public policies.

The "neoconservatives" among America's elite continue to be liberal, reformist, and public-regarding, but they are opposed to the paternalistic state. They no longer have the confidence and ambition (bordering on arrogance) of the liberals of the 1960s. They have more respect for the free market system and less confidence that government regulations will achieve their desired effects. They are more respectful of traditional values and institutions, including religion, family, and the community. They believe in equality of opportunity where everyone is free to strive for whatever they wish, but they do not believe in absolute equality, where the government ensures that everyone gets equal shares of everything. Finally, neoconservatives believe that the United States must maintain a strong national defense and that American democracy cannot survive for long in a world that is overwhelmingly hostile to American values.[3]

The neoconservatives, like all liberals, disapprove of unequal treatment suffered by racial minorities, but neoconservatives generally oppose affirmative action and busing programs which involve racial quotas. Neoconservatives are skeptical that laws, bureaucracies, regulations, and public spending can improve the nation's health, or guarantee employment, or protect the environment. Government is being "overloaded" with tasks, many of which should be left to the individual, the family, the church, or the free-market system. Government has attempted to do too much for its citizens, and by failing to meet its promises, government has lost respect and legitimacy. The War in Vietnam was not a national "crime," but instead a "tragic error." The United States must regain its military power and remain a force for good in the world.[4]

In its beginning, the neoconservative position was a reaction of a few intellectuals to the turbulence of the 1960s. The early movement included sociologists Nathan Glazer, Irving Kristol, and Daniel Bell; political scientists James Q. Wilson, Aaron Wildavsky, and Daniel Patrick Moynihan (now U.S. Senator from New York); and political sociologist Seymour Martin Lipset. They captured control of an established liberal journal, *Commentary*, and created a new journal of their own, *The Public Interest*. More recently, a neoconservative base has emerged in the American

[3]Irving Kristol, "What is a Neoconservative?" *Newsweek*, January 19, 1976, p. 87.
[4]Peter Steinfels, *The Neoconservatives* (New York: Simon and Schuster, 1979).

Enterprise Institute, a Washington policy-planning organization which has grown in recent years to challenge the unrestrained liberalism of the more prestigious The Brookings Institution.

The message of these neoconservative intellectuals may not have been heard in elite circles if the nation had not faced rampaging inflation and declining productivity. By 1980, the United States had experienced a decade-long inflation—the worst in its history. Personal savings were disappearing rapidly. The incentive to invest was crippled by high taxes. Factories and machines became outmoded. U.S. products could no longer compete with products from Europe and Japan in the world (and even the U.S.) market. Americans as a whole spent too much and saved too little. Federal tax and budget policies promoted immediate consumption instead of investment in the future. A large segment of the federal government's budget (up to three quarters of it) was declared "uncontrollable"—notably the social insurance, welfare, and pension programs. Heavy taxes discouraged work, investment, and productivity.

For forty years the liberal establishment believed that government could stimulate the economy by increasing its own spending to increase overall demand. The ideas of British economist John M. Keynes prevailed in elite circles: to offset unemployment, government should stimulate demand by increasing spending or lowering taxes and incurring added debt; to offset inflation, government should reduce spending or increase taxes and incur little or no debt. But Keynesian economics did not envision "stagflation," with both high unemployment *and* high inflation. Moreover, while politicians had no problem in spending money in periods of recession, it turned out to be impossible for them to reduce spending in periods of inflation.

A small group of younger economists began to counter Keynesian notions with their own "supply-side" economics. Supply-side economics asserts that the free market is better equipped than government to bring lower prices and more supplies of what people want and need. Government, they argue, is the problem, not the solution. Government taxing, spending, and monetary policies have promoted immediate consumption instead of investment for the future. High taxes penalize hard work, creativity, investment, and saving. According to the supply-siders, government should provide tax incentives to encourage investment and savings; tax rates should be lowered on middle and high income brackets to encourage work; government spending should be reduced; government regulations should be minimized in order to increase productivity and growth; and government should stimulate production and supply rather than demand and consumption.

America's deep economic problems convinced even the most liberal policy-planning organization, The Brookings Institution, that "persistent inflation, slowing productivity, and sluggish growth...are sources of increased concern" and that there is "deep skepticism that collective response through government institutions are likely to be effective."[5]

These newer trends in elite thinking—neoconservatism and supply-side economics—do not alter the underlying commitment to liberal, reformist values. But they represent more realistic views of what can be achieved by government, and more traditional views about the importance of personal initiative, enterprise, work, and family. These views are not limited to the Reagan Administration. They enjoy wide acceptance among the nation's top leaders in every sector of society.

EQUALITY AND LEVELING

Perhaps no issue has been so much at the heart of American political life since the nation's founding than that of equality. Today, voting rights, school busing, feminism, affirmative action, and income redistribution are all essentially questions of equality—what it is, how much we want, and how best to achieve it.

American elites, from the Founding Fathers to the current national leadership, have defined equality as *equality of opportunity*—the elimination of artificial barriers to success, fame, and wealth. *Absolute equality*—the equal division of income and wealth among people—was referred to as "leveling" by our Founding Fathers, and it has always been denounced by the nation's leadership. In 1816, Thomas Jefferson wrote:

> To take from one, because it is thought his own industry and that of his fathers has acquired too much, in order to spare to others, who, or whose fathers have not, exercised equal industry and skill, is to violate arbitrarily the first principle of association, the guarantee to everyone the free exercise of his industry and the fruits acquired by it.[6]

Elites have traditionally defended the principle of merit. At the same time, elites (more than masses) have supported efforts to eliminate artificial barriers to advancement such as race, religion, class, and sex. But support for equality of opportunity has not meant support for equality of results. Despite occasional demagogic rhetoric, redistributional ideas wither and die among national leaders when given specific contextual meanings.

Consider a *Washington Post*-Harvard University survey of 2,500 recognized national leaders.[7] These leaders were selected from eight

[5]*Brookings Annual Report 1980* (Washington: The Brookings Institution, 1981), p. 2.

[6]Cited in Richard Hofstadter, *The American Political Tradition* (New York: Knopf; 1948), p. 45.

[7]*Washington Post*, September 26, 1976.

groups: businesspersons, farm leaders, intellectuals, news media executives, Republican officials, Democratic officials, blacks, feminists, and youth. (Of course, these leaders include many individuals who would *not* be considered institutional elites according to our more rigid definition in Chapter 1.) The first question was designed to ascertain the meaning of "equality"—specifically, to learn whether American leaders idealized *equality of opportunity* in the fashion of traditional liberal thought, or *equality of results* in the fashion of modern equalitarianism. The question was "Which do you prefer: equality of opportunity—giving each person an opportunity for an education to develop his or her ability—or equality of results—giving each person a relatively equal income regardless of his or her education and ability?"

The striking outcome was that *all* of the leadership groups chose *equality of opportunity* by overwhelming margins. Even black, feminist, and youth leaders chose equality of opportunity and rejected equality of results by margins of twelve to one. Businesspersons, farm leaders, and media executives chose equality of opportunity by ninety to one.

The next question was how much inequality was thought to be "fair." Leaders were asked how much a "fair salary" would be for different occupations. The figures shown in Table 8–1 were those produced for "semi-skilled workers in an auto assembly plant" and "a president of one of the top 100 corporations."

Table 8–1   How Elites Believe Incomes Should Be Distributed

Leadership Groups	Auto Worker	Corporate Executive	Executive/Worker Ratio
Businesspersons	$16,000	$206,000	13 to 1
Farm Leaders	12,000	111,000	9 to 1
Intellectuals	17,000	119,000	7 to 1
News Media Executives	16,000	131,000	8 to 1
Republican Officials	13,000	146,000	11 to 1
Democratic Officials	16,000	128,000	8 to 1
Blacks	18,000	114,000	6 to 1
Feminists	15,000	88,000	6 to 1
Youth	13,000	105,000	8 to 1

Source: *Washington Post,* September 26, 1976, p. A8.

The most important finding of this inquiry was the belief among *all* types of leaders that inequalities ranging from six to one to thirteen to one were considered "fair." Predictably, black and feminist leaders thought business executives deserved a somewhat lower worker-executive pay ratio than did business executives themselves. But the really striking conclusion is that all elites, even minority group leaders, believed large inequalities in income to be "fair."

In short, American elites, even those representing the young, the poor, and blacks, overwhelmingly reject the idea that "fairness" requires equality of income.

FACTIONALISM AMONG ELITES

Exactly how much competition and conflict exists among America's elites? Are American elites generally cohesive, with only traditional Democratic and Republican affiliations and conventionally liberal and conservative attachments dividing them? Or are there serious conflicts among elites—serious splits which threaten the national consensus and the stability of the system itself? Are political conflicts in America merely petty squabbles among ambitious individuals, competing interest groups, or competing institutions—all of which agree on the underlying "rules of the game"? Or is American leadership seriously divided—so much so that the very framework of the political system is being shaken?

The pluralist view is that competition is a driving force in the American political system. Yet the very purpose of this system, according to pluralist political theory, is to manage competition, to channel it through the institutional structure, to modify its intensity, to assay compromises and balance conflicting interests. In short, pluralism recognizes and encourages competition as a system of checks and balances within American society.

In general, pluralists contend that competition will be limited by several forces which act to maintain an "equilibrium" in the political system. First of all, there is supposed to be a large, nearly universal *latent group* in American society which supports the constitutional system and the prevailing rules of the game. This group is not always visible, but it can be activated to administer overwhelming rebuke to any faction that resorts to unfair means, violence, or terrorism. Secondly, *overlapping group membership* is also supposed to maintain the system in equilibrium: Many individuals belong to a number of groups so that group leaderships must moderate their goals and philosophies to avoid offending members who have other group affiliations. Finally, pluralists offer the notion of *checks and balances* that arise from competition itself. No single segment of society—no single group of powerful leaders—could ever command a majority. Thus, the power of corporations is checked by government, government by parties and civic groups, the mass media by government and advertisers, and so on. These "countervailing" centers of power function to check the influence of any single segment of the nation's elite.

Elitists, of course, see a much greater cohesion and unity among various segments of the nation's leadership. Yet elitism does not imply a single, monolithic body of power-holders. Elitism does not pretend that power in society does not shift over time, or that new elites cannot emerge to compete with old elites. Indeed, it is unlikely that there ever was a society in which various individuals and factions did not compete for power and preeminence. A "circulation of elites" is clearly necessary to ensure a renewal of elite leadership through the contribution of slightly different interests and experiences that new members bring to their roles.

Elite theory contends, however, that serious splits among elites—disagreements over the fundamental values and future directions of American society—are rare. Indeed, perhaps the only really serious split in the nation's elite led to the Civil War—the split between southern planters, landowners, exporters, and slave owners, and northern manufacturers, merchants, and immigrant employees, over whether the nation's future, particularly its western land, was to be devoted to a plantation, exporting, slave economy or a free, small farmer, market economy for domestic manufactured goods. This conflict led to the nation's bloodiest war. However serious we believe our present internal conflicts to be, they do not match the passions which engulfed this nation over a century ago.

THE SUNBELT COWBOYS VERSUS
THE ESTABLISHED YANKEES

Nonetheless, elite factionalism today is evident. A major source of this factionalism among America's elite is the division between the new-rich, southern and western *cowboys* and the established, eastern, liberal *yankees*. This factional split transcends partisan squabbling among Democrats and Republicans, or traditional riffs between Congress and the President, or petty strife among organized interest groups. The conflict between *cowboys* and *yankees* derives from differences in their sources of wealth and the newness of the elite status of the *cowboys*.

Since World War II, new opportunities to acquire wealth and create new bases of power have developed as a result of technological change and adjustments in the economy. The major areas of opportunity have been:

1. Independent oil drilling operations
2. Aerospace industry
3. Computer technology, cameras, and copying machines
4. Real estate development, particularly in the "Sunbelt" from southern California and Arizona through Texas to Florida
5. Discount drugs and merchandising, fast foods, and low-cost insurance

The personal wealth of the *cowboys* is frequently unstable, compared, for example, to the established wealth of the Rockefellers, Fords, duPonts, or Mellons. Wealth that is institutionalized in giant corporations—corporations that form the basis of an industrialized economy such as autos, steel, oil, and chemicals—is likely to remain intact over generations with only minor fluctuations in value. But many of today's *new* rich have acquired their wealth in relatively new and unstable industries. Independent oil operations and the aerospace industry are highly fluctuating businesses. The computer industry has now stabilized and appears to be an integral part of a mature economy. But fortunes in real estate, drug stores, discount merchandising, and low-cost insurance can quickly disappear.[8]

By contrast, the established *yankees* are second- or third-generation descendants of the great entrepreneurial families of the Industrial Revolution (the familiar Rockefellers, Fords, Mellons, duPonts, Kennedys, Harrimans, and so forth). Other *yankees* have been recruited through established corporate institutions, Wall Street and Washington law firms, Eastern banking and investment firms, well-known foundations, and Ivy League universities.

The *cowboys* do not fully share in the liberal, social welfarism of the dominant eastern establishment. However, they do not exercise power that is in any way proportional to the overwhelming hegemony of the established *yankees*. The *cowboys* may have gained in influence in recent years—and much of the petty political fighting reported in today's press has its roots in *cowboy-yankee* factionalism—but the liberal establishment remains dominant. Most importantly, *cowboys* and *yankees* agree on the overriding importance of preserving political stability and a healthy free-enterprise economy.

The *cowboys* are "self-made" individuals who acquired wealth and power in an intense competitive struggle that continues to shape their outlook on life. Their upward mobility, their individualism, and their competitive spirit shape their view of society and the way they perceive their new elite responsibilities. In contrast, the *yankees* have either inherited great wealth or attach themselves to established institutions of great wealth, power, and prestige. The *yankees* are socialized, sometimes from earliest childhood, in the responsibilities of wealth and power. They are secure in their upper-class membership, highly principled in their relationships with others, and public-regarding in their exercise of elite responsibilities.

---

[8]Consider, for example, the case of H. Ross Perot, the only man ever to *lose* $1 billion in personal wealth. When he first publicly offered shares of his company, Electronic Data Systems, shares sold for $16.50. Perot held 9 million shares himself, amounting to a total value of over $150 million. In 1970, the value of EDS stock had risen to $162 a share, making Perot's fortune worth close to $1.5 *billion*. But the stock crashed shortly thereafter to $29 a share, leaving Perot with a mere $270 million. Apparently these fluctuations fascinated Perot, so he purchased duPont, Walston, Inc., one of the largest brokerage firms on the New York Stock Exchange, perhaps to learn more about the stock market. But Perot failed as a broker, too; duPont, Walston collapsed and Perot disappeared from the list of "people at the top." See "The Man Who Lost a Billion," *Fortune* (September 1973).

The *cowboys* are new to their position; they lack old-school ties, and they are not particularly concerned with the refinements of ethical conduct. The *yankees* frequently regard the *cowboys* with disdain—as uncouth and opportunistic gamblers and speculators, shady wheeler-dealers and influence-peddlers, and uncultured and selfish bores.

The *cowboys* are newly risen from the masses—many had very humble beginnings. But it is their experience in *rising* from the masses that shapes their philosophy, rather than their mass origins. As we would expect, they are less public-regarding and social-welfare oriented than the *yankees,* and tend to think of solutions to social problems in individualistic terms—they place primary responsibility for solving life's problems on the individual. *Cowboys* believe that they "made it" themselves through initiative and hard work, and advise anyone who wants to get more out of life to follow the same path. The *cowboys* do not feel guilty about poverty or discrimination— clearly neither they nor their ancestors had any responsibility for these conditions. Their wealth and position was not given to them—they earned it themselves and they have no apologies for what they have accomplished in life. They are supportive of the political and economic system that provided them the opportunity to rise to the top; they are very patriotic— sometimes vocally "anti-Communist"—and moderate to conservative on most national policy issues.

An examination of the backgrounds of some of the new-rich, sunbelt *cowboys* reveals their connections with the oil, defense, and real-estate industries and illuminates some of our contentions about their general qualities.

Clint Murcheson (Murcheson Brothers Investments, Dallas, Texas). Attended public schools and Trinity College, Texas. A director of the First National Bank of Dallas, and Delhi-Australian Petroleum Co. Owner of the Dallas Cowboys, a professional football team. Owns substantial interest in Atlantic Life Insurance, Transcontinental Bus, Southeastern Michigan Gas, and Holt, Rinehart & Winston Publishers. A former director of the New York Central Railroad, which he purchased with partner Sid W. Richardson.

John B. Connally. Former Secretary of the Treasury, Secretary of the Navy, governor of Texas, and administrative assistant to Lyndon B. Johnson. Wounded in the assassination fire that killed President John F. Kennedy. Attorney for oil operator Sid W. Richardson.

Sid W. Richardson. Independent oil operator. Formerly a director of New York Central Railroad. Attended University of Texas.

Roy Ash. Did not attend undergraduate college. Director, Office of Management and Budget, under Nixon. Former president and director of Litton Industries. Director of BankAmerica, Global Marine, Inc., Pacific Mutual Life Insurance. A trustee of California Institute of Technology, Marymount College, Loyola University. Formerly chief financial officer of Hughes Aircraft.

Table 8–2   A Guide to Distinguishing Yankees from Cowboys

Eastern Establishment		*Sunbelt Cowboys*
	Universities	
Harvard, Yale		University of Texas
		Air Force Academy
	Newspapers	
New York Times		*Chicago Tribune*
Washington Post		*New York Daily News*
	Music	
Leonard Bernstein		Lawrence Welk
	Books	
David Halberstam, *The Best*		George Gilder,
and The Brightest		*Wealth and Poverty*
	Movies	
Shampoo, China Syndrome		*Patton, Smokey and the Bandit*
	Magazines	
Harpers, Newsweek		*Reader's Digest,*
		U.S. News & World Report
	Food	
Quiche Lorraine		Charcoal Steak
	Foundations	
Brookings Institution		W. Clement Stone Foundation
Ford Foundation		Herman Kahn's Hudson Institute
Rockefeller Foundation		
	Intellectuals	
Herbert Marcuse		NONE
Arthur Schlesinger, Jr.		
John Kenneth Galbraith		
	Car	
Porsche		Cadillac
	Entertainment	
Concerts		Golf
Tennis		Football
	Comedians	
Woody Allen		Bob Hope
	Actors	
Alan Alda		Clint Eastwood (following
		the death of John Wayne)
	Singers	
Barbra Streisand		Johnny Cash

With apologies to Kevin Phillips' "Conservative Chic," *Harpers,* (June, 1973), pp. 66–70; whose notions of "elite liberal" and "new majority" overlap with our own idea of eastern *Yankees* and sunbelt *Cowboys*.

Yankee distrust of *cowboys* may have begun with the assassination of President John F. Kennedy in Dallas and the rash of conspiracy theories linking the assassination to reactionary Texas oil interests. President Johnson acted decisively to discredit these rumors with the appointment of the Warren Commission, composed mainly of eastern liberals, which concluded that Kennedy's death was the act of a lone assassin.

Representative of the swashbuckling style of the true sunbelt *cowboys* is the father and son construction team which heads the Bechtel Corporation. Steven D. Bechtel and his son, Steven D. Bechtel, Jr., control a little-known, family-held, corporate colossus, which is the *world's* largest construction company.[9] The senior Bechtel never obtained a college degree, but he acquired engineering know-how as a builder of the Hoover dam. Bechtel conceived of, and built, the San Francisco Bay Area Rapid Transit, and he and his son are currently building the 98-mile Washington, D.C. METRO subway system.

Simultaneously, Bechtel is building an entire industrial city—Jubayl in Saudi Arabia; a copper industry including mines, railroads, and smelters in Indonesia; and the world's largest hydroelectric system in Ontario, Canada. Bechtel was fired as the contractor for the Trans-Alaska pipeline when cost overruns first occurred; but the final price of $8 billion turned out to be eight times higher than the original estimate, and it seems in retrospect that Bechtel would have done a more cost-effective job if he had been allowed to complete the work. The Bechtel Corporation remains family owned, and therefore refuses to divulge to the SEC or other prying bureaucracies its real worth. However, the Bechtels have gone outside of the family to bring in top leadership for their far-flung enterprises: George Schultz, former Secretary of the Treasury under President Nixon, is now president of the Bechtel Corporation; and Caspar Weinberger, former Secretary of Health, Education, and Welfare under President Nixon, was a vice-president of Bechtel Corporation before he accepted the position of Secretary of Defense under President Reagan.

"BUNKY" HUNT: THE COWBOY WITH A BILLION

The late billionaire H. L. Hunt was once asked by reporters whether he was worried about his son's extravagance: (Lamar Hunt had lost over $1 million in one year as the owner of the new American League football team, the Kansas City Chiefs.) "Certainly it worries me," replied the legendary oil magnate. "At that rate he'll be broke in 250 years."

[9]See *Newsweek*, August 29, 1977, pp. 60–62.

The senior Hunt began drilling for oil in Smackover, Arkansas, in 1920. His very first well (which he won in a poker game) produced a gusher. By 1937, the independent Hunt Oil Company of Dallas, Texas, was worth millions, and at his death in 1974, H. L. Hunt was believed to be one of the richest men in America. His sons, Nelson Bunker, William Herbert, and Lamar, have continued to amass vast personal wealth. "Bunky" Hunt, who regularly refuses interviews and declines publicity, admitted to a congressional committee that he was probably worth over a billion dollars, but he added, "a billion dollars isn't what it used to be." He refused to say how much he was worth: "Senator, it's been my experience that anyone who knows how much they're worth, ain't worth very much."

Operating out of the First National Bank of Dallas, Bunky Hunt manages a vast array of businesses, including the Hunt Energy Corporation; Placid Oil; 3.5 million acres of real estate, including prime downtown Dallas properties; 100,000 head of cattle; and 700 thoroughbred horses. But in 1979, Hunt and his brother William Herbert decided on an even more ambitious scheme—to corner the world market in silver.

The Hunts began to buy silver at $6 an ounce. Their purchases were so vast that they decided to buy a leading Wall Street investment firm, Bache Halsey Stuart Shields, to facilitate their operations. When silver jumped to $11 an ounce, they contacted their oil-rich Arab friends and recommended more heavy buying. By early 1980, the Hunts had forced the price of silver to $50 an ounce and their holdings were worth an estimated $7.5 billion. However, much of their holdings were in the form of "futures contracts"—guarantees to pay a set price for silver at a certain date in the future. Rising interest rates in the U.S. attracted many investors away from silver (and gold) and into high-interest-paying bank certificates and money market funds. Increasingly the Hunts were called upon to pay cash for the unpaid portions of their futures contracts. Finally, on March 27, 1980, "Silver Thursday," the Hunts and their Bache brokers were unable to meet their debts. Panic ensued on Wall Street, as well as in the Federal Reserve System, the U.S Treasury, and the Commodities Future Trading Commission. The price of silver tumbled to $10 an ounce. Bache was barely saved from bankruptcy, and many investors lost millions. A $1.1 billion loan was made to the Hunts to keep them from dumping their silver on the market and further depressing the price. Their scheme to corner the silver market failed. Bunky Hunt was forced to go back to being an ordinary billionaire. But, as the Wall Street investor put it, "No one has to put on a benefit dinner for Bunker Hunt." Hunt's irrepressible style was unchanged by the episode: "I may lose money, but I never lose sleep."[10]

---

[10]See Roy Rowan, "A Talkfest with the Hunts," *Fortune*, August 11, 1980.

The Watergate Affair and the subsequent movement to impeach President Nixon also involved *cowboy-yankee* conflict. Early in the affair, the Eastern liberals were content merely to chastise the President; there was little open talk of impeachment. The President appointed a *yankee,* Elliot Richardson (Harvard Law School, clerkship under Supreme Court Justice Felix Frankfurter, prestigious Boston law firm, prior government service as Secretary of HEW and Secretary of Defense), as attorney general to replace Richard Kleindienst (Arizona attorney and former assistant to Senator Barry Goldwater). Richardson appointed as special prosecutor, *yankee* Archibald Cox (Harvard law professor, U.S. solicitor general under Kennedy and Johnson) to conduct the Watergate investigation. But when President Nixon fired Cox over the use of taped presidential conversations, and Richardson resigned, the eastern establishment turned against the president.

Eastern liberals in both parties charged that President Nixon had surrounded himself with southern and western, sunbelt "wheeler-dealers" whose opportunism and lack of ethics created the milieu for Watergate. Liberals attacked the President's closeness to John Connally and his personal friendships with Charles "Bebe" Rebozo (who started life as a gas station attendant, opened a successful tire recapping business, expanded into Florida real estate, and later established the Key Biscayne Bank) and Ralph Abplanalp (inventor of the spray valve used on aerosol cans and co-owner of Nixon's Key Biscayne and San Clemente properties). Easterners decried the unwholesome influence of many White House staffers whose careers were tied to southern and western interests: H.R. "Bob" Haldeman (California public relations), John Erlichman (Seattle lawyer), Ronald Ziegler (California public relations), Herbert Klein (California press executive), and Frederick Dent (South Carolina textile millionaire).

The *New York Times,* voice of the eastern establishment, published an article specifically blaming Watergate on the *cowboys:*

> The Nixonian bedfellows, the people whose creed the President expresses and whose interests he guards, are, to generalize, the economic sovereigns of America's Southern rim, the "sunbelt," that runs from Southern California, through Arizona and Texas down to the Florida Keys....They are "self-made" men and women in the sense that they did not generally inherit great riches....whether because of the newness of their position, their frontier heritage, or their lack of old school ties, they tend to be without particular concerns about the niceties of business ethics and morals, and therefore to be connected more than earlier money would have thought wise, with shady speculations, political influence-peddling, corrupt Nixons, and even organized crime....

Other scandals are sure to follow, for it seems obvious that the kind of milieu in which the President has chosen to immerse himself will continue to produce policies self-serving at best, shady at average, and downright illegal at worst....the new-money wheeler-dealers seem to regard influence-peddling and back-scratching as the true stuff of the American dream.[11]

Of course, this charge overlooks the fact that former Attorney General John Mitchell, who as chairperson of the Committee to Re-Elect the President was directly responsible for campaign tactics, possesses impeccable Eastern establishment credentials: senior partner, top Wall Street law firm of Mudge Rose Guthrie Alexander & Mitchell; and specialist in tax-free municipal bond investing (a favorite tax shelter for establishment fortunes).

THE PREDOMINANCE OF ESTABLISHED WEALTH

Despite the rise of many new persons of wealth in America, established eastern sources of wealth and power continue to dominate national life. Indeed, there is some evidence of a decline in the rate of new elite formation in the course of the twentieth century. Most of America's great corporate families built their empires in the period between the Civil War and World War I. The Industrial Revolution propelled many new waves to the top of the national elite structure. This was a period of rapid industrial expansion, the growth of new sources of wealth, and corresponding changes in the elite structure. But today the nation's economy is mature; large corporate and governmental institutions control most of the nation's resources; and opportunities for the accumulation of great personal wealth are more limited. Table 8–3 presents estimates by C.

Table 8–3   Social Origins of the Super-Rich, 1900–1970

Social Origin	1900	1925	1950	1970
Upper Class	39%	56%	68%	82%
Middle Class	20	30	20	10
Lower Class	39	12	9	4
Not Classified	2	2	3	4

Sources: Estimates for 1900, 1925, and 1950 are from C. Wright Mills, *The Power Elite* (New York: Oxford University Press, 1950), pp. 104–105. The percentages are derived from biographies of the 275 people who were and are known to historians, biographers, and journalists as the richest people living in the United States—the 90 richest in 1900, the 95 richest in 1925, and the 90 richest in 1950. Estimates for 1970 are from our own analysis of biographies of the nation's 66 richest Americans, *Fortune* magazine, July 1968. At the top of the 1900 list is John D. Rockefeller; at the top of the 1925 list is Henry Ford; at the top in 1950 is H.L. Hunt; at the top in 1970 is J. Paul Getty.

[11]Kirkpatrick Sale, "The World Behind Watergate," *The New York Times Book Review,* May 3, 1973.

Wright Mills of the social backgrounds of the nation's richest men in 1900, 1925, and 1950; we have added our own estimates for 1970. Only 39 percent of the richest men in America come from the upper social class in 1900; but 68 percent of the richest men were born to wealth in 1950 and 82 percent in 1970. Mills estimates that 39 percent of the richest men in 1900 had struggled up from the bottom compared to only 4 percent in 1970.

SUMMARY

Elitist and pluralist scholars disagree over the extent and significance of conflict among national leaders. Pluralists observe disagreements over specific programs and policies; they contend that this competition is a significant aspect of democracy. Competition among elites makes policies and programs more responsive to mass demands, because competing elites will try to mobilize mass support for their views. Masses will have a voice in public policy by choosing among competing elites with different policy positions. Moreover, competitive elites will check and balance each other and help prevent abuses of power. In contrast, elitist scholars observe a fairly broad consensus among national leaders on behalf of fundamental values and national goals. Elitists contend that the range of disagreement among elites is relatively narrow and generally confined to means rather than ends.

It is our own judgment, based on our examination of available surveys of leadership opinion as well as public statements of top corporate and governmental executives, that consensus rather than competition characterizes elite opinion. Despite disagreements over specific policies and programs, most top leaders agree on the basic values and future directions of American society.

The established liberal values of the nation's leadership include a willingness to take the welfare of others into account as a part of one's own sense of moral well-being, and a willingness to use governmental power to correct the perceived wrongs done to others—particularly the poor, blacks, and other minorities. Popular notions of corporate and financial leaders as exploitative, reactionary robber barons are based on nineteenth-century stereotypes.

Disagreement among various sectors of national leaders— businesspersons, Democratic and Republican politicians, bureaucrats, mass media executives, and labor leaders—is confined to a relatively narrow set of issues—the oil depletion allowance, federal versus state-local control of social programs, inheritance taxes, and the proper range of income differences. There is widespread agreement on the essential components of welfare-state capitalism.

Nonetheless, there is evidence of elite factionalism. In recent years, the major faultline among the nation's leaders is the division between the new-rich southern and western *cowboys* and the established eastern liberal *yankees*. The *cowboys* have acquired their wealth since World War II in independent oil operations, the aerospace and computer industries, sunbelt real estate from California through Texas to Florida, and discount stores. These *cowboys* do not fully share the liberal values of the established *yankees*. They are self-made persons of wealth and power—individualistic, highly competitive, and politically conservative. The *yankees* have enjoyed wealth for generations, or slowly climbed the rungs of the nation's largest corporations, law firms, banks, and foundations. They have acquired a sense of civic responsibility, and they look upon the *cowboys* as unprincipled gamblers, shady wheeler-dealers, and uncultured influence-peddlers.

The *yankees* continue to dominate positions of power in America. Two presidents—Johnson and Nixon—with close ties to southern and western, new-wealth *cowboys,* have been forced from office. In both cases opposition from eastern establishment *yankees,* particularly those in the mass media, played an important role in their loss of power.

9

How institutional leaders make public policy

POLICY AS ELITE PREFERENCE OR GROUP INTERACTION?

Are the major directions of public policy in America determined by a relatively small group of like-minded individuals interacting among themselves and reflecting their own values and preferences in policy-making? Or are the major directions of American policy a product of competition, bargaining, and compromise among a large number of diverse groups in society? Does public policy reflect the demands of "the people" as demonstrated in elections, opinion polls, and interest-group activity? Or are the views of "the people" easily influenced by communications flowing downward from elites? Are the "proximate policy-makers"— the president, Congress, the courts—truly representatives of their constituents' views in public policy? Or are these public officials relatively free from constituency pressure on most issues and more responsive to elitist views?

The elitist model of the policy process would portray policy as the preferences and values of the dominant elite. According to elitist political theory, public policy does not reflect demands of "the people," but rather the interests, sentiments, and values of the very few who participate in the policy-making process. Changes or innovations in public policy come about when elites redefine their own interests or modify their own values. Of course, elite policy need not be oppressive or exploitative of the masses. Elites may be very "public-regarding," and the welfare of the masses may be an important consideration in elite decision-making. Yet the central feature of the model is that *elites* make policy, not masses. The elite model views the masses as largely passive, apathetic, and ill-informed about policy. Public opinion is easily manipulated by the elite-dominated mass media, so that communication between elites and masses flows downward. The "proximate policy-makers" knowingly or unknowingly respond primarily to the opinions of elites.

No serious scholar today claims that the masses make policy—that each individual can directly participate in all of the decisions that shape his or her life. The ideal of the New England town meeting where the citizenry convenes itself periodically as a legislature to make decisions for the whole community is irrelevant in today's large, complex industrial society. Pure democracy is and always has been, a romantic fiction. Social scientists acknowledge that all societies, even democratic societies, are governed by elites.

By contrast, the pluralist model of policy-making portrays the process as a give-and-take among many diverse groups in society. Few individuals can participate directly in policy-making, but they can join groups that will press their demands upon government. The interest group is viewed as the principal actor in the policy-making process—the essential bridge between the individual and government. Public policy at any time reflects an equilibrium of the relative influence of interest groups. Political scientist Earl Latham describes public policy from the pluralist viewpoint as follows:

> What may be called public policy is actually the equilibrium reached in the group struggle at any given moment, and it represents a balance which the contending factions or groups constantly strive to tip in their favor.... The legislature referees the group struggle, ratifies the victories of the successful coalition, and records the terms of the surrenders, compromises, and conquests in the form of statutes.[1]

The individual can play an indirect role in policy-making by voting, joining interest groups, and working in political parties. Parties themselves are viewed as coalitions of groups: the Democratic Party a coalition of labor, ethnic groups, blacks, Catholics, central-city residents, black intellectuals, and southerners; the Republican Party a coalition of middle-class, white-collar workers, rural and small-town residents, suburbanites, and Protestants. According to this model, mass demands flow upward through the interest groups, parties, and elections to the proximate policy-makers.

[1]Earl Latham, "The Group Basis of Politics," in *Political Behavior*, ed. Heinz Eulau, Samuel J. Eldersveld, and Morris Janowitz (New York: Free Press, 1956), p. 239.

intellectual community. The foundations determine broad policy objectives—strategic arms limitations, relations with the Soviet Union and China, defense strategies, urban renaissance, the quieting of racial violence in cities, population control, improved public health care systems, and so forth. The foundations provide the initial "seed money" to analyze social problems, to determine national priorities, and to investigate new policy directions. At a later period in the policy-making process, massive government research funds will be spent to fill in the details in areas already explored by these initial studies.

Universities necessarily respond to the policy interests of foundations, although of course they also try to convince foundations of new and promising policy directions. Nonetheless, research proposals originating from universities which do *not* fit the previously defined "emphasis" of foundation interests are usually lost in the shuffle of papers. While university intellectuals working independently occasionally have an impact on the policy-making process, on the whole intellectuals who would be heard must respond to policy directions set by the foundations, corporations, and government agencies that underwrite the costs of research.

The *policy-planning groups* are the central coordinating points in the entire elite policy-making process. They bring together people at the top of the corporate and financial institutions, the universities, the foundations, the mass media, the powerful law firms, the top intellectuals, and influential figures in the government. They review the relevant university- and foundation-supported research on topics of interest, and more importantly they try to reach a consensus about what action should be taken on national problems under study. Their goal is to develop *action recommendations*—explicit policies or programs designed to resolve or ameliorate national problems. At the same time, they endeavor to build consensus among corporate, financial, media, civic, intellectual, and government leaders around major policy directions.

Certain policy-planning groups—notably the Council on Foreign Relations, the Business Roundtable, the Committee on Economic Development, and The Brookings Institution—are influential in a wide range of key policy areas. Other policy-planning groups—the Population Council (world population control), Resources for the Future (environmental concerns), and the Urban Institute (urban problems), for example—specialize in certain policy issues. The well-known "think tanks"—the RAND Corporation, the Stanford Research Institute, the Hudson Institute—are a crossbreed between a research organization and a policy-planning group. Their research is more "action-oriented" than typical university research, yet it falls short of the consensus building and policy implementation exercised by true policy-planning groups such as the CFR, the Business Roundtable, and The Brookings Institution. Generally, the "think tanks" submit their reports to foundations and policy-planning groups for further discussion before efforts at policy implementation begin.

Corporate representatives—company presidents, directors, or other high officials—sit on the boards of trustees of the foundations, universities, and policy-planning groups. The personnel interlocking between corporation boards, university trustees, foundation boards, and policy-planning boards is extensive. (We have described interlocking among the Rockefeller, Ford, and Carnegie Foundations, and the Council on Foreign Relations, the Business Roundtable, the Committee on Economic Development, and The Brookings Institution in Chapter 5.)

Policy recommendations of the key policy-planning groups are then distributed to the mass media, federal executive agencies, and the Congress. The mass media play a vital role in preparing public opinion for policy change. They also encourage political personalities to assume new policy stances by allocating valuable network broadcast time to those who will speak out in favor of new policy directions.

If policy recommendations call for *major* departures from current programs or policies, or if they are sufficiently innovative and therefore not widely understood, an additional consensus-building step may be utilized—that performed by the presidential commission. The President's Advisory Commission on Civil Disorders, chaired by Governor Otto Kerner of Illinois, followed in the wake of the urban violence of the 1960s. The President's Commission on the Causes and Prevention of Violence, chaired by Milton S. Eisenhower, brother of the former President, considered the rising problems of political assassination and violence in society. The President's Commission on Campus Unrest, chaired by millionaire Republican Governor William Scranton of Pennsylvania, was the government's response to campus disturbances. The continuing U.S. Commission on Civil Rights provides symbolic assurance that the government "cares" about minorities; it has been headed for many years by the Rev. Theodore Hesburgh, president of Notre Dame University. These presidential commissions are designed more for "window dressing" than actual policy development. The membership of such commissions usually includes a few prestigious individuals at the top, but many members are chosen simply as stereotypical representatives of labor, blacks, women, students, and other "political" appointments. The commissions may contract for university research or simply hear testimony from prominent persons before making their recommendations. But their recommendations are clearly predictable: they reflect sometimes word for word the previous reports of the established policy-planning groups. Nonetheless, presidential commissions offer the public "symbolic reassurance" that the government and the nation's leadership are *concerned* about a particularly vexing problem. However, their record in developing and implementing really innovative solutions to national problems has been poor.

A more fruitful path in policy development is for federal executive agencies to respond directly to policy recommendations from policy-planning groups. Very often agencies do so initially by contracting with universities for supporting research in the same subject areas in which the foundations and policy-planning groups have already been working. This new research is not so much to discover alternative policies, but rather (1) to confirm the need for change, and (2) to deal with the details of the new policy direction. The results of much of this research are often foregone conclusions, since the same university intellectuals and "think-tank" members who had initially received grants from foundation and policy-planning groups are now employed by federal agencies to continue their work. Thus, the initial "seed money" sown by foundations and corporations is now supplanted by massive government subsidies. It is as though government agencies, aware of support from those at the top of the policy-planning groups, now feel free to support research in approved areas.

The White House staff, congressional committee staffs, and top executive administrators, who usually maintain close contact with policy-planning groups, are contacted with increasing frequency by representatives of such groups, foundation heads, and corporate representatives, as the time for government action draws near. Frequently before the results of government-sponsored research are available, federal executive agencies, with the assistance of policy-planning groups, will prepare legislation for the Congress to implement policy decisions. Particular versions of bills will pass between executive agencies, the White House, policy-planning groups, and the professional staffs of the congressional committees that will eventually consider the bills. The groundwork is laid for making policy into law. Soon the work of the people at the top will be reflected in the actions of the "proximate policy-makers."

THE POLICY-PLANNING ESTABLISHMENT

The policy-planning organizations are clearly at the center of this "oligarchic" model of national policy-making. We have already documented their financial support and interlocking directorships with the nation's largest industries, banks, utilities, insurance companies, and the mass media (see Chapter 5). We observed that David Rockefeller serves as chairman of the Council on Foreign Relations with establishment figures such as Robert V. Roosa, Peter G. Peterson, W. Michael Blumenthal, George P. Schultz, and others. We observed that Clifton C. Garvin, Exxon chairman, heads the Business Roundtable with Walter Wriston (Citicorp), Frank T. Cary (IBM), Rawleigh Warner (Mobil), Richard Shinn (Metropolitan), and others. We observed that Robert V. Roosa headed The Brookings Institution board along with Robert S. McNamara, Frank T.

Cary, John deButts, and so on. We also observed how the policy-planning organizations have recruited and developed leaders for top executive positions in government: Cyrus Vance, Michael Blumenthal, Zbigniew Brzezinski, Paul Warnke, Henry Kissinger, Harold Brown, among many others (see Chapter 5).

Now let us turn to some of the policy decisions in which the leading policy-planning organizations—the Council on Foreign Relations, the Business Roundtable, the Committee on Economic Development, and The Brookings Institution—have been influential.

Council on Foreign Relations.   Political scientist Lester Milbraith observes that the influence of CFR throughout government is so pervasive that it is difficult to distinguish CFR from government programs: "The Council on Foreign Relations, while not financed by government, works so closely with it that it is difficult to distinguish Council actions stimulated by government from autonomous actions."[2]

In the Kennedy and Johnson Administrations, the Council took the lead in determination of U.S. policy in Southeast Asia—including both the initial decision to intervene militarily in Vietnam and the later decision to withdraw. Council members in the Kennedy-Johnson Administration included Secretary of State Dean Rusk, National Security Adviser McGeorge Bundy, Assistant Secretary of State for Far Eastern Affairs William P. Bundy, C.I.A. Director John McCone, and Under Secretary of State George Ball. The Council consensus up to November 1967 was clearly in support of the U.S. military commitment to South Vietnam. (Of all top establishment leaders, only George Ball dissented from the war as early as 1965.) Following the Tonkin Gulf Resolution and the introduction of U.S. ground combat troops in February 1965, President Lyndon Johnson created a private, informal group of CFR advisers, with the assistance of CFR chairman John J. McCloy, which later became known as the "Senior Advisory Group on Vietnam." The group was not an official governmental body and it included more private elites than public officeholders. Twelve of the fourteen members of the Senior Advisory Group were CFR members; only Johnson's close personal friend Abe Fortas and General Omar Bradley were *not* CFR members. As the war continued unabated through 1967, the Council, at the urging of George Ball, recruited Professor Hans Morganthau of the University of Chicago to conduct a new private study, "A Reexamination of American Foreign Policy." Following the Tet offensive in February 1968, President Johnson called a special meeting of his Senior Advisory Group. The Group met for two days, March 25 and 26, during which time key members Douglas

---

[2]Lester Milbraith, "Interest Groups in Foreign Policy," in *Domestic Sources of Foreign Policy*, ed. James Rosenau (New York: Free Press, 1967), p. 247.

Dillon, Cyrus Vance, Arthur Dean, Dean Acheson, and McGeorge Bundy switched from "hawks" to "doves." They presented their new consensus to the President. Five days later, on March 31, 1968, President Johnson announced a de-escalation of the war and his personal decision to retire from public office.

At this point, the CFR, which was doubtlessly relieved that Johnson and his immediate advisers were left as the scape-goats of the Vietnam disaster, immediately launched a new group, the "Vietnam Settlement Group," headed by Robert V. Roosa and Cyrus Vance. The group devised a peace proposal allowing for the return of prisoners and a stand-still ceasefire, with the Viet Cong and Saigon dividing the territory under their respective controls. Secretary of State Kissinger avoided directly attributing U.S. policy to the CFR plan,[3] but the plan itself eventually became the basis of the January 1973 Paris peace agreement.

Following Vietnam, the CFR, under David Rockefeller's tenure as chairman, began its "1980s Project." This was an ambitious program even for so powerful a group as the CFR. But money from the Ford, Lilly, Mellon, and Rockefeller Foundations provided the necessary resources. The project officially began in 1975 and lasted until 1980, and it included:

1. An international campaign on behalf of "human rights"
2. A series of alternative approaches to nuclear stability, including a new strict policy toward nuclear proliferation
3. An effort to restrict international arms sales
4. A study of "North-South global relations"—relations between richer and poorer countries

Upon taking office in 1977, the Carter Administration set all of these policies in motion. It restricted international arms sales; it halted development of the "fast breeder" nuclear reactor; it encouraged private and World Bank loans to less developed countries; and, most importantly, it initiated a world-wide "human rights" campaign in which U.S. trade and aid were curtailed in countries that did not live up to human rights standards. Not only did the Carter Administration adopt the CFR program in full, but it also brought CFR members into the government to administer these programs.

It would be unfair to say that the CFR dominated the Carter Administration. The CFR *was* the Carter Administration. The Carter

---

[3]Although the CFR had supported Henry Kissinger early in his career, Kissinger believed that many CFR members were overly critical of him as Secretary of State. One CFR member remarked: "Kissinger owed his career to the Council, but he never set foot here the whole time he was in office. He is, as you know, extremely arrogant." Leonard Silk and Mark Silk, *The American Establishment* (New York: Basic Books, 1980), p. 208.

Administration included prominent CFR members such as Cyrus Vance (Secretary of State), Harold Brown (Secretary of Defense), Walter Mondale (Vice-President), Zbigniew Brzezinski (National Security Adviser), W. Michael Blumenthal (Secretary of the Treasury), Sol Linowitz (negotiator of the Panama Canal Treaty), Andrew Young (U.N. ambassador), and Paul Warnke (negotiator of the SALT II Agreement).

But the CFR itself, still under Rockefeller's direction, was aware of the crumbling foreign and military policies of the United States during the Carter Administration. In 1980, the CFR issued a stern report citing "sharp anguish over Americans held hostage by international outlaws" (Iran) and "the brutal invasion of a strategic nation" (Afghanistan).[4] It described U.S. defenses as "a troubling question." More importantly, the CFR announced the end of the "1980s Project," with its concern for "human rights," and initiated a new study program—on Soviet Union and U.S.-Soviet relations. Even before Carter left office, leading CFR members had decided that the "human rights" policy was crippling U.S. relations with its allies but was not affecting policies in communist countries. Moreover, the CFR apparently decided that "detente" with the Soviet Union should be re-examined. The CFR recognized "the relentless Soviet military build-up and extention of power by invasion, opportunism, and proxy," and recommended that the U.S.-Soviet relationship "occupy center stage in the coming decade."[5] Thus, elite support for a harder line in foreign and defense policy had been developed through CFR even before Ronald Reagan took office.

The CFR announced its new hard line toward the Soviet Union in a 1981 report, *The Soviet Challenge: A Policy Framework for the 1980s*. It recommended a comprehensive, long-term military build-up by the United States, and it even argued that arms control should no longer be the "centerpiece" of U.S. policy toward the Soviets. It also recommended that the U.S. be prepared to use force in unstable areas of the world such as the Persian Gulf.

The Reagan Administration, like those which preceded it, is relying heavily on CFR advice. However, because of some conservative objections to the "internationalism" of the Council on Foreign Relations, CFR members on the Reagan team have not publicized their membership. Indeed, during the 1980 campaign, CFR and Trilateral Commission member George Bush was forced to resign from both organizations to deflect right-wing attacks that he was part of the CFR "conspiracy" to subvert U.S. interests to an "international government." Nonetheless, Secretary of State Alexander Haig, Defense Secretary Caspar Weinberger, Treasury Secretary Donald Regan, and C.I.A. Director William Casey were

---

[4]Council on Foreign Relations, *Annual Report 1979–80*, p. 11.
[5]*Ibid.*, p. 12.

CFR members. David Rockefeller remains as chairman of the CFR, and Henry Kissinger remains a director.

The Trilateral Commission.   A discussion of the CFR would be incomplete without some reference to its multinational arm, the Trilateral Commission. The Trilateral Commission was established by CFR Board Chairman David Rockefeller in 1972, with the backing of the Council and the Rockefeller Foundation. The Trilateral Commission is a small group of top officials of multinational corporations and governmental leaders of industrialized nations, who meet periodically to coordinate economic policy between the United States, Western Europe, and Japan. According to David Rockefeller, a small, private group of international bankers, business leaders, and political figures—about 290 in all—can assist governments in a wide variety of decisions. "Governments don't have time to think about the broader, longer-range issues," says Rockefeller, in typically elitist fashion. "It seemed to make sense to persuade a group of private, qualified citizens to get together to identify the key issues affecting the world and possible solutions."[6] One outgrowth of the Trilateral Commission is the notion of regular summit meetings with the heads of Western European nations, the United States, and Japan to discuss economic policy.

The Business Roundtable.   The Business Roundtable was established in 1972 "in the belief that business executives should take an increased role in the continuing debates about public policy." The organization is composed of the chief executives of the 200 largest corporations in America. Their firms pay membership fees of up to $50,000 per year; this gives the Roundtable an initial operating budget of nearly $10 million. DuPont chairman Irving Shapiro summarized the purposes of the Roundtable: "We wanted to demonstrate that there are sensible human beings running big companies, people who can think beyond their own interests."[7]

The real impetus to the formation of the Business Roundtable, however, was the worsening inflation of the 1970s, a series of oil crises and resulting public criticism of the oil companies, and the growing consumer and environment movements which threatened big business with costly regulations. The Roundtable was created at a time when big business believed it should draw its wagons together in a circle.

The initial success of the Roundtable was the defeat of the proposed Federal Consumer Protection Agency. The Roundtable then went on to successfully lobby against public financing of congressional election campaigns and against common-site picketing by construction unions. Irving

[6]*Newsweek*, March 24, 1980, p. 38.

[7]*Time*, April 13, 1981, p. 76.

Shapiro of DuPont was the Roundtable's chairman until 1981, when Clifford Garvin of Exxon took over the reins of leadership.

A Roundtable brochure acknowledges that "A principle strength of the Roundtable is the extent of participation by the chief executive officers of the member firms." The organization has fifteen task forces on various national policy issues: antitrust, energy, environment, inflation, government regulation, health, social security, taxation, welfare, and so on. Congress members are impressed when Frank T. Cary, chairman of IBM, appears at a congressional hearing on business regulation; or when Theodore F. Brophy, chairman of GTE, speaks to a congressional committee about taxation; or when Robert A. Beck, chairman of Prudential, talks to congress members about social security. In the Reagan inner circle of friends, Justin Dart, chairman of Dart and Kraft, and Joseph Coors, the Colorado brewer, can present the Roundtable views directly to the President.

The Roundtable has been at the forefront of "deregulation," tax cutting, budget cutting, and "re-industrialization." They have argued successfully that proposed environmental regulations should undergo economic impact analysis in order to learn what the cost of compliance really is and whether this cost is worth whatever improvement the regulations bring. The Roundtable has generally supported tax cuts and budget cuts. As one of Reagan's personal friends (Holmes Tuttle) reported: "The morning after the Inauguration, Justin Dart and I sat down with the President and gave him our impression of the budget. We kept saying the same thing: cut, cut, and then cut some more."[8] Apparently, Reagan received the message. Another primary interest of the Roundtable is speeding up depreciation of buildings, plants, and equipment. Theodore Brophy of GTE has personally led the fight to get faster tax write-offs for business.

Chairman Irving Shapiro explains: "The guts of the Roundtable is the fact that the chief executive officer is the man who participates"—who does the direct lobbying. The Roundtable takes very specific positions on important pieces of legislation affecting business and the economy. In contrast, the Committee on Economic Development (CED) generally develops more comprehensive, long-range policy positions. As Fletcher Byrom, Koppers Company chairman and chairman of the CED explains: "I happen to be on the policy committee of the Roundtable as well as being chairman of the CED .... The Roundtable is taking a very pragmatic short-term approach to specific legislation at the present time. The CED is trying to understand the external issues that are going to have an impact on society."[9]

[8]*Ibid.*, p. 77.
[9]Silk and Silk, *The American Establishment*, p. 259.

Council on Economic Development.   The CED was created in 1942 as an outgrowth of the realization that business would be required to work closer with government in World War II production and in avoiding economic depression after the war. The CED was initially composed of businesspersons who viewed the New Deal as an essential reform to save the capitalist system and their place in it. Early CED members were considered more progressive and far-sighted than the more conservative and less influential businesspersons in the National Association of Manufacturers (NAM). As business gradually moved away from the discredited "public be damned" attitudes of the nineteenth-century robber barons and assumed a new, liberal, public-regarding, social consciousness, a new organization was required to reflect these views. The once powerful NAM became a discredited voice of conservatism, and the CED became the voice of top corporate enterprise.

CED's founder, Paul Hoffman, served as chairman from 1942 to 1948. (Hoffman had been chairman of the board of Studebaker-Packard Corporation; a trustee of the Ford Foundation and the University of Chicago; and a director of New York Life Insurance Co., Time, Inc., and Encyclopedia Britannica.) Another key figure in the formation of the CED was William Benton. (Benton was a former U.S. Senator from Connecticut; former Assistant Secretary of State; chairman of the board of Encyclopedia Britannica; a trustee of the University of Chicago and the American Assembly; and a member of CFR.) The early membership of CED was drawn heavily from the Business Advisory Council of the Department of Commerce, which President Roosevelt had established during the Depression to bring businesspeople into his administration. From the academic world, the CED brought in Robert Calkins, who was dean of the School of Business at Columbia; later Calkins went on to become president of The Brookings Institution.

The CED grew in influence when one of its original trustees, Thomas B. McCabe, chairman of the board of Scott Paper Company, was appointed by President Truman to be chairman of the board of the Federal Reserve System, which directs U.S. monetary policy. McCabe served as FRS chairman from 1948 to 1951, and later became a governor of the New York Stock Exchange.

The first important accomplishment of the CED was the Employment Act of 1946, creating the Council of Economic Advisers and officially committing the U.S. government to fiscal and monetary policies devised to avoid depression, maintain full employment, and minimize inflation. At this time, the CED was heavily interlocked with an organization called the National Planning Association. This latter group did the actual lobbying for the Employment Act. The NPA was then headed by Charles E. Wilson, president of GE. (This Wilson was then referred to as "Electric Charlie" to distinguish him from Charles E. Wilson, president of General Motors and

later Secretary of Defense, who was called "Engine Charlie.")
According to the CED itself:

> The Committee for Economic Development has a special mission that no other business-related organization performs. At CED, business leaders actively engage in the policy process by combining their practical day-to-day experience with the findings of objective research. Volunteering their time, CED's Trustees meet with academic and business experts and staff to develop statements on national policy. Only the Trustees have the final say on CED's policy recommendations. These two hundred Trustees—mostly board chairmen, corporate presidents, and university presidents—make up this independent, nonprofit, and nonpartisan research and educational organization.[10]

The CED immodestly claims that "recommendations made by CED have a penetrating impact on the development of the consensus from which national and international policies emerge."[11] The immodesty, however, may be an honest appraisal of its influence. The CED program "Achieving Energy Independence" (December 1974) contained many of the components of the energy package presented to Congress by President Carter, including energy conservation measures, standby fuel rationing authority, synthetic fuels development, and oil price deregulation. The CED proposed a public-service jobs program with temporary public-service employment funds allocated to cities with especially high unemployment rates. The program was passed in 1974 as part of the Comprehensive Employment and Training Act (CETA). It was the CED which recommended to both Presidents Ford and Carter a "go slow" approach on nuclear energy, a halt to commercial fuel processing plants, and prevention of the sale of nuclear plants to non-nuclear countries by the U.S. and European nations.[12] The CED recommended federal assumption of current federal-state-local welfare programs into a single reformed income maintenance program.[13]

Even before the Reagan Administration came into office, the CED had issued several policy statements calling for deregulation of business activity,[14] tax incentives for business investment,[15] and rebuilding a sound economy.[16] These ideas became the core of Reagan's "A Program for

[10]Committee for Economic Development, *Annual Report 1980* (New York: CED, 1981), p. 2.

[11]Committee for Economic Development, *Report of Activities, 1976* (Washington, D.C.: CED, 1977), p. 3.

[12]"Nuclear Energy and National Security" (Washington, D.C.: CED, 1976). See also CED, "Report on Activities, 1976" (Washington, D.C.: CED, 1977).

[13]"Welfare Reform and Its Financing" (Washington, D.C.: CED, 1976).

[14]"Redefining Government's Role in the Market System" (New York: CED, 1979).

[15]"The Nation's Capital Needs" (New York: CED, 1979).

[16]"Fighting Inflation and Rebuilding a Sound Economy" (New York: CED, 1980).

Economic Recovery,"[17] which initially outlined his budget and tax cutting proposals. CED chairman Fletcher Byron (chairman of Koppers Company) testified before Congress on behalf of the President's program, as did Franklin Lindsay (chairman of Itek Corp.), J. Paul Lyet (chairman of Sperry Corp.), and Thomas A. Vanderslice (chairman of GTE). Current CED policies call for (1) "an industrial strategy...with the market rather than the government determining how resources are allocated"; (2) improving productivity; (3) dampening the inflationary spiral; and (4) changing the social security system, private pension plans, and individual savings plans "to make the nation's retirement system sound and affordable."

The Brookings Institution.   The Brookings Institution remains the dominant policy-planning group for American domestic policy. This is true despite the growing influence of conservative think tanks under the Reagan Administration. Since the 1960s, The Brookings Institution has overshadowed the CED, the American Assembly, the American Enterprise Institute, the Heritage Foundation, and all other policy-planning groups. Brookings staffers dislike its reputation as a "liberal think tank," and they deny that Brookings tries to set national priorities.[18] Yet Brookings has been very influential in planning the war on poverty, welfare reform, national defense, and taxing and spending policies.

The Brookings Institution began as a modest component of the progressive movement of the early twentieth century. A wealthy St. Louis merchant, Robert Brookings,[19] established an Institute of Government Research in 1916 to promote "good government," fight "bossism," assist in municipal reform, and press for economy and efficiency in government. It worked closely with the National Civic Federation and other reformist, progressive organizations of that era. Brookings himself was appointed to the War Production Board by President Woodrow Wilson.

The original trustees of Brookings included Frederic H. Delano (wealthy banker and railroad executive, a member of the first Federal Reserve Board, and an uncle of President Franklin Delano Roosevelt), James F. Curtis (banker and assistant Secretary of the Treasury under President Taft), Arthur T. Hadley (president of Yale University): Herbert Hoover (then a self-made millionaire engineer and later Secretary of

---

[17]Office of the President, "A Program for Economic Recovery," February 1981 (Washington: Government Printing Office, 1981).

[18]Brookings staffer Gilbert Y. Stiener specifically attacked the description of the Institution found in this book. See Gilbert Y. Stiener, "On Thomas R. Dye's Presidential Address," *Journal of Politics,* 41 (February 1979), pp. 315–319.

[19]Brookings also served as chairman of the board of trustees of Washington University in St. Louis for twenty years, building a small college into a major university.

Commerce and President of the United States), and Felix Frankfurter (Harvard law professor, later to become Supreme Court Justice).

The first major policy decision of The Brookings Institution was the establishment of an annual federal budget. Before 1921, the Congress considered appropriations requests individually as they came from various departments and agencies. But The Brookings Institution proposed, and the Congress passed, the Budget and Accounting Act of 1921, which created for the first time an integrated federal budget prepared in the executive office of the President and presented to the Congress in a single budget message. This notable achievement was consistent with the early interests of the Brookings trustees in improving economy and efficiency in government.

In 1927, with another large gift from Robert Brookings as well as donations from Carnegie, Rockefeller, and Eastman (Kodak), the Brookings Institution assumed its present name. It also added Wall Street lawyer Dean Acheson to its trustees; he remained until his appointment as Secretary of State in 1947. For many years, the full-time president and executive officer of Brookings was Robert D. Calkins, former dean of the School of Business at Columbia and former CED director.

In 1952, under the leadership of Robert Calkins, the Institution broke away from being "a sanctuary for conservatives" and recruited a staff of in-house liberal intellectuals. The funds for this effort came mainly from the Ford Foundation; later a Ford Foundation staff worker, Kermit Gordon, was named Brookings Institution president. (He served until his death in 1977.) First under Calkins and later under Gordon, Brookings fashioned itself as a policy-planning organization and rapidly gained prestige and prominence in elite circles. When Republicans captured the presidency in 1968, Brookings became a haven for unemployed liberal Democratic intellectuals and bureaucrats. "In the late sixties and early seventies, Brookings took on the appearance of a government-in-exile as refugees from the Johnson Administration found new offices in the Brookings edifice..."[20] Charles L. Schultze, former chairman of the Council of Economic Advisers, began the publication of an annual "counter-budget" as a critique of the Nixon budgets. These are published each year under the title "Setting National Priorities." President Kermit Gordon, drawing on his experience as budget director under President Johnson, pressed forward with the notion of an alternative to the presidential budget. Gordon persuaded Charles Schultze and Alice Rivlin at Brookings to develop a proposal for a new congressional budget and Congressional Budget Office. In 1974, Congress obligingly established new budgetary procedures, and created new and powerful House and

[20]Silk and Silk, *The American Establishment*, p. 154.

Senate Budget Committees, and a new joint Congressional Budget Office headed, of course, by Brookings staffer Alice Rivlin.

The Brookings Defense Analysis Project was begun in 1969 and resulted in a series of studies which, in the words of a Brookings report, "informed and stimulated debate in the Congress, the executive branch and the press." Perhaps the most important recommendation to emerge from the Defense Analysis Project was the recommendation to drop the B-1 bomber from the U.S. arsenal. Brookings made its B-1 report in February 1976; it was read by President Carter and announced as national policy in July 1977 despite strong recommendations of military advisers to retain the bomber. But Brookings clearly overpowered the "military-industrial complex."

Brookings, however, is clearly part of the larger Washington establishment:

> Above all, Brookings is part of the Washington system. Its purpose is to influence public policy, and to be influential it must have a highly developed sense of the possible and accept the status quo in its essentials.[21]

Brookings people are encouraged to move in and out of top government posts. The current Brookings president, Bruce MacLaury, has said:

> In principle it is good to have people moving in and out of the government. This is the advantage which Brookings has over a place like Yale: that people have gotten their hands dirty.[22]

Before the Reagan Administration took office, Brookings was re-thinking many of the long-standing tenets of the liberal establishment. Arthur M. Okun (former chairman of the Council of Economic Advisers and a Brookings staffer from 1969 to his death in 1980) urged that "we face up to our lack of progress in the seventies. The economic record of the past decade is the second worst of the century—inferior to all but the horrible 1930's."[23] Okun called for "prudent restraint in the federal budget," higher interest rates, government deregulation, tax reductions on new plants and equipment, and "timely tax cuts." Brookings acknowledged the need for "supply-side" economic measures, but it tempered its enthusiasm by warning that "reduced social expenditures are even less likely to hold the key to improved economic performance than the discredited emphasis on countercyclical fiscal policy."[24] Brookings also

[21]*Ibid.*, p. 157.
[22]*Ibid.*, p. 158.
[23]*Brookings Bulletin*, 16 (Winter 1980), p. 1.
[24]*Brookings Annual Report 1980* (Washington: Brookings, 1981), p. 3.

challenged the social security program, arguing that social security benefits should not be treated as if they were "rights" immune from reductions.[25] In short, while Brookings has recently moved in a conservative direction, it remains the most liberal of the policy-planning organizations.

For many years, Republicans dreamed of a "Brookings Institution for Republicans" which would help offset the liberal bias of Brookings itself. In the late 1970s, that role was assumed by the American Enterprise Institute (AEI). The American Enterprise Association, as it was first called, was founded in 1943 by Lewis H. Brown, chairman of the Johns-Manville Corporation, to promote free enterprise. William J. Baroody, Sr., a staffer at the U.S. Chamber of Commerce, became executive director in 1962 and adopted the name American Enterprise Institute. William J. Baroody, Jr. assumed the presidency of AEI after his father. In 1976, the AEI provided a temporary haven for many Ford Administration refugees, including Treasury Secretary William E. Simon, Transportation Secretary Carla Hills, and AEI's "Distinguished Fellow," former President Gerald R. Ford. More importantly, however, the AEI began to attract distinguished "neoconservative" scholars, including sociologist Irving Kristol, economist Murray Weidenbaum (now chairman of the Council of Economic Advisers), and political scientists Seymour Martin Lipset and Jeane Kirkpatrick (now U.N. ambassador). The AEI appealed to both Democrats and Republicans who were beginning to have doubts about big government. The AEI began the publication of two excellent journals—*Public Opinion* and *Regulation*. President William Baroody, Jr. distinguished the AEI from Brookings:

> In confronting societal problems those who tend to gravitate to the AEI orbit would be inclined to look first for a market solution . . . while the other orbit people have a tendency to look for a government solution.[26]

But Robert V. Roosa, Brookings chairman and senior partner in the Wall Street investment firm of Brown Brothers Harriman and Company, resents the implication that Brookings is "liberal," while the AEI is "conservative."

> AEI is selling against Brookings. They don't have to do that—they have a role to fill . . . . We do some things on the conservative side—and more now . . . . We say to corporations "we're on your side too."[27]

[25]Martha Derthick, *Policymaking for Social Security* (Washington: Brookings, 1979).
[26]Silk and Silk, *The American Establishment,* p. 179.
[27]*Ibid.*

A collective portrait of the directors of CFR, the Business Roundtable, CED, and The Brookings Institution confirms the impressions derived from our brief biographies. The biographies "flesh out" the statistics in Table 9–1, and "naming names" reminds us that the leaders of the policy-planning organizations are real people. But the aggregate figures on corporate, governmental, university, and civic organization interlocking, as well as the education and social character of these individuals, also deserve attention.

First of all, it is clear that the policy-planning organizations do in fact provide structured linkages with the corporate world. The directors of

Table 9–1 The Policy-Planning Directors: A Collective Portrait

Positions Ever Held	CFR N = 22	CED N = 61	Brookings N = 18	Roundtable N = 44	Total N = 145
Corporate directorships					
Average number	3.2	4.1	5.0	4.3	4.1
(% with none)	(18.2%)	(4.9%)	(11.1%)	(0%)	(6.2%)
Government offices					
Average number	3.0	1.0	1.2	0.4	1.2
(% with none)	(4.5%)	(65.6%)	(50.0%)	(75.0%)	(51.9%)
University trusteeships					
Average number	1.0	1.2	1.0	1.3	1.2
(% with none)	(31.8%)	(32.8%)	(38.9%)	(27.3%)	(31.7%)
Civic association offices					
Average number	5.2	4.8	5.7	5.3	5.1
(% with none)	(0%)	(1.1%)	(0%)	(6.8%)	(2.7%)
Total institutional affiliations					
(average)	12.4	11.1	12.4	11.3	11.6
EDUCATION					
Percent college education	100.0%	100.0%	100.0%	100.0%	100.0%
Percent prestigious university*	81.8%	62.3%	77.7%	52.3%	58.6%
Percent law degree	22.7%	23.0%	11.1%	11.4%	17.9%
Percent graduate degree					
(including law)	90.9%	52.5%	66.7%	47.7%	58.6%
SOCIAL CHARACTER					
Percent female (number)	9.0%(2)	0	11.1%(2)	0	2.7%
Percent black (number)	4.5%(1)	0	5.5%(1)	0	1.3%
Average age	57.5	62.1	57.7	58.9	59.9
Private club membership					
Average number	2.8	2.8	3.4	3.0	2.9
(% with none)	(36.4%)	(27.8%)	(27.8%)	(34.1%)	(31.0%)

Source: Marquis, *Who's Who in America 1980–81*. Data on eight directors were not available.
*Harvard, Yale, Chicago, Stanford, Columbia, M.I.T., Cornell, Northwestern, Princeton, Johns Hopkins, Pennsylvania, and Dartmouth.

these four policy-planning organizations averaged over four corporate directorships each; only 6 percent of the policy-planning directors were *not* members of corporate boards. In the CFR, only Graham T. Allison, J.F. Kennedy School Dean at Harvard, and Lane Kirkland, AFL-CIO president, reported holding *no* corporate directorships. *All* Roundtable directors are corporate directors; indeed, one must be a corporate chief executive officer as a condition of membership. On the Brookings board, only one college professor, together with Lane Kirkland, reported holding *no* corporate directorships.

Second, the directors of the policy-planning organizations have considerable government experience. They averaged 1.2 government posts during their careers; about half of all of the directors reported some governmental experience. All of the CFR directors (except Atlantic Richfield chairman Robert Anderson) held governmental posts at one time or another in their careers. Half of the Brookings directors had served in government. This is an important comment on the four organizations: Clearly the CFR and Brookings directors are more experienced in governmental affairs than the directors of the Business Roundtable or the CED.

Third, the policy-planning directors maintain an active interest in education. The average director held 1.2 university trusteeships; only 32 percent of our directors had *not* held a university trusteeship.

Fourth, it is clear that the policy-planning directors also form a bridge between their organizations and a wide range of civic and cultural organizations. The average director held five reported posts (not merely memberships) in civic and cultural associations. These included, for example, the Metropolitan Museum of Art in Lincoln Center; the Rockefeller, Ford, and Carnegie Foundations; and other policy-planning groups such as the Urban Institute, American Assembly, and Resources for the Future. Only 3 percent did *not* report holding official posts in civic or cultural organizations.

The coordinating function of the policy-planning directors is made strikingly clear when we observe that the directors averaged over eleven institutional positions each! Certainly, the policy-planning organizations provide extensive linkages with the corporate, governmental, university, and civic and cultural institutions.

If we investigate their educational backgrounds, we find that the policy-planning directors are distinctively "Ivy League." Over three quarters of the directors of the CFR, CED, Business Roundtable, and The Brookings Institution graduated from just twelve prestigious universities. Over 20 percent of the policy-planning directors are lawyers. More importantly, perhaps, is the prevalence of postgraduate degrees among the policy-planning directors, including law degrees and an impressive number of M.B.A.'s and Ph.D.'s from prestigious universities. Over half of the directors held advanced degrees, and this figure does *not* include the numerous honorary degrees that are regularly bestowed upon them. This finding supports speculations by other writers of the growing importance of expertise in policy-planning.

Finally, we might observe that only 3 percent of the policy-planning directors are women, and 1 percent are black, but this itself is a recent development. A check against earlier information on the directors of the CFR, CED, and The Brookings Institution showed that as late as 1971 there were *no* women or blacks on the governing boards of these organizations.

In addition to their impressive educational credentials, and a great deal of experience in corporate, governmental, university, and civic affairs, the policy-planning directors bring considerable experience in life itself to their jobs—their average age is sixty. However youthful the *staffs* of the policy-planning organizations may be, overall direction of these organizations is secure in the hands of experienced individuals of public affairs. Membership in private clubs (emphasized as a coordinating device by some writers) was common: The average director reported 2.8 club memberships. Only about one third did *not* report any club memberships.

In brief, the policy planners have a great deal of experience in directing affairs in the corporate, governmental, university, and civic worlds. They are extraordinarily well-educated, with the vast majority holding advanced degrees and over 75 percent of these obtained from prestigious Ivy League universities. And, of course, the policy-planning directors are overwhelmingly white, male, and middle-aged.

THE ROLE OF THE "PROXIMATE POLICY-MAKERS"

The activities of the "proximate policy-makers"—the President, the Congress, federal agencies, congressional committees, White House staff, and interest groups—in the policy-making process have been described in countless books and articles. The term *proximate policy-maker* is derived from political scientist Charles E. Lindbloom, who uses it merely to distinguish between citizens and elected officials: "Except in small political systems that can be run by something like a New England town meeting, not all citizens can be the immediate, or *proximate,* makers of policy. They yield the immediate (or proximate) task of decision to a small minority."[28] In typically pluralist fashion, Lindbloom views the activities of the proximate

---

[28]Charles E. Lindbloom, *The Policy-Making Process* (Englewood Cliffs, N.J.: Prentice-Hall, Inc., 1968), p. 30.

policy-makers as the *whole* of the policy-making process. But our oligarchic model of public policy-making views the activities of the proximate policy-makers as only the *final phase* of a much more complex process. This is the open, public stage of policy-making, and it attracts the attention of the mass media and most political scientists. It is much easier to study than the private actions of corporations, foundations, universities, policy-planning groups, and mass media executives. Most "pluralists" concentrate their attention on this phase of public policy-making and conclude that it is simply a process of bargaining, competition, and compromise among governmental officials.

Undoubtedly, bargaining, competition, persuasion, and compromises over policy issues continue throughout this final phase of the policy-making process—the law-making phase. This is particularly true in the formulation of domestic policy; by contrast, the President is much freer to pursue elite recommendations in foreign and military policy areas without extensive accommodation of congressional and interest-group pressures. Of course, many elite recommendations fail to win the approval of Congress or even of the President in the first year or two they are proposed. Conflict between the President and Congress, or between Democrats and Republicans, or liberals and conservatives, and so forth, may delay or alter somewhat the final actions of the "proximate policy-makers." Indeed, important policy changes—welfare reform, for example—can be postponed for years by bickering in the Congress. Other important policy innovations—national health care, for example—can be delayed by the conflicting ambitions of a Republican President and a Democratic senator.

But the agenda for policy consideration has been set by other elites *before* the "proximate policy-makers" become actively involved in the policy-making process. The major directions of policy change have been determined, and the mass media have prepared the public for new policies and programs. The formal law-making process concerns itself with details of implementation: Who gets the "political" credit, what agencies get control of the program, and exactly how much money will be spent? These are not unimportant questions, but they are raised and decided within the context of policy goals and directions that have already been determined. These decisions of the "proximate policy-makers" tend to center about the *means* rather than the *ends* of public policy.

PUBLIC POLICY-MAKING: A CASE STUDY—POPULATION CONTROL

Following World War II, American scientists became increasingly aware that the world's rapidly growing population would some day threaten the very existence of humanity. But before 1952, there was little elite awareness of population problems, and hence no government activity in the field. The only group in either the public or private sector actively concerned with population control was the Planned Parenthood Federation of America, which had been created by Margaret Sanger, a pioneer in America's feminist movement. Planned Parenthood provided birth control information materials to indigent females, but its attempts to promote birth control as public policy were unsuccessful. Indeed, the subject of birth control was a political taboo. As late as 1959, President Eisenhower said he "could not imagine anything more emphatically a subject that is *not* a proper political or governmental activity or function or responsibility" than family planning.

But more advanced segments of the nation's elite began to take notice of early scientific warnings about the world population explosion. Several Rockefeller Foundation study grants had produced disquieting facts and projections regarding population growth in the 1940s. In 1952, John D. Rockefeller III convened a Conference on Population Problems at Williamsburg, Virginia. Rockefeller invited thirty participants, most of whom were physical or social scientists from universities in the United States, together with some federal officials, Rockefeller Foundation representatives, and staff members of the Planned Parenthood Federation. The Williamsburg Conference ended with a recommendation to establish a new body to formulate population policy for the nation. Given the political sensitivities surrounding the issue of birth control, the new body was to be a private rather than a public agency.

Accordingly, Rockefeller, buttressed by the scientific consensus expressed at the Williamsburg Conference, formed the Population Council. The Council was funded by generous grants from the Rockefeller Foundation and later the Ford Foundation. It quickly assumed a leadership role in the development of national population control policy. It supported population research, including an energetic program in contraceptive product development and family-planning programs. The Population Council gathered together an eminent group of medical and social scientists as its staff members and consultants. It mobilized the nation's universities through research grants, contracts, and fellowships from both the Population Council and the Rockefeller and Ford Foundations. Population study centers were established at Harvard, Johns Hopkins, Columbia, University of California at Berkeley, University of North Carolina, Michigan, and Tulane.

At the same time, efforts were begun to restructure public opinion regarding population control through the use of the mass media. Hugh Moore, chairman of the board of the Dixie Paper Cup Company and the St. Lawrence Seaway Development Corporation, and a director of the Planned Parenthood Federation, set out to remold public opinion. Moore published a pamphlet called "The Population Bomb," which has been described as an exaggerated but compelling document. A series of full-page newspaper advertisements appeared periodically in the *New York Times* and other leading newspapers warning of "the population bomb" and signed by prominent Americans from industry and finance and the professionals of the academic and intellectual community. Soon image-conscious scientists were turning out popular scare books about population growth: Paul Ehrlich produced his popular, best-selling *The Population Bomb*.[29]

Moore also created a permanent lobbying group in Washington—the Population Crisis Committee—headed by a well-known American banker and public servant, General William H. Draper, Jr. Draper was senior partner of a New York investment banking firm, a former chairman of the board of Combustion Engineering Corporation, and a former vice-president of Dillon, Reed, and Company, a New York investment firm headed by Douglas Dillon. He had also served as Under Secretary of the Army in the Truman Administration. The Population Crisis Committee itself consisted of an impressive array of major corporate executives, retired ambassadors and generals, members of leading law firms, government officials, and prominent university figures.

While the Planned Parenthood Federation of America had historically led the way in the fight for population control, it was soon reduced to a supportive role after the entry into the field of these two elite-backed organizations—the Population Council and the Population Crisis Committee. The Federation became a national network for the dissemination of information and policy positions from national elites to the community level. It created hundreds of local affiliates, each characterized as a "junior-league-type" organization. Later, a somewhat more youth-oriented organization, Zero Population Growth, was organized by publicist Paul Ehrlich ZPG was principally a campus-based organization composed of faculty and students in large universities. It had little influence, and it declined when the ZPG fad evaporated from campuses.

In 1965, the national government under President Johnson committed itself to developing a population policy. A major role was assigned to the Agency for International Development (AID). A Population Office was created in the AID; millions of dollars were authorized for population activities in AID programs; and a position of special assistant to the Secretary of State for population matters was created. On the domestic side, centers for population research and family planning were created in the Department of Health, Education, and Welfare (now the Department of Health and Human Services). The federal government began to fund family-planning services as a part of federal public health activities. Gradually, the funding of population research and family-planning

---

[29]Paul Ehrlich, *The Population Bomb* (New York: Ballantine, 1964).

services was shifted from the private sector to the federal government. But the role of the Population Council had been significant in implementing the growing concern of corporate and financial elites about public policy in this field.

The first presidential message on population was submitted by Richard M. Nixon to the Congress in 1969. The President committed the nation to the support of family planning in all nations and defined the U.S. population problem as unwanted children in poor families. Congressional activity followed in the wake of presidential, corporate, foundation, and university leadership. The first two pieces of significant population legislation were enacted in 1970—the Family Planning Services and Population Research Act of 1970; and an Act to Establish a Commission on Population Growth and the American Future. The Family Planning Services and Population Research Act provided grants to state and local governments for family-planning projects and services. Priority was given to low-income families. Funds were provided for research on developing better means of contraception and providing better family-planning services by the nation.

The Commission on Population Growth in the American Future was established to formally convene top leadership from various sectors of America's society. The Commission was headed by John D. Rockefeller III, and included representatives of corporate and financial institutions, foundations, universities, and the Population Council and Planned Parenthood, together with representatives of blacks, women, and youth. The Commission was asked to examine population growth and internal migration within the United States to the end of the twentieth century, and to assess the impact of projected population changes on government services, the economy, resources, and the environment, with an eye to recommending how the nation can best cope with these impacts. In short, the Commission's mandate was "to formulate policy for the future."

The Commission made its final report in 1972; it is the strongest statement to date on population control:

> The Commission believes that all Americans regardless of age, marital status, or income, should be enabled to avoid unwanted births. The major efforts should be made to enlarge and improve the opportunity for individuals to control their own fertility, aiming toward the development of a basic ethical principle of only wanted children being brought into the world.[30]

[30]The Commission was an excellent example of a structured forum for elite interaction. Corporate and financial elites were represented, of course, by John D. Rockefeller III as chairman; and by R.B. Hansberger, chairman of the board of Boise-Cascade Corp.; John R. Mire, president of the National Bureau of Economic Research; George D. Woods, director of the First Boston Corp. The foundations were represented by David E. Bell, vice-president of the Ford Foundation; Bernard Berelson, president of the Population Council.

These recommendations were developed by a "tight little community." A foundation staff member reported that

> research is a tight little professional community.... The determination of priorities is made by members of the professional community in intimate dialogue with one another.... Ford and Rockefeller pick up special things that NIH cannot do; for example, the more flexible things.... Product research falls in AID.... It is directed at contraceptive development and is applied, rather than the basic research that NIH does....[31]

The pattern of interaction is clear:

> ... there is a movement in and out of one role or another, academia to government, to foundations, etc.... Channels of communication develop ... and can lead to specialization in particular issues.... One man can have great influence ... a "Mafia-like" structure has existed....[32]

The consensus that we have observed in this case study uniting the Rockefellers with the intellectual elite, corporate leaders, congresspersons, organized labor, civic and cultural leaders, universities and foundations is the *liberal notion of improving the quality of life by using government power* to control population growth. All are convinced that rational planning and government action is required to improve conditions of life at home and abroad. They view political stability and reduction in international and domestic violence as desirable by-products of reduced population growth. They believe that lower fertility is an essential requirement for higher levels of individual and societal well-being. Energetic government intervention is seen as essential to achieving the good society. Most (but not all) would prefer to achieve lower fertility through government manipulation of incentives and disincentives, voluntary family planning, and the dissemination of technology, rather than by direct government coercion.

Population policy-making in America also provides a classic example of the *non*-decision. By focusing on population growth as the obstacle to improving the quality of life of the world's population, the more threatening question of *inequalities in the distribution of wealth* between rich and poor nations and peoples can be bypassed. Hunger, disease, and violence are portrayed as a product of too many people rather than of inequality in the distribution of resources among people. Some "radical" critics of current population policy argue that fundamental social changes must occur *before* fertility can be reduced. Standards of living among the poor must be

---

[31]Peter Bachrach and Elihu Bergman, *Power and Choice* (Lexington, Mass.: D.C. Heath and Co., 1973), p. 79.
[32]*Ibid.*

raised, wider opportunities for individual fulfillment must be provided, and women must be given a wider variety of roles and opportunities, so that large families will no longer be an economic or psychological necessity. But these questions are seldom addressed by an American elite predisposed to view population growth *within* the established social, economic, and political system.

Many of the nation's most important public policies are made by the Supreme Court rather than the president or Congress. So it was in population policy—the most significant decision about the future of the nation's population was the Supreme Court's momentous decision recognizing abortion as a constitutional right of women. In the historic decisions of *Roe* v. *Wade* and *Doe* v. *Bolton* (1974), the Court determined that the fetus is not a "person" within the meaning of the Constitution, and the fetus' right to life is not guaranteed by law. Moreover, the Court held that the liberties guaranteed by the 5th and 14th Amendments encompass the woman's decision about whether or not to terminate her pregnancy. The Supreme Court decided that the Texas criminal abortion statutes prohibiting abortions in any state of pregnancy except to save the life of the mother were unconstitutional; that during the first three months of pregnancy the abortion decision must be left wholly to the woman and her physician; that during the second three months of pregnancy the state may not prohibit abortion but only regulate procedures in ways reasonably related to maternal health; and that only in the final three months of pregnancy may the state prohibit abortion except where necessary for the preservation of life or health of the mother.

In this sweeping decision the Supreme Court established abortion not merely as permissible under law, but as a constitutional right immune from the vagaries of popularly elected legislatures. Abortion, previously regarded as a serious crime, became a constitutional right. Such far-reaching policy declaration would have been unthinkable a few years ago. But the patient efforts of a small group of the nation's top leaders over decades resulted in this startling reversal of traditional policy.

The current "Right-To-Life" movement, which opposes abortion itself as well as federal funding for family planning, is a *mass* movement with relatively little elite support. The "Right-To-Life" movement has called for a constitutional amendment to protect the unborn fetus, and it has opposed federal funding for abortions (the Hyde Amendment). Many "pro-lifers" are very intense in their commitment, and they have succeeded in halting federal funds for abortion under Medicaid. But it is not likely that this mass movement can alter the basic direction of elite-sponsored policy—including the guarantee of a constitutional right to an abortion for women in the United States and the encouragement of family planning throughout the world.

Pluralist scholars focus their attention on the activities of "the proximate policy-makers"—the President, Congress, and the courts. They observe competition, bargaining, and compromise among and within these public bodies over specific policies and programs. They observe the role of parties, interest groups, and constituents in shaping the decision-making behavior of these proximate policy-makers. But it is quite possible that the activities of the proximate policy-makers are merely the final phase of a much more complex structure of national policy formation.

Our "oligarchic model" of national policy-making attempts to trace elite interaction in determining the major directions of national policy. It portrays the role of the proximate policy-makers as one of implementing through law, the policies that have been formulated by a network of elite-financed and elite-directed policy-planning groups, foundations, and universities. The proximate policy-makers act only after the agenda for policy-making has already been set, the major directions of policy changes have been decided, and all that remains is the determination of programmatic specifics.

The initial resources for research, study, planning, and formulation of policy come from donations of corporate and personal wealth. These resources are channeled into foundations, universities, and policy-planning groups. Moreover, top corporate elites also sit on the governing boards of these institutions to help determine how their money will be spent. The policy-planning groups—such as the Council on Foreign Relations, the Committee on Economic Development, and The Brookings Institution—play a central role in bringing together individuals at the top of the corporate and governmental worlds, the foundations, the law firms, and the mass media, in order to reach a consensus about policy direction. The mass media, in addition to participating in policy formulation, play a vital role in preparing public opinion for policy change. Special presidential commissions, governmental study groups, or citizens' councils can also be employed to mobilize support for new policies.

Our examination of population control policy was designed to illustrate our oligarchic model. We do not expect every major policy decision to conform to this model. However, we believe the model deserves consideration by students of the policy-making process.

10

Institutional elites in America

INSTITUTIONAL POWER IN AMERICA

Power in America is organized into large institutions, private as well as public—corporations, banks, utilities, governmental bureaucracies, broadcasting networks, law firms, universities, foundations, cultural and civic organizations. The nation's resources are concentrated in a relatively few large institutions and control over these institutional resources is the major source of power in society. The people at the top of these institutions—those who are in a position to direct, manage, and guide institutional programs, policies, and activities—compose the nation's elite.

The *systematic* study of the nation's institutional elite is still in an exploratory stage. Although a great deal has been written about "the power elite," much of it has been speculative, impressionistic, and polemical. Serious difficulties confront the social scientist who wishes to move away from anecdote and ideology to serious scientific research on national elites—research that "names names," attempts operational definitions, develops testable hypotheses, and produces some reliable information about national leadership.

The first task confronting social science is to develop an operational definition of national elite. Such a definition must be consistent with the notion that great power resides in the institutional structure of society; it must also enable us to identify by name and position those individuals who possess great power in America. Our own definition of a national institutional elite produced 7,314 elite positions. Taken collectively, individuals in these positions controlled half of the nation's industrial assets; half of all the assets in communications, transportation, and utilities; half of all banking assets; two thirds of all insurance assets; and they directed the nation's largest investment firms. They commanded nearly half of all assets of private foundations and universities, and they controlled the television networks, wire services, and major newspaper chains. They dominated the nation's top law firms and the most prestigious civic and cultural associations and occupied key federal government posts in the executive, legislative, and judicial branches and the top military commands.

Our selection of positions of institutional power involved many subjective judgments, but it provided a starting place for a systematic inquiry into the character of America's elite structure. It allowed us to begin investigation into a number of important questions: Who are the people at the top of the institutional structure of America? How did they get there? What are their backgrounds, attitudes, and values? How concentrated or dispersed is their power? Do they agree or disagree on the fundamental goals of society? How much cohesion or competition characterizes their interrelationships? How do they go about making important policy decisions or undertaking new policy directions?

HIERARCHY AND POLYARCHY
AMONG INSTITUTIONAL ELITES

Before summarizing our data on institutional elites, it might be helpful to gain some theoretical perspectives on our findings by suggesting *why* we might expect to find evidence of either hierarchy or polyarchy in our results.

European social theorists—notably Weber and Durkheim—provide theoretical explanations of why social structures become specialized in advanced societies, and why coordination mechanisms are required. These theorists suggest that increasing functional *differentiation* of elites occurs with increasing socioeconomic development. In a primitive society, it is difficult to speak of separate economic, political, military, or administrative power roles; in primitive life, these power roles are merged together with other roles, including kinship, religion, and magical roles. But as separate economic, political, bureaucratic, and military institutions develop, and specialized power roles are created within these institutions, separate elite groups emerge at the top of separate institutional structures. The increased division of labor, the scale and complexity of modern social organizations, and specialization in knowledge, all combine to create functional differentiation among institutional elites. This suggests polyarchy among elites in an advanced society such as the United States.

Yet even though specialized elite groups are required to direct relatively autonomous institutional sectors, there must also be some social mechanisms to coordinate the exercise of power by various elites in society. This requirement of *coordination* limits the autonomy of various institutional elites. Thus, specialization acts to bring elites together, as well as to force them apart. Social theory does not necessarily specify *how* coordination of power is to be achieved in modern society. Nor does it specify *how much* unity is required to maintain a relatively stable social system or, conversely, how much competition can be permitted. Certainly there must be *some* coordination if society is to function as a whole. The amount of coordination can vary a great deal, however, and the mechanisms for coordination among elites differ from one society to another.

One means of coordination is to keep the relative size of elite groups small. This smallness itself facilitates communication. If there are relatively few people who actually direct institutional activity, then these people can have extraordinary influence on national policy. What's more, the small size of these groups means that institutional leaders are known and accessible to each other. Of course, policy-planning groups, governmental commissions, and advisory councils, or informal meetings and conferences, are instrumental in bringing "specialists" together. But how small *is* America's elite? C. Wright Mills, wisely perhaps, avoids any estimate of the size of "the power elite"; he says only that it is "a handful of men."[1] Floyd Hunter estimates the size of "top leadership" to be "between one hundred and two hundred men."[2] We have already indicated that our definition of the elite produces an estimated size of over 7,000 individuals— considerably more than implied in the power elite literature, but still few enough to permit a great deal of personal interaction.

Another coordinating mechanism is to be found in the methods by which elites are recruited. The fact that elites who are recruited to different institutional roles share the same social class and educational backgrounds should provide a basis for understanding and communication. Social homogeneity, kinship links, similarity of educational experience, common membership in clubs, common religious and ethnic affiliations, all help to promote unity of outlook. Yet at the same time we know that a certain amount of "circulation of elites" (upward mobility) is essential for the stability of a social system. This means that some heterogeneity in social background must be tolerated. But again social theory fails to quantify the amount of heterogeneity that can be expected.

[1]C. Wright Mills, *The Power Elite* (New York: Oxford, 1956), p. 7.
[2]Floyd Hunter, *Top Leadership, U.S.A.* (Chapel Hill: University of North Carolina Press, 1959), p. 176.

A related mechanism for coordination is common career experiences. If elite members were drawn disproportionately from one career field—let us say industry or finance—there would be greater potential for unity. But again, social theory does not tell us how much, if any, commonality in career lines is functionally requisite for coordination of specialized elites.

Still another form of coordination is a general consensus among elites on the rules to resolve conflicts and to preserve the stability of the social system itself. Common values serve to unify the elites of various institutional systems. Moreover, agreement among elites to abide by the rule of law and to minimize violence has a strong utilitarian motive, namely to preserve stable working arrangements among elite groups. Finally, unifying values also legitimize the exercise of power by elites over masses, so the preservation of the value system performs the dual function of providing the basis of elite unity, while at the same time rationalizing and justifying for the masses the exercise of elite power. Unfortunately, social theory does not tell us *how much* consensus is required among elites to facilitate coordination and preserve a stable social system. Social theory tells us that elites must agree on more matters than they disagree, but it fails to specify how broad or narrow the range of issues can be.

Because social theory suggests *both* convergence and differentiation among institutional elites, it is possible to develop competing theoretical models of the social system—models which emphasize either hierarchy or polyarchy. For example, the notion of the "power elite" developed by C. Wright Mills implies *hierarchy* among economic, political, and military power-holders. The idea suggests unity and coordination among leaders of functionally differentiated social institutions. Mills speculates that a large-scale, centralized, complex, industrial society *necessitates* coordination:

> At the pinnacle of each of the three enlarged and centralized domains, there have arisen those higher circles which make up the economic, the political, and the military elites. At the top of the economy, among the corporate rich, there are the chief executives; at the top of the political order, the members of the political directorate; at the top of the military establishment, the elite of soldier-statesmen clustered in and around the Joint Chiefs of Staff in the upper echelon....each of these domains of power—the warlords, the corporation chieftains, the political directorate—tend to come together, to form the power elite of America.[3]

Thus, the hierarchical or "elitist" model rests upon the theoretical proposition that increasing complexity, both internal and external—that is, the demands of relations with other societies—requires a high degree of coordination and consequently a great concentration of power.

In contrast, the *polyarchical* or "pluralist" model emphasizes differ-

[3]Mills, *The Power Elite*, pp. 8–9.

entiation in institutional structures and leadership positions—with different sets of leaders and different institutional sectors of society and with little or no overlap, except perhaps by elected officials responsible to the general public. According to this view, elites are largely "specialists," and leadership roles are confined to a narrow range of institutional decisions. These specialists are recruited through separate institutional channels— they are not drawn exclusively from business or finance. Further, the functional specialization of institutional elites results in competition for power, a struggle in which competing elites represent and draw their strength from functionally separate systems of society. How do pluralists assume coordination is achieved among elites? The argument is that functionally differentiated power structures lead to an equilibrium of competing elites. Resulting checks and balances of competition are considered desirable to prevent the concentration of power and assure the responsibility of elites.

In short, social theory postulates both hierarchy *and* polyarchy among elites in the social system. It is the task of systematic social science research to determine just *how much* convergence or differentiation exists among elites in the national system.

WHO'S RUNNING AMERICA?
SUMMARY OF FINDINGS

Our findings do not all fit neatly into either an hierarchical, elitist model of power, or a polyarchical, pluralist model of power. We find evidence of both hierarchy and polyarchy in the nation's institutional elite structure. Let us try to summarize our principal findings regarding the questions posed at the beginning of this volume.

1. Concentration of Institutional Resources

The nation's resources are concentrated in a relatively small number of large institutions. Half of the nation's industrial assets are concentrated in 100 manufacturing corporations; half of U.S. banking assets are concentrated in the 50 largest banks; and half of our assets in transportation, communications, and utilities are concentrated in 50 corporations. Two thirds of the nation's insurance assets are concentrated in just 50 companies; 50 foundations control 40 percent of all foundation assets; 25 universities control 50 percent of all private endowment funds in higher education; 3 network broadcasting companies control 90 percent of the television news; and 10 newspaper chains account for one third of the nation's daily newspaper circulation. It is highly probable that 30 Wall Street and Washington law firms exercise comparable dominance in the legal field; that 15 Wall Street investment firms dominate decision-making in securities; and that a dozen cultural and civic organizations dominate music, drama, the arts, and civic affairs. Federal government alone now accounts for 21 percent of the gross national product and two thirds of all government spending. More importantly, concentration of resources in the nation's largest institutions is increasing over time.

In 1950 the largest 100 manufacturing corporations controlled only 39.8 percent of all manufacturing assets, compared to 55.0 percent in 1980. The development of television network broadcasting over the past twenty-five years has concentrated news dissemination (recall that a healthy majority of Americans get the news solely from TV) in just three corporations. Centralization of governmental functions at the national level has proceeded at a rapid pace since the 1930s. Similar trends in nationalization and concentration of resources in a small number of institutions is evident in other sectors of society.

2. Individual Versus Institutional Resources

The resources available to individuals in America are infinitesimal in comparison with the resources available to the nation's largest institutions. Personal wealth in itself provides little power; it is only when wealth is associated with top institutional position that it provides the wealth-holder with any significant degree of power.

Managerial elites are gradually replacing owners and stockholders as the dominant influence in American corporations. Most capital investment comes from retained earnings of corporations and bank loans, rather than from individual investors.

Nonetheless, personal wealth in America is unequally distributed: the top fifth of income recipients receive over 40 percent of all income, while the bottom fifth receives about 5 percent. This inequality is lessening very slowly over time.

3. The Size of the Nation's Elite

Approximately 6,000 individuals in 7,000 positions exercise formal authority over institutions that control roughly half of the nation's resources in industry, finance, utilities, insurance, mass media, foundations, education, law, and civic and cultural affairs. This definition of the elite is fairly large numerically, yet these individuals constitute an extremely small percentage of the nation's total population—less than three-thousandths of 1 percent. However, this figure is considerably larger than that implied in the "power elite" literature.

Perhaps the question of hierarchy or polyarchy depends on whether one wants to emphasize numbers or percentages. To emphasize hierarchy, one can comment on the tiny *percentage* of the population that possesses such great authority. To emphasize polyarchy, one can comment on the fairly large *number* of individuals at the top of the nation's institutional structure; certainly there is room for competition within so large a group.

4. Interlocking Versus Specialization

Despite concentration of institutional resources, there is clear evidence of specialization among institutional leaders. Eighty-five percent of the institutional elites identified in our study were "specialists," holding only one post of the 7,000 "top" posts. Of course, many of these individuals held other institutional positions in a wide variety of corporate, civic, and cultural organizations, but these were not "top" positions as we defined them. Governmental leadership is *not* interlocked with the corporate world.

However, the multiple "interlockers"—individuals with six or more top posts—not surprisingly turn out to be "giants" in the industrial and financial world. Another finding is that there is a good deal of "vertical" overlap—top position-holders who have had previous experience in other top corporate, governmental, and legal positions—more so than there is "horizontal" (concurrent) interlocking. Over one quarter of governmental elites have held high corporate positions, and nearly 40 percent of the corporate elites have held governmental jobs. Yet even this "vertical overlapping" must be qualified, for most of the leadership experience of corporate elites was derived from *corporate* positions, and most of the leadership experience of governmental elites was derived from *government and law.*

There are, however, important concentrations of combined corporate, governmental, and social power in America. Large corporations such as AT&T have many interlocking director relationships with industrial corporations, banks, utilities, and insurance companies. There are identifiable groupings of corporations by interlocking directorships; these groupings tend to center around major banks and regions of the country. In addition, there is concentration of power among the great, wealthy, entrepreneurial families—the Rockefellers, Mellons, duPonts, Fords. Doubtlessly, the most important of these concentrations is in the Rockefeller family group, which has an extensive network in industrial, financial, political, civic, educational, and cultural institutions.

5. Inheritors Versus Climbers

There is a great deal of upward mobility in American society, as well as "circulation of elites." We estimate that less than 10 percent of the top corporate elites studied inherited their position and power; the vast majority climbed the rungs of the corporate ladder. Most governmental elites—whether in the executive bureaucracy, Congress, or the courts—

also rose from fairly obscure positions. Elected political leaders frequently come from parochial backgrounds and continue to maintain ties with local clubs and groups. Military leaders tend to have the largest percentage of rural, southern, and lower-social-origin members of any leadership group.

6. Separate Channels of Recruitment

There are multiple paths to the top. Our top elites were recruited through a variety of channels. Governmental leaders were recruited mainly from law and government; less than one in six was recruited from the corporate world. Military leaders were recruited exclusively through the military ranks. Most top lawyers rose through the ranks of the large, well-known law firms, and mass media executives were recruited primarily from newspaper and television. Only in the foundations, universities, and cultural and civic associations was the formal leadership drawn from other sectors of society.

7. Social Class and Elite Recruitment

Individuals at the top are overwhelmingly upper- and upper-middle-class in social origin. Even those who climbed the institutional ladder to high position generally started with the advantages of a middle-class upbringing. Nearly all top institutional elites are college-educated, and half hold advanced degrees. Elites are notably "Ivy League": 54 percent of top corporate leaders and 42 percent of top governmental leaders are alumni of just 12 well-known private universities. Moreover, a substantial proportion of corporate and government leaders attended one of just thirty private "name" prep schools.

Very few top corporate or governmental elites are women, although more women are now being appointed to top corporate boards. A greater number of women serve in top positions in the cultural world, but many of these women do so because of their family affiliation.

It is clear that very few blacks occupy any positions of authority in the institutional structure of American society. We estimated that in 1980 only about ten blacks served as directors of the nation's corporations, banks, or utilities. One black served on the Cabinet (HUD Secretary Samuel R. Pierce), and one on the Supreme Court (Thurgood Marshall). The Ford Foundation has a black president (Franklin A. Thomas).

Corporate elites are somewhat more "upper-class" in origin than are governmental elites. Governmental elites had slightly lower proportions of private prep school types and Ivy Leaguers than corporate elites, and governmental elites were less eastern and urban in their origins than corporate elites. Governmental leaders in our study had more advanced professional degrees (generally law degrees) than did corporate elites.

8. Conflict and Consensus Among Elites

Elites in all sectors of American society share a consensus about the fundamental values of private enterprise, limited government, and due process of law. Moreover, since the Roosevelt era, elites have generally supported liberal, public-regarding, social welfare programs—including social security, fair labor standards, unemployment compensation, a graduated income tax, a federally aided welfare system, government regulation of public utilities, and countercyclical fiscal and monetary policies. Elite consensus also includes a desire to end minority discrimination—and to bring minority Americans into the mainstream of the political and economic system. Today's liberal elite believes that it can change people's lives through the exercise of governmental power—eliminate racism, abolish poverty, uplift the poor, overcome sickness and disease, educate the masses and generally *do good*.

While American politics continue in this liberal tradition, there has been a growing disillusionment among elites with government interventions in society, and a reaffirmation of the role of the home, the community, and the free market in shaping society. The "neoconservatives" are still liberal and public regarding in their values, but inflation, Watergate, civil unrest, and Vietnam have combined to dampen their enthusiasm for large, costly government programs.

Elites from all sectors of society (even leaders of blacks, women, and youth) believe in equality of opportunity rather than absolute equality. Elites throughout American history have defended the principle of merit. Absolute equality, or "leveling," has always been opposed by the nation's leadership.

Elite disagreement does occur *within* this consensus over fundamental values. However, the range of disagreement is relatively narrow and tends to be confined to means rather than ends. Specific policy disagreements among various elite groups occur over questions such as the oil depletion allowance, federal versus state and local control of social programs, tax reform, specific energy and environmental protection proposals, and specific measures for dealing with inflation and recession.

9. Factionalism Among Elites

Traditional "pluralist" theory emphasizes competition between Democrats and Republicans, liberals and conservatives, labor and management, and other conventional struggles among interest groups. "Elitist" theory, on the other hand, emphasizes underlying cohesion among elite groups, but still admits of some factionalism. A recognized source of factionalism is the emergence of new sources of wealth and new "self-made" individuals who do not fully share the prevailing values of established elites. In America,

Post-World War II society reveals new bases of wealth and power developed in independent oil-drilling operations, the aerospace industry, computer technology, real estate development in the sunbelt (from southern California to Florida), discount drugs and merchandising, fast foods, and low-cost insurance. We have labeled these new elites "the sunbelt *cowboys.*"

The *cowboys* are not as liberal or public-regarding, or as social-welfare–oriented as are the *yankees,* our label for the established institutional elites. The *cowboys* tend to think of solutions to social problems in much more individualistic terms, and they are generally moderate to conservative on most national policy issues.

Despite the self-importance of many new persons of wealth, established eastern institutional wealth and power continues to dominate national life. The rate of new elite formation is lower today than in previous time periods, and new wealth is frequently unstable and highly sensitive to economic fluctuations.

10. An Oligarchic Model of National Policy-Making

Traditional pluralist theory focuses attention on the activities of the "proximate policy-makers" in the policy-making process, and the interaction of parties, interest groups, President and Congress, and other public actors in the determination of national policy. In contrast, our "oligarchic model" of national policy-making views the role of "the proximate policy-makers" as one of deciding specific means of implementing major policy goals and directions which have *already been determined* by elite interaction.

Our "oligarchic model" assumes that the initial resources for research, study, planning, organization, and implementation of national policies are derived from corporate and personal wealth. This wealth is channeled into foundations, universities, and policy-planning institutions, where corporate representatives and top wealth-holders exercise ultimate power on the governing boards. Thus, the foundations provide the initial "seed money" to analyze social problems, to determine national priorities, and to investigate new policy directions. Universities and intellectuals respond to the research emphases *determined by the foundations* and produce studies that conform to these predetermined emphases. Influential policy-planning groups—notably the Council on Foreign Relations, the Business Roundtable, the Committee on Economic Development, and The Brookings Institution—may also employ university research teams to analyze national problems. But their more important function is consensus building among elites—bringing together individuals at the top of corporate and financial institutions, the universities, the foundations, and the top law firms, as well as the leading intellectuals, the mass media, and influential figures in government. Their goal is to develop action recommendations—explicit policy recommendations have general elite support. These are then communicated to the "proximate policy-makers" directly and through the mass media. At this point federal executive agencies begin their "research" into the policy alternatives suggested by the foundations and policy-planning groups. The role of the various public agencies is thus primarily to fill in the details of the policy directions determined earlier. Eventually, the federal executive agencies, in conjunction with the intellectuals, foundation executives, and policy-planning—group representatives, prepare specific legislative proposals, which then begin to circulate among "the proximate policy-makers," notably White House and congressional committee staffs.

The federal law-making process involves bargaining, competition, persuasion, and compromise, as generally set forth in "pluralist" political theory. But this interaction occurs *after* the agenda for policy-making has been established and the major directions of policy changes have already been determined. The decisions of proximate policy-makers are not unimportant, but they tend to center about the *means* rather than the *ends* of national policy.

WHO'S RUNNING AMERICA?
THEORY AND RESEARCH

Systematic research on national leadership is still very much in the exploratory phase. Indeed, most of the serious social science research on elites in America has concentrated on local communities. Frequently, analysts have extrapolated the knowledge derived from *community* power studies to *national* power structures. As a result, much of our theorizing about power in America rests on inferences derived from the study of community life. Yet to assume that national elites are comparable to community elites not only violates the laws of statistical sampling, but also runs contrary to commonsensical understanding of the size and complexity of institutions at the national level.

We do not yet have sufficient evidence to confirm or deny the major tenets of "pluralist" or "elitist" models of national power. Our research on institutional elites produces evidence of both hierarchy and polyarchy in the nation's elite structure. If we were forced to summarize our views of the elitist-pluralist debate in the light of our findings, we could do no better than to draw upon a brief statement that appears near the end of G. William Domhoff's book, *The Higher Circles:*

> If it is true, as I believe, that the power elite consists of many thousands of people rather than several dozen; that they do not meet as a committee of the whole; that there are differences of opinion between them; that their motives

are not well known to us beyond such obvious inferences as stability and power; and that they are not nearly so clever or powerful as the ultraconservatives think—it is nonetheless also true, I believe, that the power elite are more unified, more conscious, and more manipulative than the pluralists would have us believe, and certainly more so than any social group with the potential to contradict them. If pluralists ask just how unified, how conscious, and how manipulative, I reply that they have asked a tough empirical question to which they have contributed virtually no data.[4]

But we shall avoid elaborate theorizing about pluralism, polyarchy, elitism, and hierarchy in American society. Unfortunately, theory and conceptualization about power and elites has traditionally been so infected with ideological disputation that it is presently impossible to speculate about the theoretical relevance of our data on institutional leadership without generating endless, unproductive debate.

Our purpose has been to present what we believe to be interesting data on national institutional elites. We will leave it to our readers to relate this data to their own theory or theories of power in society. We do believe, however, that systematic understanding of power and elites must begin with operational definitions, testable hypotheses, and reliable data if we ever expect to rise above the level of speculation, anecdote, or polemics in this field of study.

[4]G. William Domhoff, *The Higher Circles* (New York: Random House, 1970), p. 299.

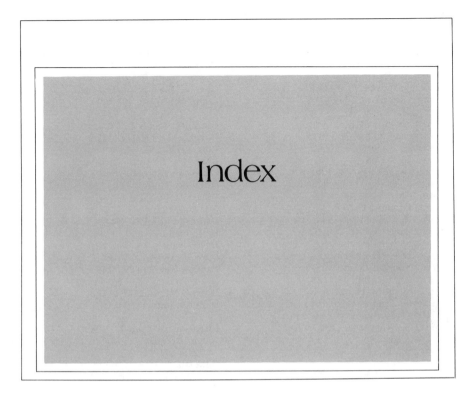

Index

LEADERSHIP INDEX

GENERAL INDEX